DOMINIC LYNE
CYCLE-2

Also by Dominic Lyne:

Prose
The Mushroom Diaries
Ink Spills and Five Notes of Suicide
Best Friends Forever (with Jeff Michalik)

Poetry
Visions of Wormwood

Cycle-2 Series
Paradise is Nowhere
Lying Wasted Under a Broken Coda
The Silent Scream

DOMINIC LYNE
CYCLE - 2
SCREAMS OF SILENCE

Published by **Degraded Discord**
An Imprint of **DPL Publishing**, 2012

Text and Illustrations copyright © Dominic Lyne, 2012
www.dom-lyne.co.uk

ISBN: 978-0-9561612-8-4

For everyone who has played a part in my journey through this world, I thank you.

CONTENTS

CYCLE-2.1: PARADISE IS NOWHERE

CYCLE-2.2: LYING WASTED UNDER A BROKEN CODA

CYCLE-2.3: THE SILENT SCREAM

CYCLE-2.4: EYES OF INSANITY

BOOK ONE
CYCLE-2
PARADISE IS NOWHERE

PART ONE

THE DREAM

Some dreams linger with you. Images burnt on your subconscious like photographs. Visions. Thoughts. Memories. The truth of emotion hidden behind silent screams. A cut in the head, and it all bleeds out onto the paper. This is my vision. This is my dream.

Dom Lyne, September 2010

That day comes. The final moments. Curled on the floor and you scream.

Scream out into the heavens in despair. Praying, hoping someone will

listen. Words like ink spills spitting against reality. Tearing the canvas

with their bitter blades.

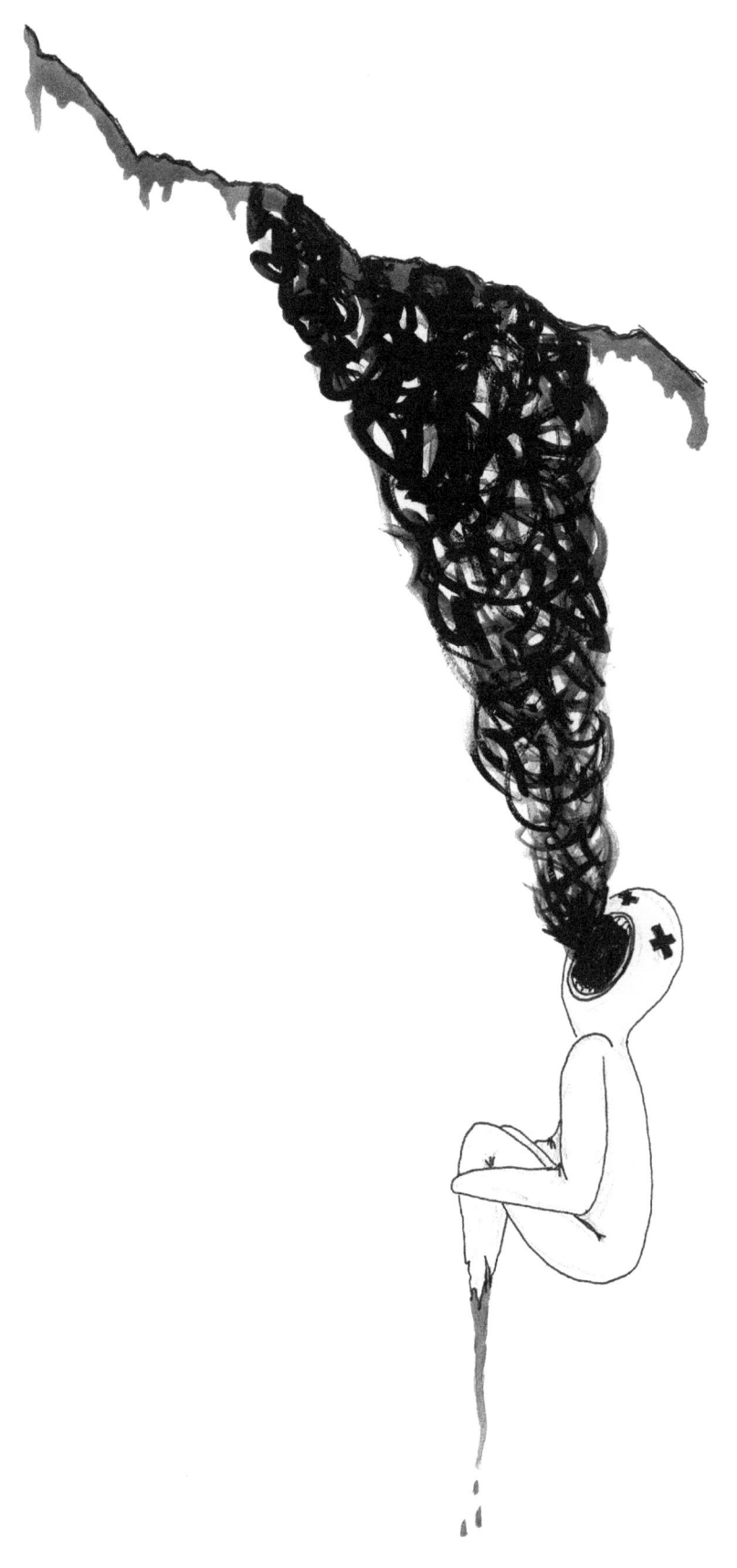

Then what? When silence answers what are we expected to do? Spinning around on this ball of dirt like evolved apes, searching desperately for a reason to our existence. Destroying from what we were born just to escape the darkness.

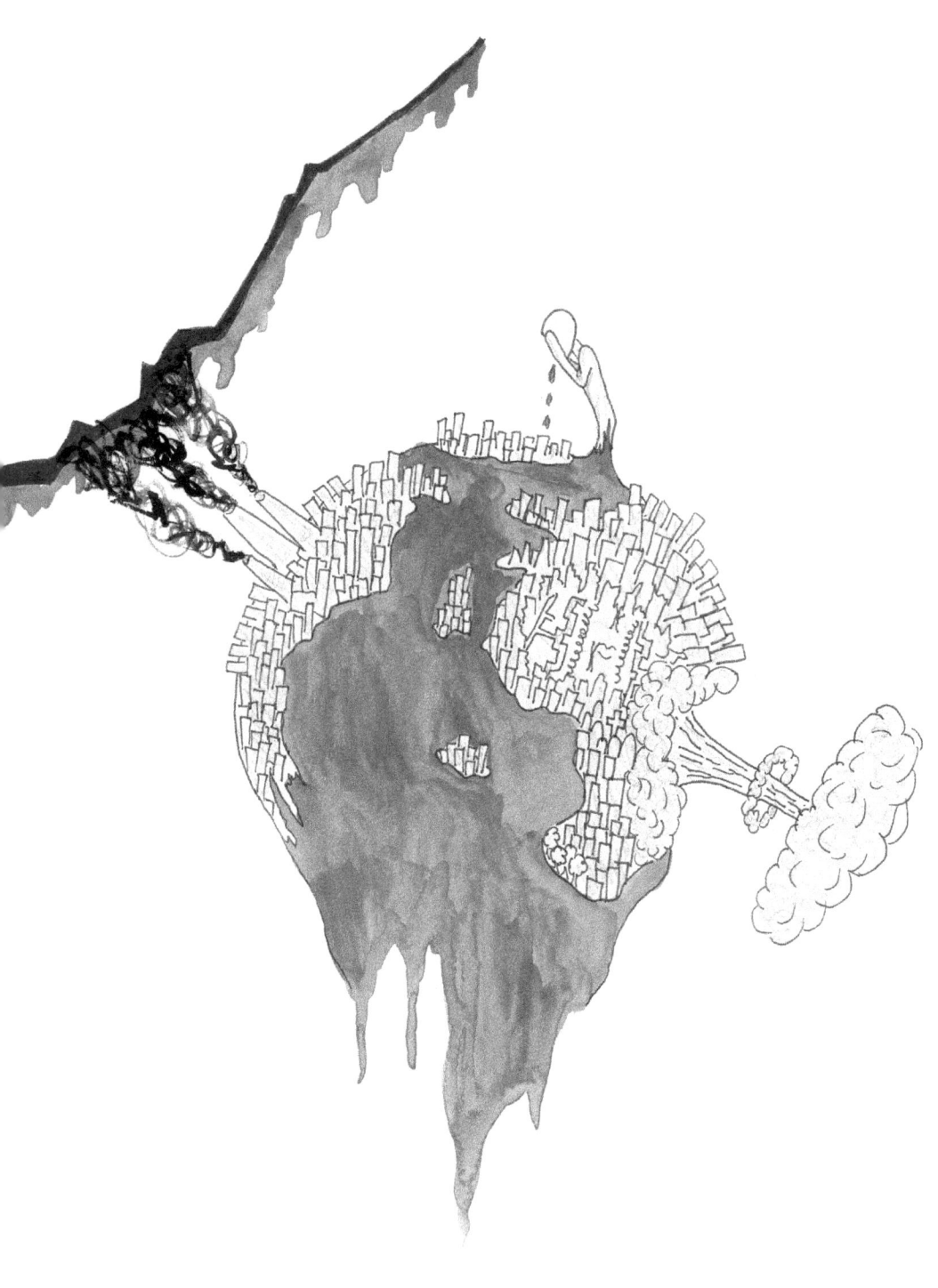

Nature screams in pain. Her roots deep, torn painfully from its core. Metal replacing organic. Warmth replaced by cold steel. She reacts, pours forth the darkness from which she came. Regretting growing the apple that gave man its sense of self importance. From beauty came cancer, and from cancer came death.

From the fruit came hate, love, death. A Pandora's box wrapped up in

sweetness. Mankind threw away everything to claim everything with a

reward of nothing. A dead world governed by dead souls fed by greed.

Lies the currency of our time.

So what of us? The individual on the battle lines. Conform or die. A slave against our natures. Filling our worlds with pointless trinkets to remind us we exist, that we have a presence. All forgettable. Memories bleed into the void and we sleep in our ignorance.

The dead cry beneath our feet. Their bodies long since crumbled to dust. Locked in fear as they realise there is nothing. No God, no Heaven, no Hell. Just the darkness pulling them towards it. The dead have no future to call their own, just memories fading like candles. Melting, distorting. Dying.

Open your eyes. Open them. Wake up and rip your messiah off his cross and demand the severed head of his god. Then we'll see who's listening now. Ignore his screams like he did the festering pile at his feet. But in all honesty, can we blame him?

Back to your room. Alone. Your dreams lost and forgotten. The silent

kiss of the barrel in your mouth. One click salvation. Blood pours

from your nose and you slump to the floor. Soul exited through the

hole in the back of your head. No more sorrow. No more chances. No

escape.

Picture the scene. Tommy boy's body hangs from the ceiling as his spirit sits on the bed watching it. Rosie girl looks at the pile of pills in front of her and wonders "what's the point?" The way has been lost, and now the darkness returns to us all.

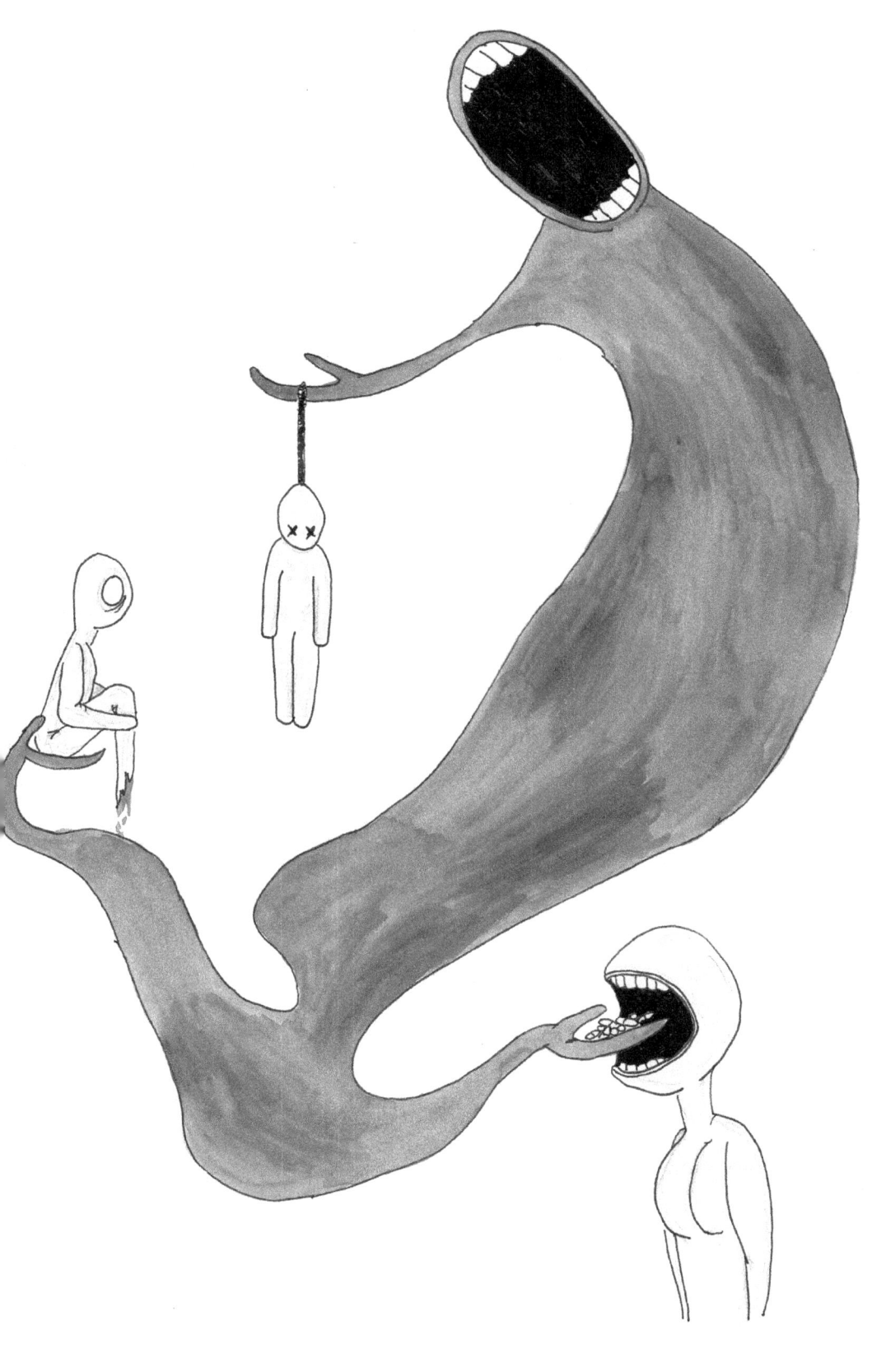

Crawling in from the sides. The great void. We were born from the infinite blackness and that is where we shall all return. We all shall learn the secret of the dead. The promise of life is the knowledge that it will end. We exist in Hell; there is only this Hell, what more could there be?

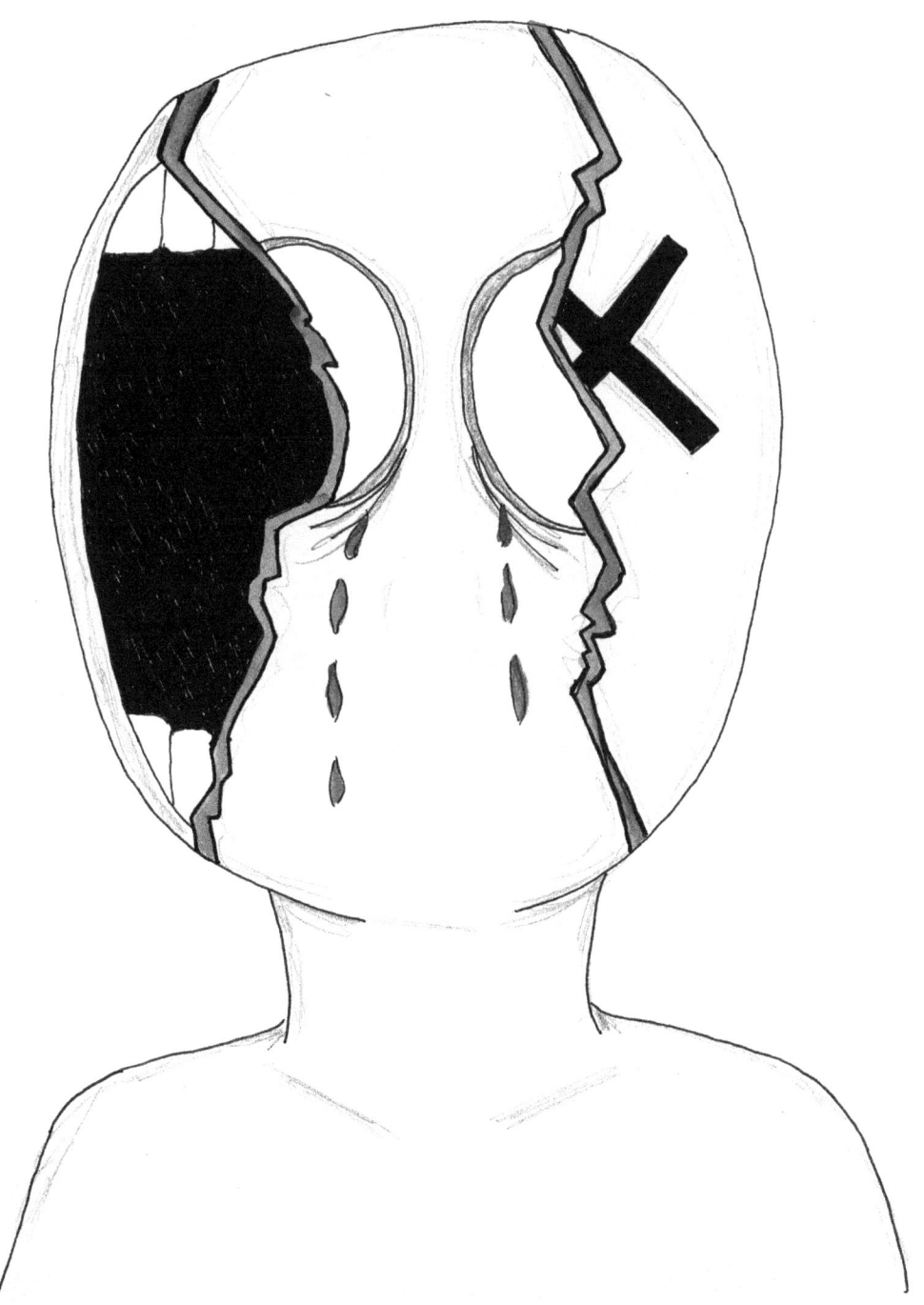

A headless girl watches over a garden of snow. Death holds her hand and tells her the time has come. Her body explodes, billions of stars erupt into the sky and everyone wakes up. They wake in the darkness. There was only the darkness, there was only the void.

And this, whatever *this* is, was but a dream.

PART TWO
THE PAIN

Pain. Constant pain. Everything hurts. The heart bleeds, the mind screams. So much noise exploding in the cage that is the head. Bleed it out on to a page. Transfer those shouts onto paper.

Dom Lyne, October 2010

How to define your life when all of a sudden you're told to change because of a name given. Everything you've been for over ten years dismissed and you're expected to change. A scream even more lost than before.

Structured by the depths of a distortion rather than reality itself. Fantasies. Defined by your addictions, by all the sex, the pills, cigarettes and needles. The screaming at the world because no one can understand. The pain too much to word. The voices in your head constantly needing to be silenced, numbed.

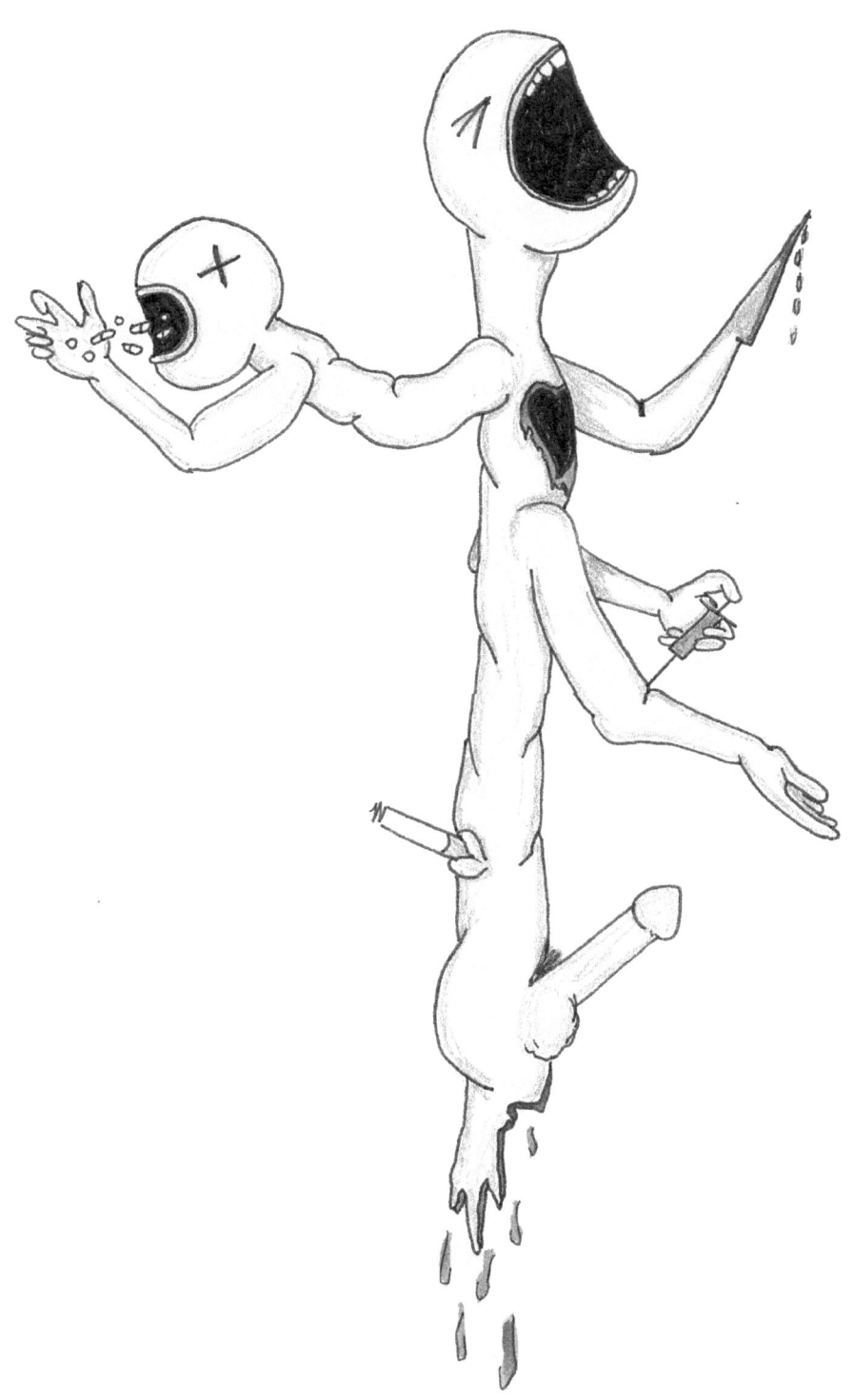

What would any of you know? How could you possibly understand the

depths of this pain? The daily torment inside this head, the self hatred.

The complete and utter sense of loss, loneliness and fear. Fear of the

darkness, the void of being alone.

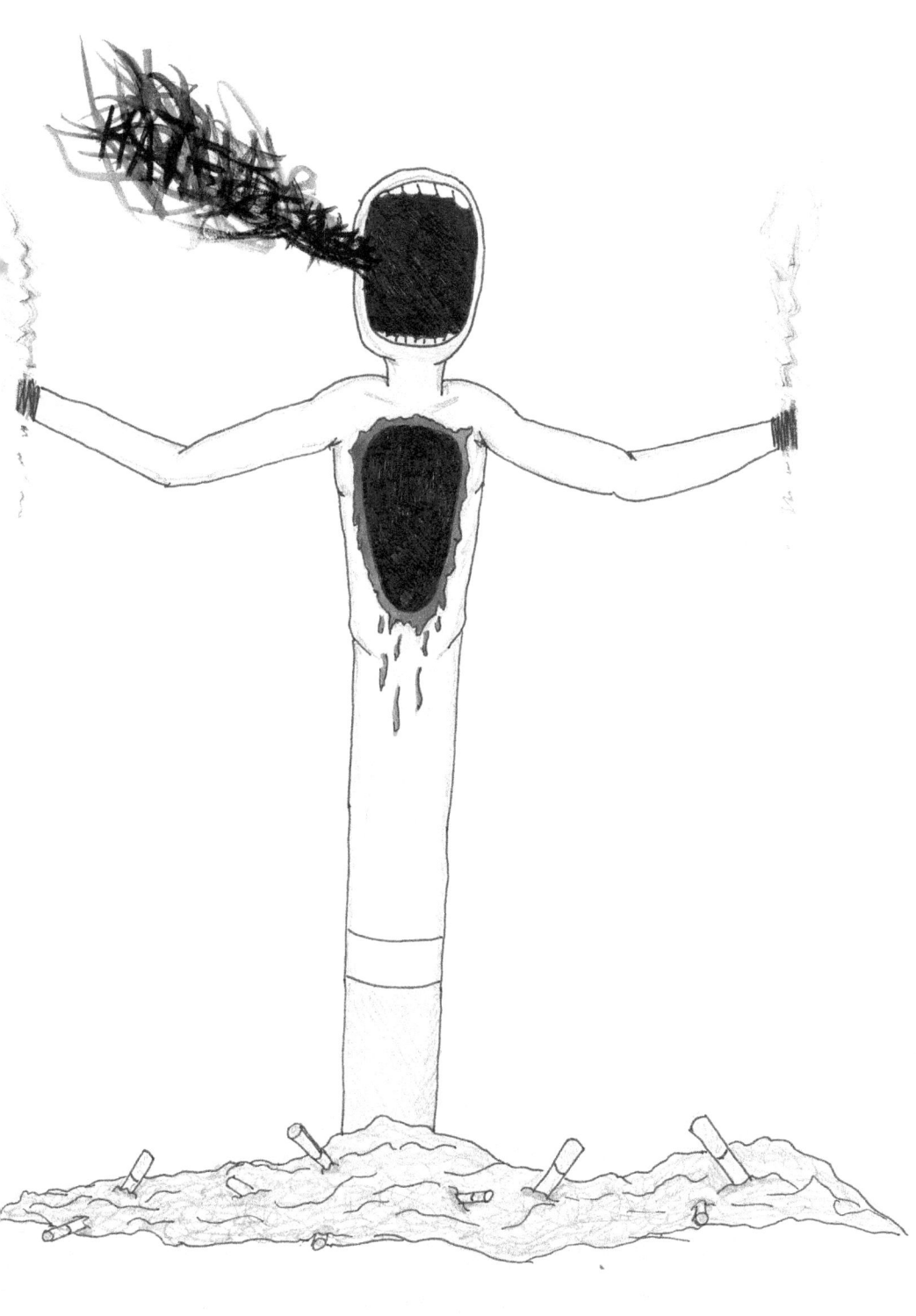

The overwhelming need to be loved, wanted; the pain of never being able to return it. The fear that surrounds everything. So you turn to the things that will only leave on your terms. The drugs never say 'no'; the vodka never breaks a shattered heart. They kiss you and silence all the noise and tell you how much nicer that feels.

A life torn between darkness and the light. Love and hate. Peace and war. A life embraced in either Heaven or Hell, unable to connect to your greyscale world. Unable to see, to understand. Lost and lonely, surrounded by angels or demons. Truth and lies.

To run, should you run? Run to something or from it? It's all a matter of hope. Hope and longing our saviours, our enemies. To dream, to feel that darkness. A pill to take it all away. This is coma. This is the Otherside. Hold the mirror to reality and what do you see? Us. The broken, the lost. The hopeless hopefuls. Dead or dying in our own heads. How could any of you understand?

The fractures, our hearts cracked and cutting glass into the mass of weeping sores that we call a soul. Never healing, never ending pain. Constant, each day a new cut, another piece lost.

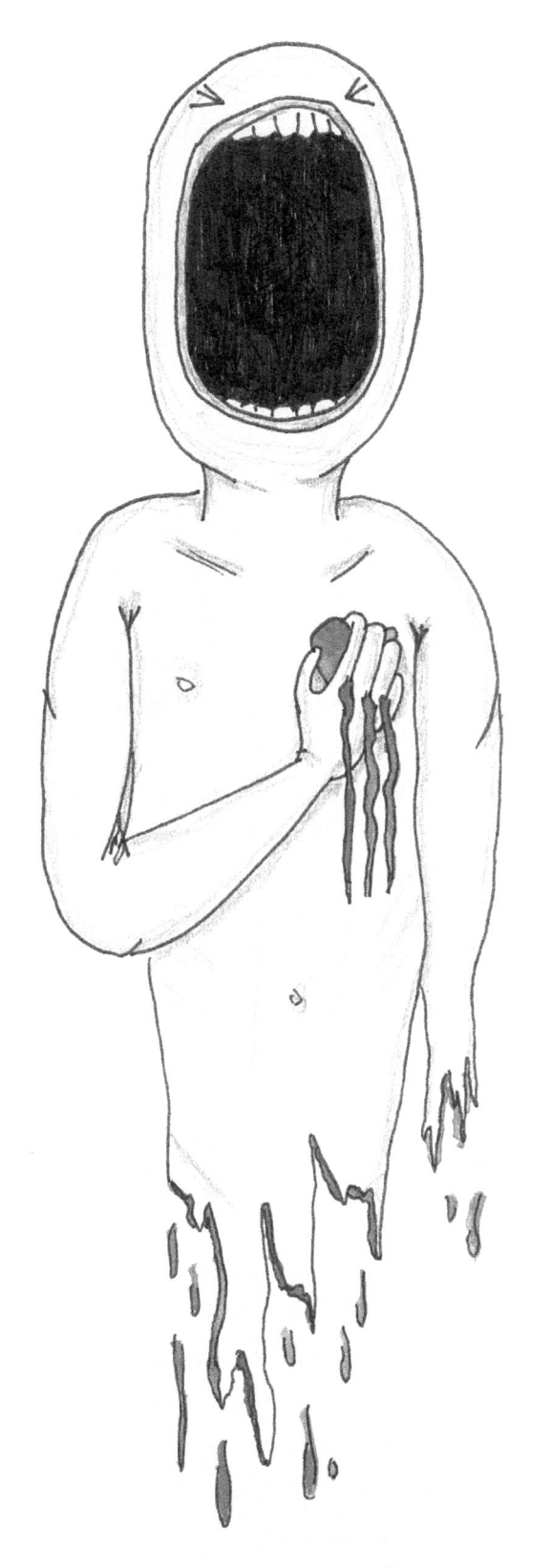

So turn to the needle, inject right into the main vein and let it kiss its way up the arm with its calm. Peace of mind can't be bought but it can be substituted.

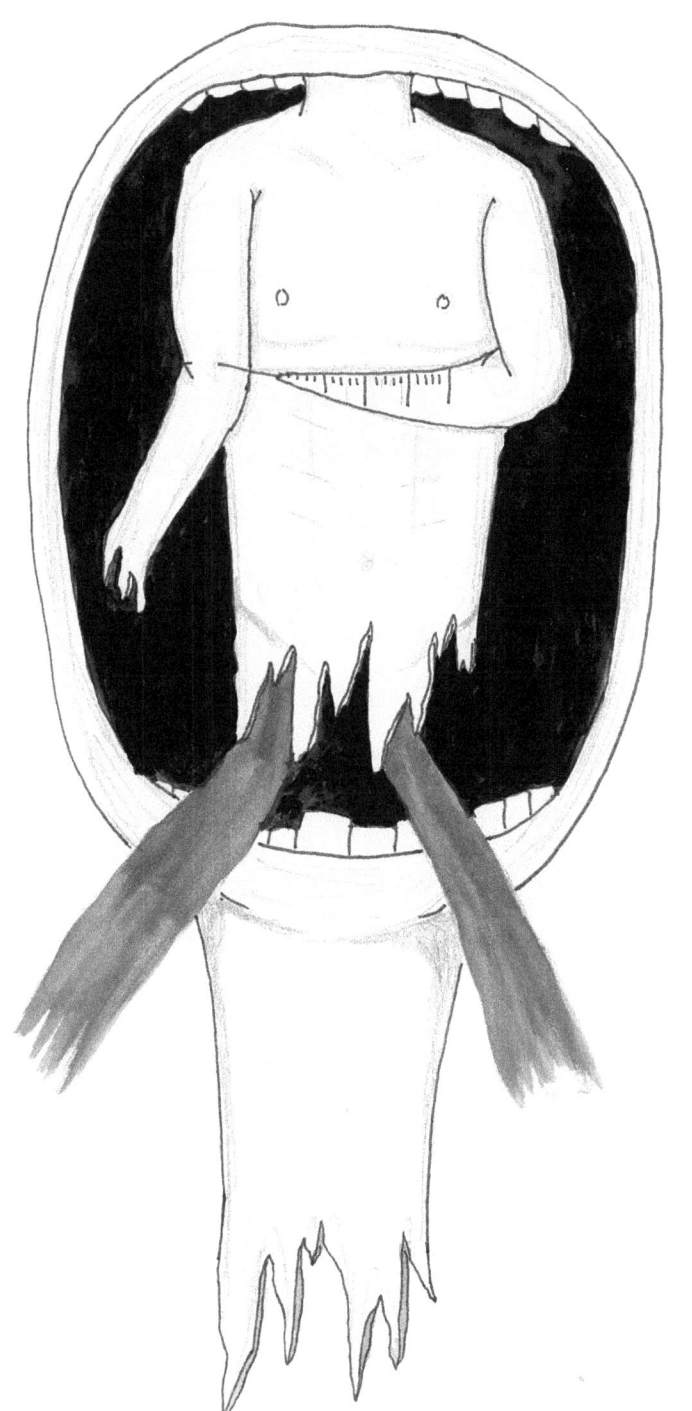

Numb our senses. The ultimate in self-harm. Our lives mapped out

by the lines on our skin. You couldn't understand, you wouldn't want

to. Tucked away safely at home you'll never feel the kiss of darkness.

Filled with hopes and dreams you'll never feel the fear of emptiness.

So you put us down. Make us feel even more worthless than we do already. Slicing our skins using words with the precision of an executioner. Forcing your world through the glass regardless of the cost. Destroying what you don't understand.

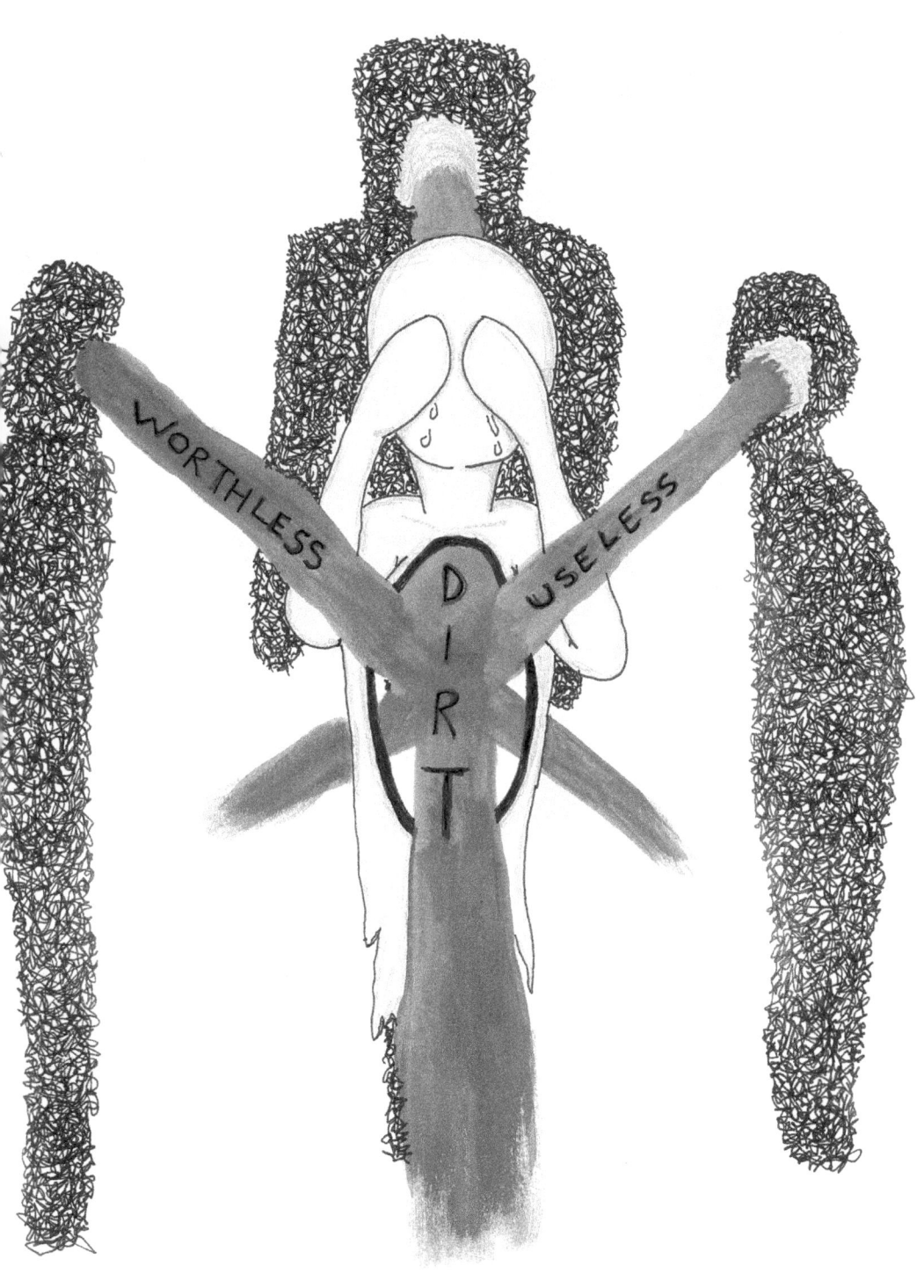

We are the abandoned, the abused. Disposed and useless. Forgotten toys from the past left to rot unwanted in silence. Huddled together under dead trees for warmth and comfort. You need not speak, just touch my hand so I know that you are there.

Take me in your arms so I don't die alone.

PART THREE
THE FEAR

We all have fears. We all have ghosts we must face up to. These fears become more concrete when they are unknown futures. Changes which are to be made. Who will I become? What will I lose?

This was delayed by a night of K, vodka and weed.

Dom Lyne, November 2010

Scared, shaking. Unable to sleep. Feel every breath, each heartbeat.

Closed eyes see only shadows. Figures looking between realms.

Reality, dream; Dream, reality. Which one is real when you exist in the middle?

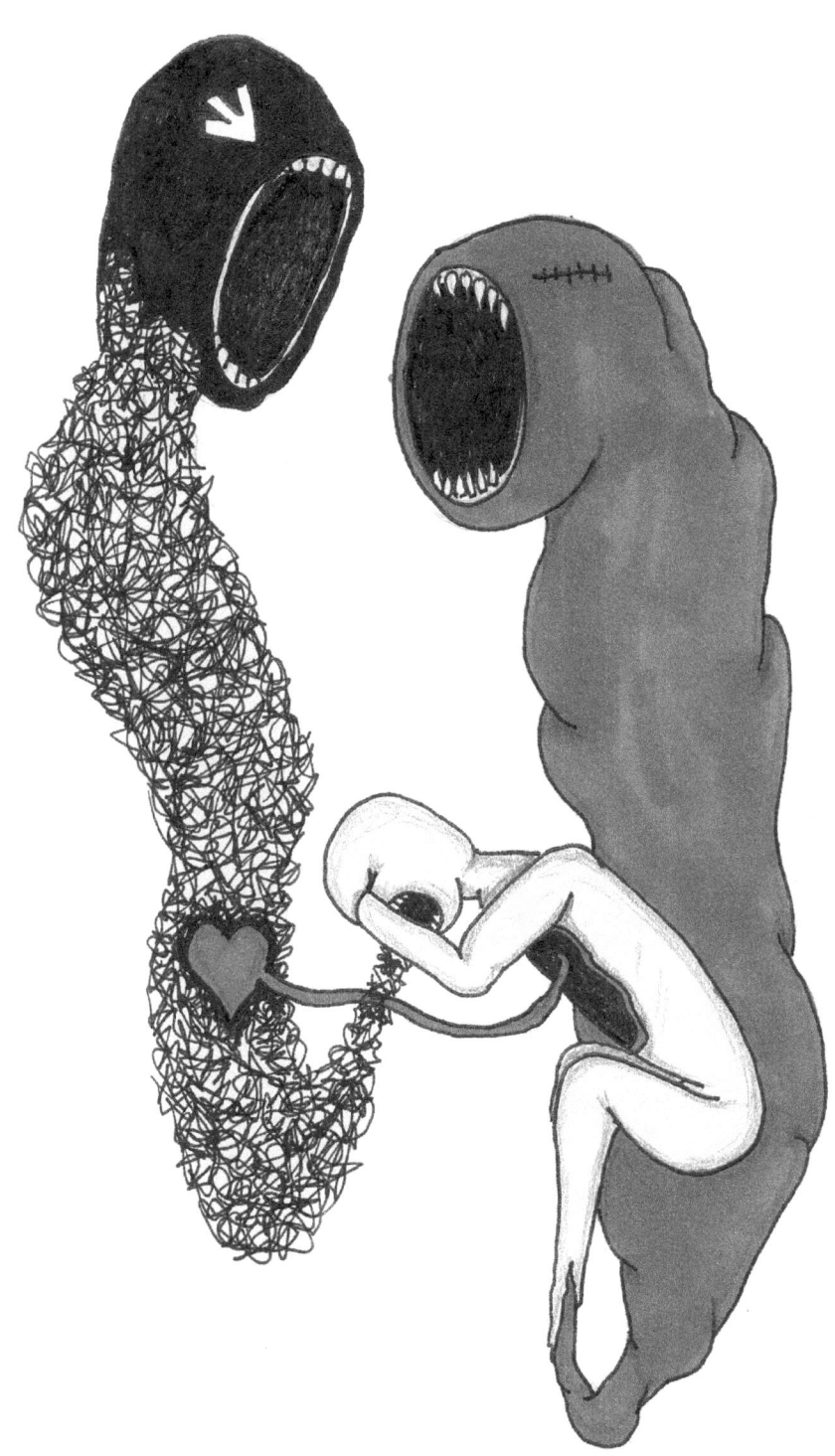

Disconnected. Constant. Black shadows bleed in from the corners. Confusion. One day it might snap. Then what? Where will that leave you?

So this life has been built on error? A fantasy built alongside your world. Change? I don't want to. Who will I be? What will I become? Most important of all, what will be the sacrifice? What will I lose?

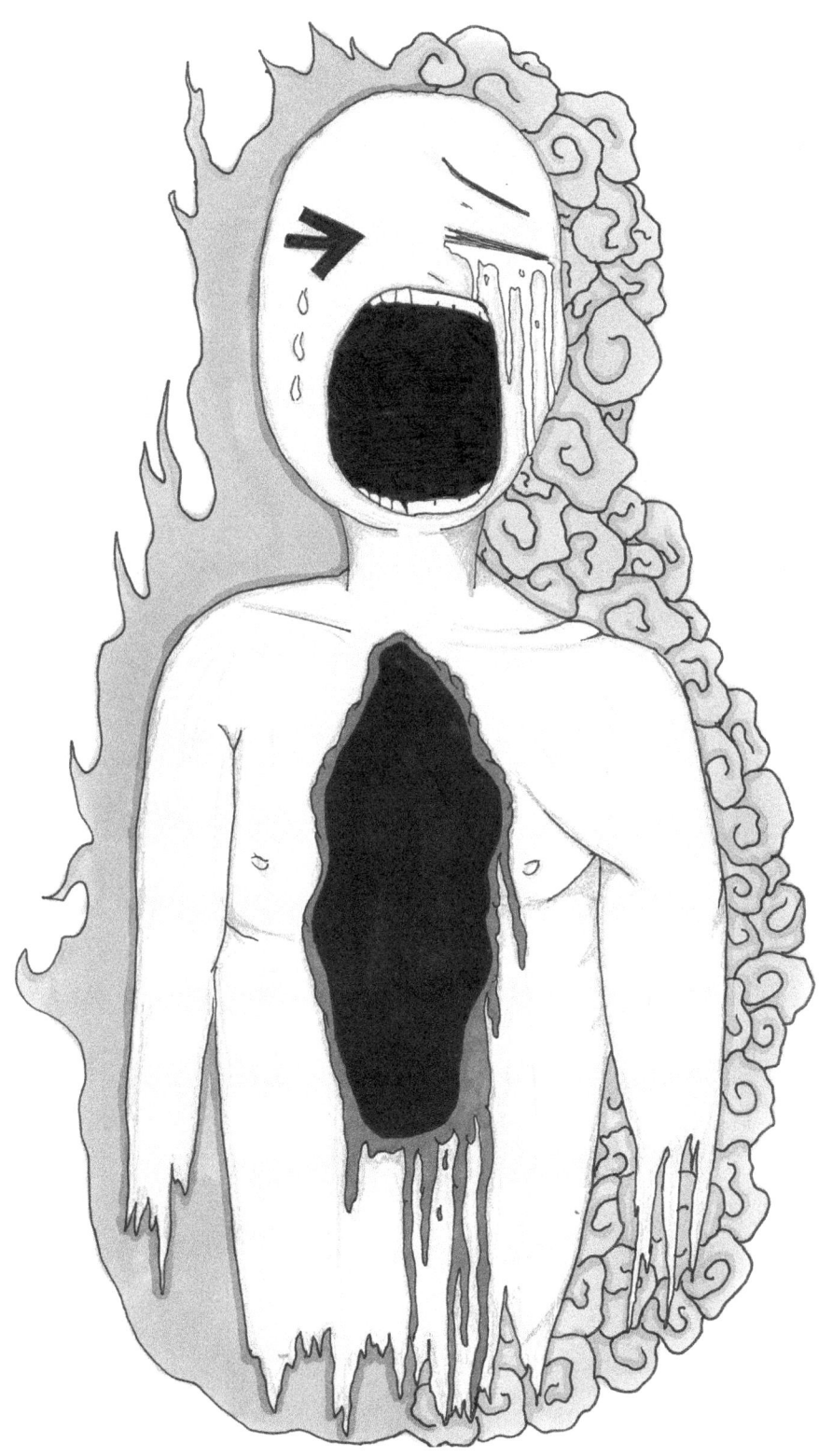

I don't want to relearn. Why can't I just exist on the hill looking down on your evil cities? Cities filled with people, actions and ideals that disgust me. Rats running around in stinking piles of coins, dressed as though they are gods. Here's your ego, you wear it on your sleeve.

Cry. Curl into a ball and cry. Always crying. Always screaming.

Pathetic boy in your world; main character in my own. Hero or villain?

That's just a point of view. §Outsider. Watcher. Winged death.

Why do you all get to live as you wish? Why are your dreams more

acceptable because you fit into the social normality? Why am I told

to be someone different because of mine? We just grew in different

worlds. Right?

Snap back to my world. My reality. None of you could exist here.

Wrapped in cotton wool you'd never be able to stand here naked to the

pain, the noise. The constant uncertainty. You all need structure, order.

Here there is only chaos.

Sit as king on a throne, my guardian behind me. My companion, my pain, my fears, my death. The figure in the shadows watching, absorbing everything. The manifestation of my inner world in yours. Can you sense its presence?

Let us not talk of love; that biggest fear of all. That creator of pain.

I could never love someone as much as I need to feel loved. Could

I? Never will I open myself completely. Your world uses that as a

weapon.

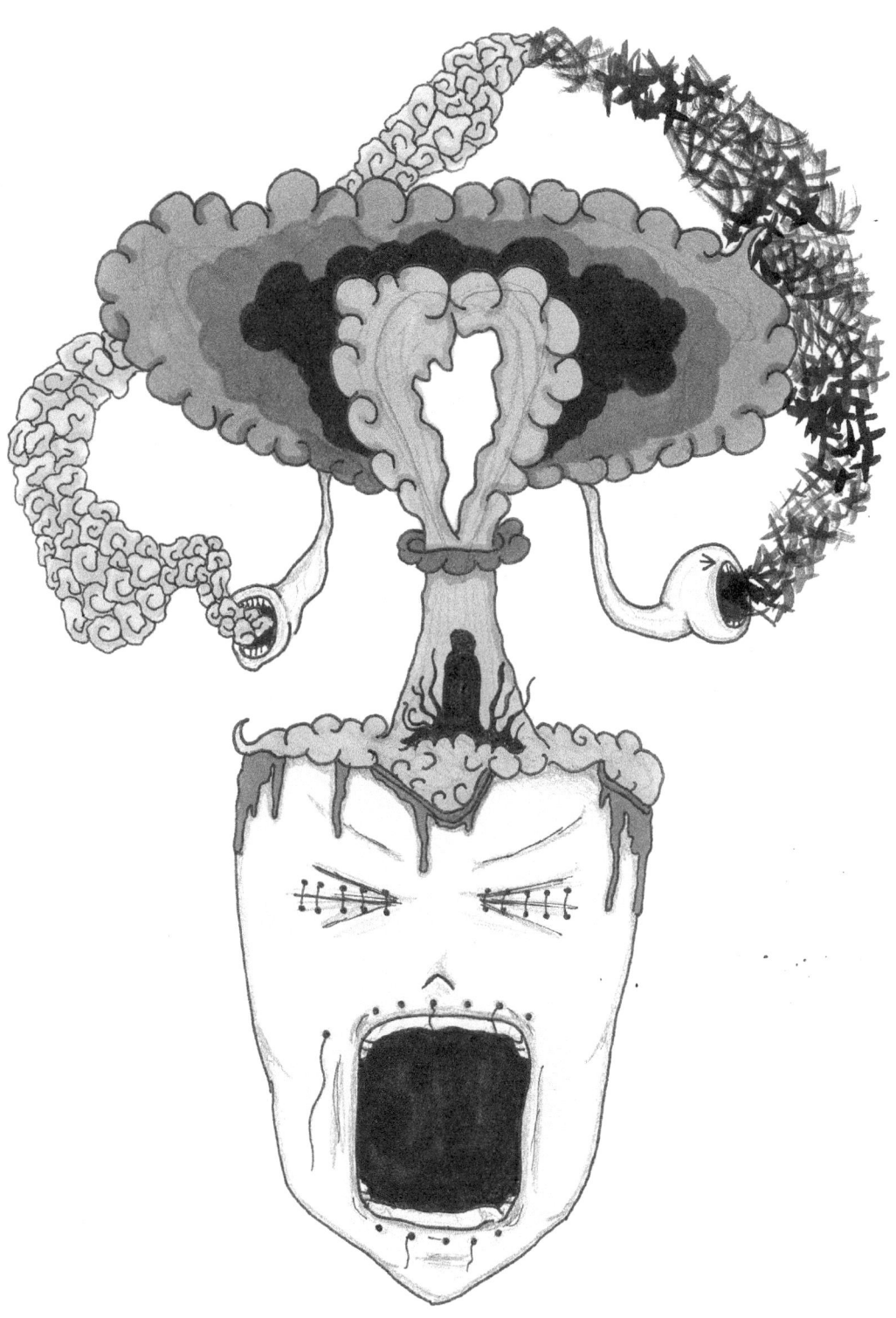

Time is running out. The world grows old and frail. I don't want to
be part of all this. The planet of bloodshed. The planet of war and
arrogance. You all make me sick. Make me sick. Your sickness feeds
mine and I can never return because I was never here to begin with.

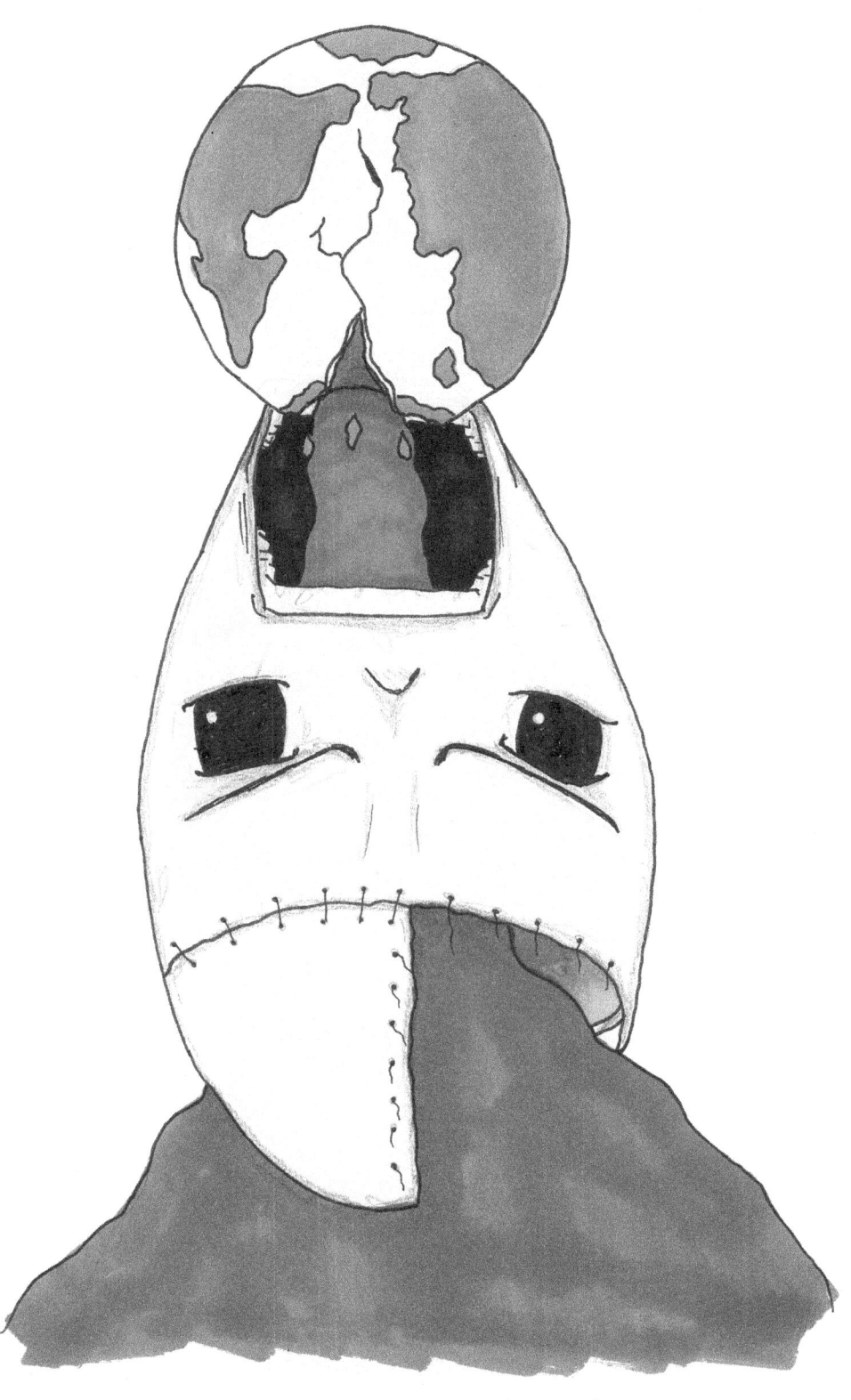

For I am a ghost. A voice in a memory. All the seeds have been sown

and now my weed will strangle all your corn.

I am the voice in the Dark. I have fear because I am fear.

BROKEN
INVISIBLE
DIRT
ANGER
FEAR
NOTHING
I AM A GHOST
FORGET ME

PART FOUR
THE FUTURE

Who knows what the future holds? Who knows where we are going to be in the final moments of our existence. How would you feel if the next few years of your life will be planned out for you by others? Think about that and then try to think how we feel.

Dom Lyne, December 2010

So what now? Where does everything go from here? A future? The future? Your future for me? Who wants future when the present is so painful?

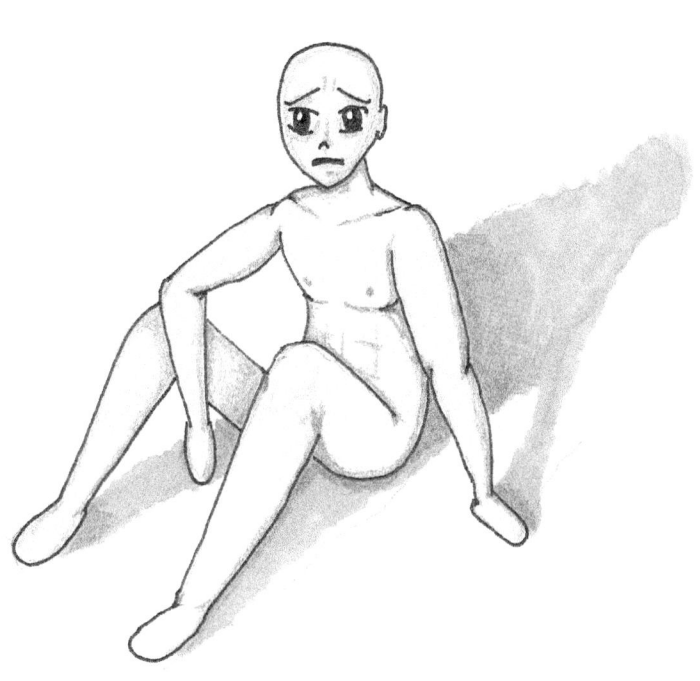

Too many unanswered questions. The void between two worlds being pulled together against their will. Is this what I need? Is this what I want? Will I actually be able to find my place in your world?

Your world, the place where pain, death and injustice roam freely.

Breathing deceitful whispers into the ears of blinded drones. There is

no place for true difference here.

I'll tell you what I want to do. I want to rip this world apart; tear it to

pieces with words. Bring its rotten carcass closer to its last breath and

stand over it as I watch it burn to ash.

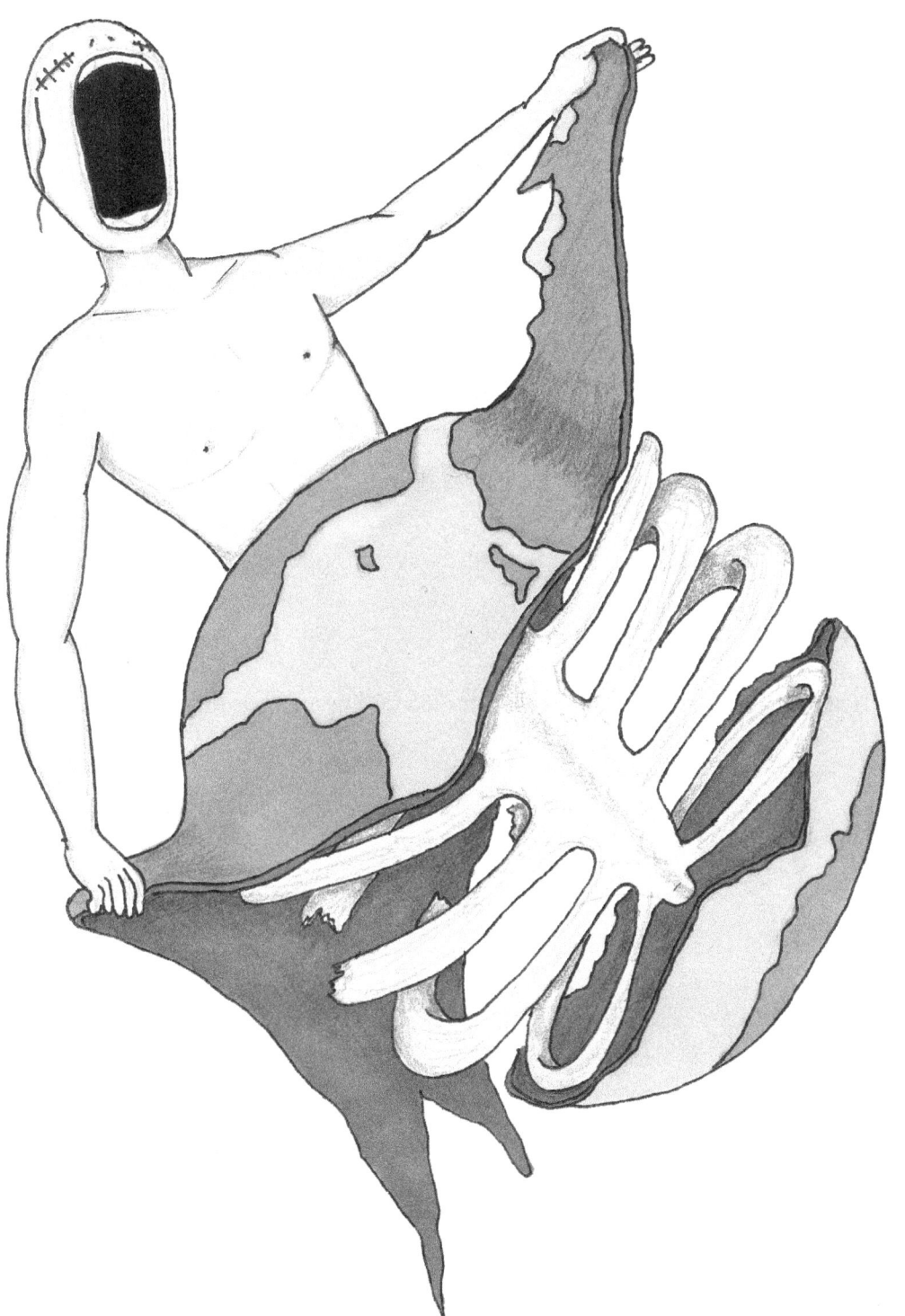

See this pen? With it I want to wash away your beauty, your innocence.

I want to corrupt your souls and pull your minds through the gutter,

leaving stains that will never wash clean. The images locked hidden

for eternity.

THERE IS NO
BEAUTY
THAT CAN'T
BE LOST
OR TAKEN

I want to tear open the crack and let the darkness seep through. This would be my world. A planet of nightmares, of screams and noise. Demons resting on all your shoulders.

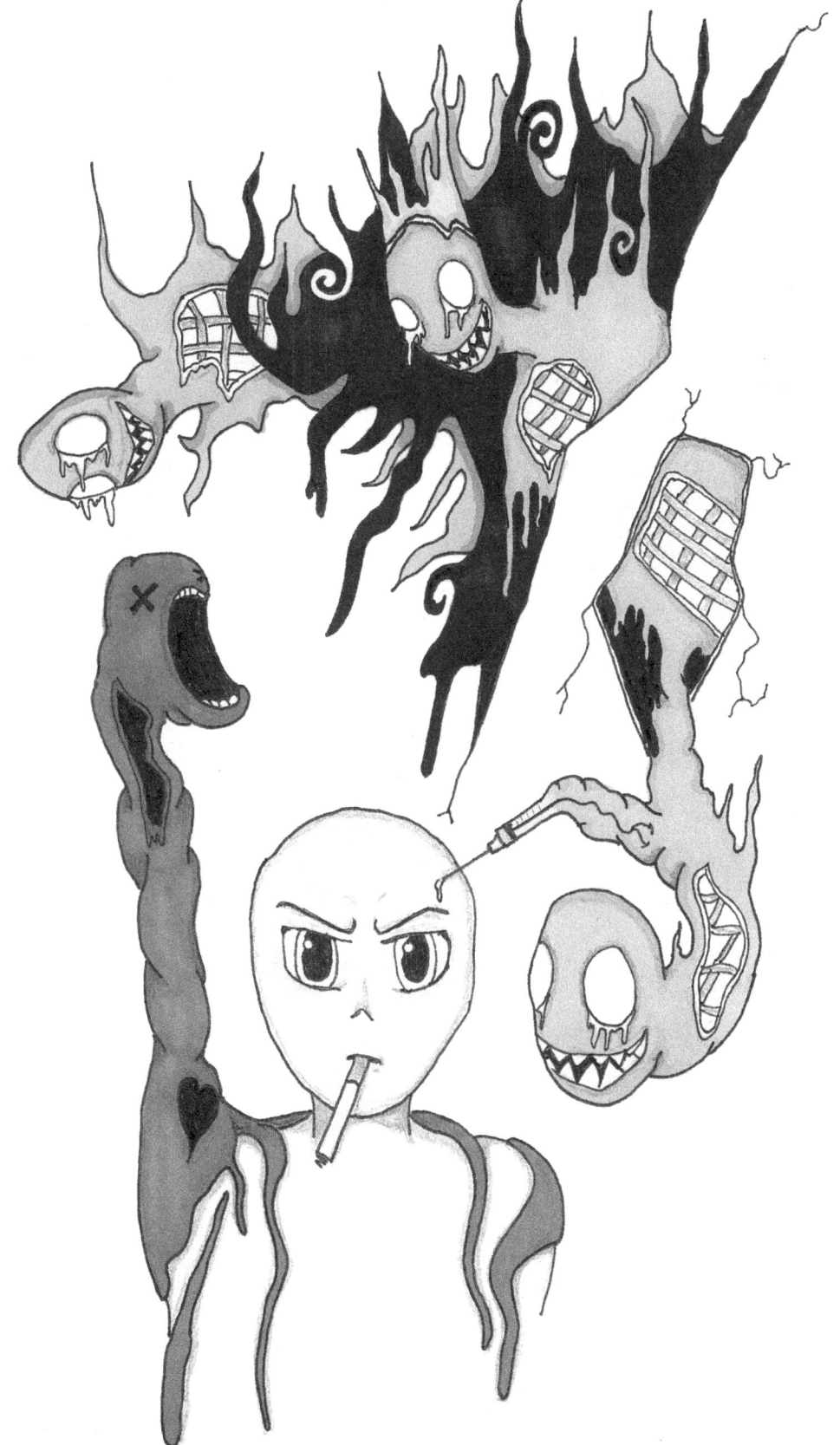

Think I can change? Can you really make a person change through a 'treatment'? Forcing order to chaos just so it slots into a box the correct way, then gift wrap it back to society. The broken are broken, fix them and they eventually break again. Hope is ever so changeable.

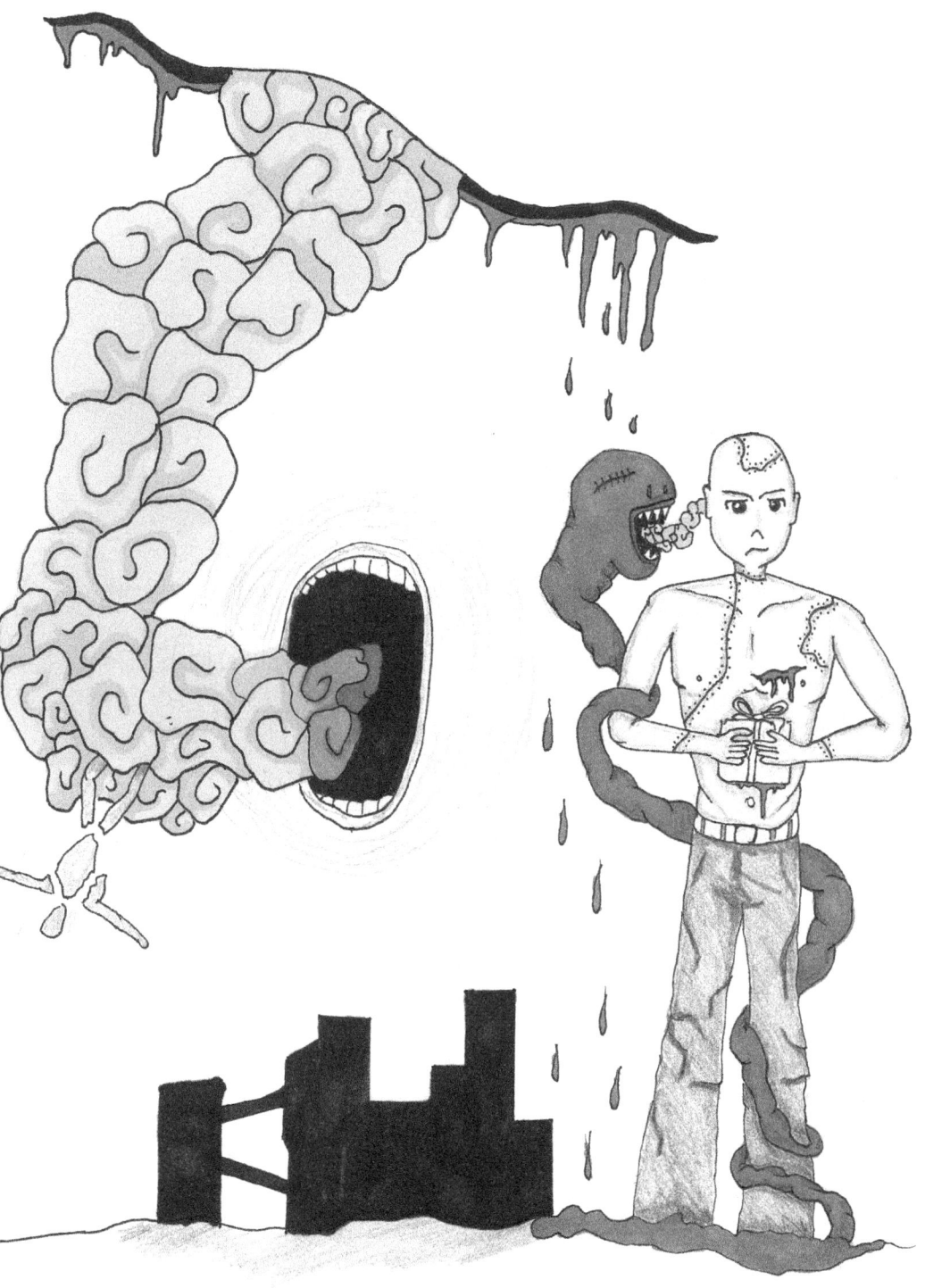

The future is a black cloud, an unknown. Ever changing. It is uncertain.

Every second pulls us closer into its arms. Days, months, years. Hopes

turn to disappointment, love to hate, life to death.

Prove me wrong. Prove to me that everything is wonderful. Don't just say it and expect me to agree, show me. Show me a better way. Show me one thing that could change my whole view. Hard task isn't it?

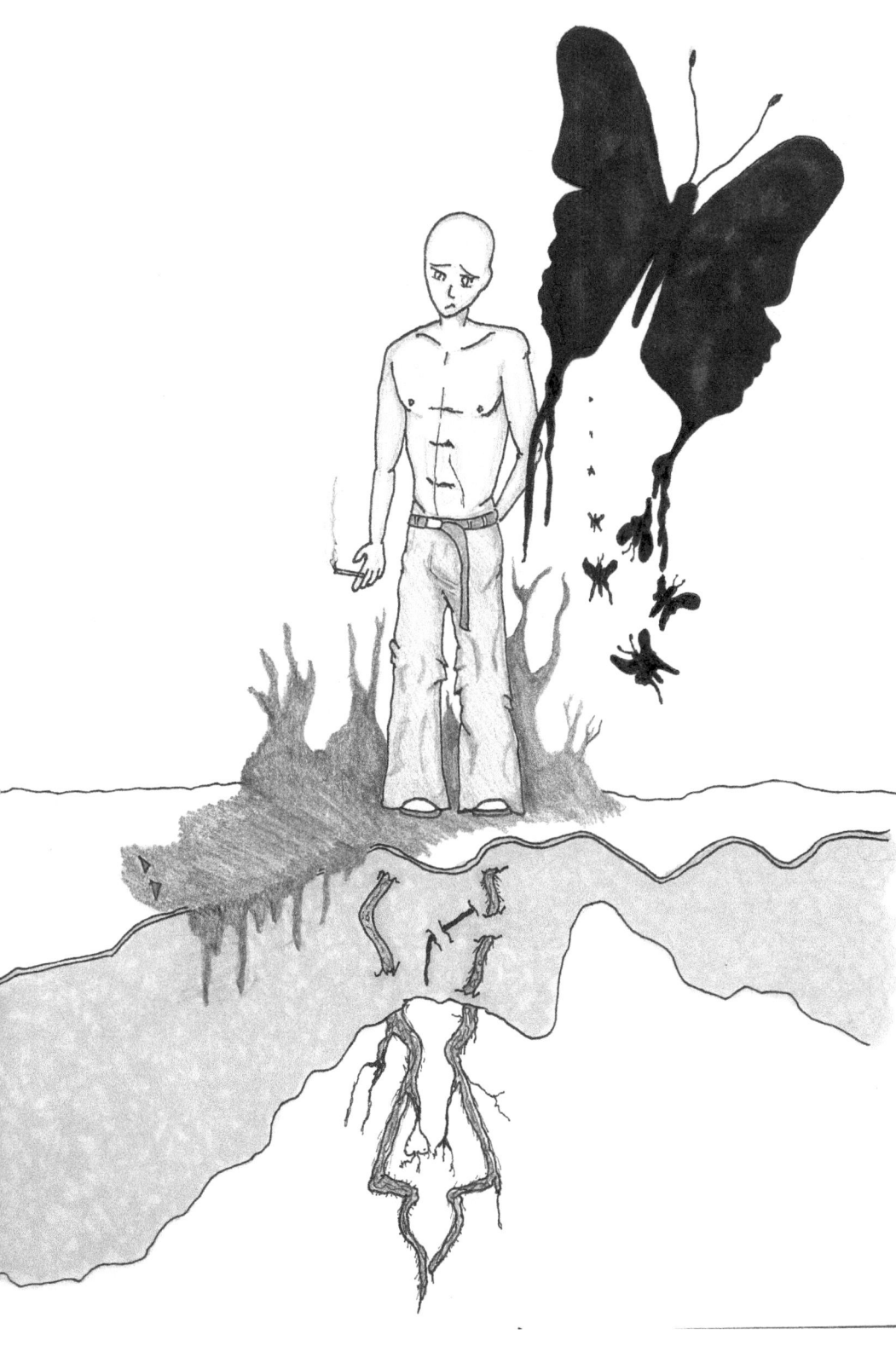

The world spins, rotates. Day becomes night. You close your eyes and sleep. Which do you truly prefer? What if you had the choice? Dream or reality? Ever thought that it's jealousy that forces you to want me to fit in.

I live on the otherside. I don't play by your rules and never have. This is my world. I decide its cast. I control it and make it what it is, or at least I try. If dreams came true, you'd all be dead.

We all rot in the end. That is the conclusion.

CYCLE-2

LYING WASTED UNDER A BROKEN CODA

2010
JULY

So, you think you're invincible? Maybe I did. Survived so many years getting through it my way but now my body says 'no'. When the mental becomes physical in the most disgusting of rashes then that's when you need to take action.

One little bit of stress and 'whoosh', hello elephantiasis. Makes you hate yourself even more than you do already. Then you get the panic attacks, the claustrophobia. Pressure making you want to flee the scene of where you are.

So maybe now it's the time I finally take a bow and accept I've been beaten. After ten years of coping I can't take anymore. I need help, proper help. Eep, I'm scared. Maybe they'll tell me I'm totally fine, maybe they won't. Let's see shall we…

Soul

Bleed

For What
Comes Out
Something Must
Go Back In

Death get
fat

Feels like I've committed myself. Fifteen minutes sat across from a doctor and I've been prescribed meds and put forward for psychological therapy. Fun. Certified mental heath case. Who'd of thought it? After ten years of dealing with the darkness, I've finally cracked. This is the point I may realise that if I had gone and got it seen to years ago, I'd have lived a happy existence. Nah, what fun would that have been? I've enjoyed it, the darkness touching my soul, damn you body for not keeping up, no actually damn you for giving up! You're meant to be my partner in crime and you've let me down.

So where do I find myself? The Black Cap, sat with a pint of Peroni whilst I can still drink. Great, so you're not meant to drink whilst on these fucking pills. Let's see how long that lasts. 'Alcohol is a depressant.' 'Yeah Doc, you're right, but it damn sure does a good job at numbing the pain.'

That's my problem I guess, I'm so good at numbing pain rather than actually dealing with it. On a side tangent, painful is looking at the guy in front's builder's crack. Not pleasant, although it is rather smooth, he just moved... eww, that sums it up totally. Commando is such a bad look for him. When you see that ass, think how many cocks have gone up it.

So where was I? Oh yeah, numbing pain. Maybe this will be an epiphany. A way forward. I've admitted defeat. Damn you! Damn you!

'The fact you've acknowledged your problem and brought yourself here is a good sign. It shows that there's hope for you.'

Gee, thanks. Hope. Wot the fuck is hope all about? Hope is changeable. It's uncertain, it's a possibility.

Okay, he's not commando, but he does have the ugliest pair of boxers I've ever seen. They probably cost £2.50 or something lame like that.

Pint number two. Moved away from the gorilla and his butt showing lover – I'm only assuming they're lovers, they look like they could be. Drinking alone. Hello self. Pfft, that's probably the reason all this therapy will conclude is the cause of all this. Loneliness. The lost and lonely all pilled into 'happiness' so that they maintain their use to society. I'm surprised I didn't swear at the doc. I almost did but I cut it short.

Gorilla man and bare butt boy just kissed. I was right, lovers.

Shit. Is this the point after twenty-seven years that I start learning about myself? Do I really want to know?

Cheers thanks. God, I'm alone and got no one outside the obvious family to talk to about it. Don't know if I really want this second pint. Drinking it anyway. Haven't eaten properly since… dunno, just had a few pathetic meals at the market.

In all honesty I'm actually truly scared. I don't want to be on meds but I now don't have a choice. If I don't take them I'm gonna keep flaring up in a rash and that'll make me feel shitter.

Oh my God! That guy has cool boxers, smiley faces and stuff like that. I want them.

'Occasionally thoughts of suicide or self harm may occur, or may increase in the first few weeks of treatment for depression…'

Ooh fun. Can't wait.

So, first day on the meds, didn't start too well given that I took them after four pints of beer and a shag. Hmmm, so much for 'responsible' drinking. Anyway, how do I feel? Well, apart from losing track in my conversations, I don't feel any different. Still think the same and react the same.

That's the strange thing, I feel no different, no change in attitude at all. I know they said it would take a few weeks but meh, I was kinda expecting something. The only change that I can note is that after three pints of San Miguel, one bottle of Budwiser and five vodkas and lemonade I don't feel drunk at all. Nothing. Usually by this point I'd be a bit wankered. But no, nothing.

So yeah, so much for not drinking whilst on these pills. Oops, fucked that right from the start.

28 JULY 2010

Been up since 7:30. I can't say I feel any different. No change in thought, I react the same. Daydream off into the same thoughts. I know these pills aren't meant to be miracles but they haven't even made my feelings worse as the packaging warns. Guess it's only day two of being on them. Pfft. I can't even say if it's stopped the rash because I haven't been stressed out enough to cause it. Haha.

Sat in McDonalds this morning, eating their processed meat and mutantly perfect shaped eggs, and I got my usual feeling in my head, like my mind is going to just snap, like I'm gonna simply awake from a coma aged five and have to live a whole new life. It's all a bit weird. I'm paying more attention to myself than I normally do, it's like I'm understanding how I am not just what I feel. Still can't stop thinking that way. Maybe the only way to change someone's nature is to give them a new brain.

Deep sigh I guess. Settled, today has been alright in the shop. New people next door. Talking to the lady keeps my mind off shit coz it's just random talk, none of the usual 'it's so bad today' bollocks you get here. "STARS WHEN YOU SHINE, YOU KNOW HOW I FEEL."

GAH! WELL HORNY. MY BONER WON'T GO AWAY! WANK... WANK...
CUM!!!

I guess this is something I'll have to get used to again. Being alone. Constantly. Life goes on and I'm not a part of it. Locked in an ivory tower I view the world through a frosted window. Disconnected. Singular. Solitary. Some things are actually too much to bear. Living a life in silence is one of them.

The invisible boy. No one sees him. He's a ghost. A memory. What happens to a memory? It fades, it corrupts and withers. An autumnal leaf fallen, rotten away to dust. A leaf falling off a dead rose, one for every cut on the heart, for every bitter word that slices the skin like a scalpel blade. Red raw and never healing. If you could see my soul, all you'd see is a mass of weeping sores.

I can see more of my scars across my torso. That old road map of pain forcing itself into my subconscious. The start is always visible at the end. Full circle. Don't pray from me, I'm already dead. Gone. Curled up and lost. Hidden somewhere in this stupid head of mine. Screaming my way through the never ending maze in my brain and finding only dead ends for all that effort.

I once hoped you would listen. It's pretty clear now you don't, won't, never have. So much belief in a foolish notion.

Falling, falling. Falling

IF YOU HAVE
NOTHING
TO BEGIN WITH
YOU HAVE
NOTHING
TO LOSE.

After the initial glum awakening, I'm actually in a good mood this morning. Like woke up in one. Now that's a first I guess. Maybe it's the pills or maybe it's just a good mood. If it's the former then how pathetic is that? Happiness I can't get normally granted by a small pill.

I keep getting boners. I thought the libido was meant to be cut.

Oh it was just a natural high. One bad encounter with *him* and I'm shaking like shit, no different. One good mood squashed flat on its face because *he* couldn't talk to me civil, like I was just an inconvenience. An hour and a half later and I'm still freaking out.

Deep breath. In... out... everything is okay.

No crashing and burning. Stop it. Fucking stop it Dom. Get a hold of yourself. It's all gonna be fine. We've been heading to this point for ten years. This is the salvation we wanted, needed. Maybe. This is the ultimate low. It's getting no better or worse, so let's just try and stay positive.

We'll be okay...

EVERYTHING WILL BE OKAY.

fucking hell... finger on neck and count to four.

One... two... three... four...

119

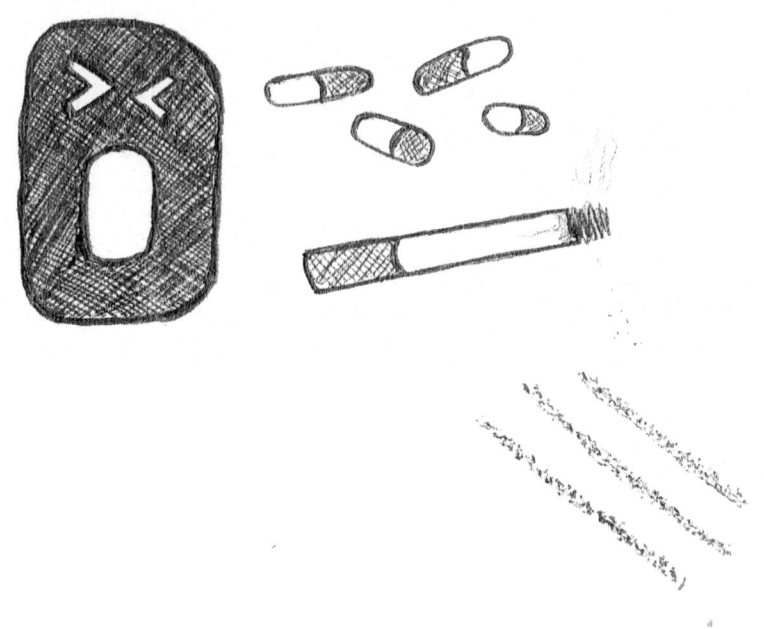

Pfft… today I just can't be arsed. Didn't sleep much last night… no surprise there and now I just wanna stay in bed for once and not have to face the stupid world outside.

Can't believe how alone I feel. I've actually got no one around me. *He's* gone and just pushed me aside all over a freak out where I pretty much just said exactly what his ex said, but for him to say it is justified, for me to is just like shitting on your grandmother's grave for no reason other than 'because I could.' So yah, talk to me like crap and step away from the broken child. Pfft, give me a fucking break.

So I'll just exist here, with nothing, with no one. Just the forgettable entity. Dom the ghost. Dom the inconvenience. Ahh, fuck off all of you.

Bad day today. Just couldn't be arsed.

I CREATE
MY BEST
WHEN I AM
AT MY WORST

SLEEP

BRING ME THE HEAD OF GOD
AND WE'LL SEE WHO'S LISTENING
NOW.

ALONE...
           ALWAYS FUCKING ALONE

Really couldn't give a SHIT
                    today

Him: *I'm just mad you're drinking but then it's not my problem eh. Stick to what you said and take care of yourself for a change, I'll keep my nose out.*

Me: Thanks

Him: *I know you're not well but it's hard for me when you can barely look at me, let alone talk to me. I'm just gonna shut up, I'm making myself angry.*

Me: I can barely look at anyone coz I feel so insignificant. I have nothing of any worth and I have no one. I'm alone. I deserve it coz I'm such a stupid and shit person but that never stops it hurting. At the end of the day no one needs to have to deal with me. I'm worthless so why waste energy?

Him: *You're not worthless to me, or the business, so I will never treat you so. And self-punishment is no way to be treating yourself. What has happened in the past is irrelevant. You're a beautiful person and you need to find out for yourself why. But you are.*

Me: I'm not a beautiful person. If I was I wouldn't keep ending up in the same place. I'm just there, an inconvenience that won't fuck off. I'm disposable.

Him: *Then if that's what you really believe then change. Don't waste another breath even saying it. Put it behind you and look forward.*

Me: I did and look where I ended up. Full fucking circle. Nothing. Maybe that's me. Nothing. I have nothing.

Him: *You have a home, a business with huge potential, talent, health, looks, friends and family. That's not nothing.*

Me: I have a home I don't pay for. The business is yours. Wot good is talent when no one cares? Health is debatable; looks are nonexistent. Friends are pretty much the same. And family are the only reason I'm still here.

I fucking hate all this 'if you don't like it you can change it' bollocks. Like I haven't tried to change, I just end up locked in the same fucking situation. *Here*. On my fucking own.

If I'm myself, no one likes me. If I'm someone else, no one likes me. Who the hell am I meant to be? A puppet for everyone? Use me, mould me, I'm yours to abuse.

124

WTF is wrong with me? Am I that bad a person?

Fuck it
it's all bullshit at the
end of the day

2010
AUGUST

YOU KNOW THERE'S A PROBLEM
WHEN RADIOHEAD SOUNDS
LIKE HAPPY MUSIC!

"I don't do boyfriends."
never has a throw away comment made
something so clear.

fuck... i bet he has.
just a feeling. i maybe
wrong...
... i mean i have,
so where's the problem?
i'm just a fuck
up!

Maybe love doesn't exist. Maybe I've spent my life chasing a concept.
An illusion.

Always wanting what I can't have.

Question:

To Dom, I'm just as freak as you and I'm 16. Were you the way
you are today when you had my age?'

Answer:

Oh yes, exactly the same.

ANOTHER DAY
DONE

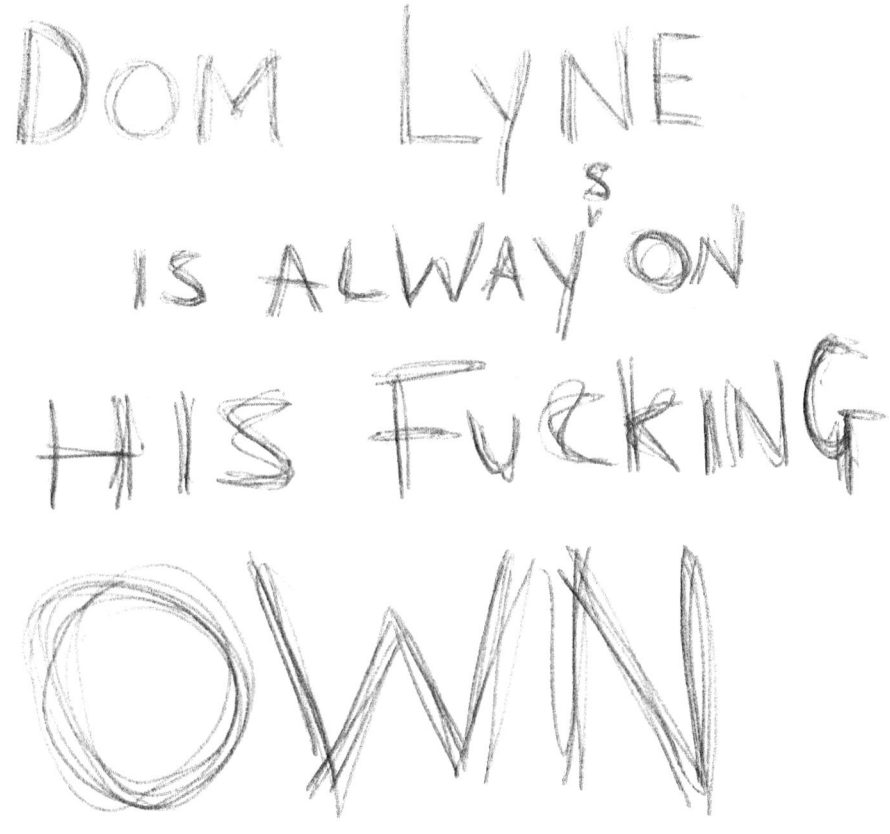

I got angry today. I threw a lighter but it kept bouncing so I threw a glass. It shattered. I almost trashed the flat but I stopped myself from doing that.

Fuck, cunt, shit, wank.

03 AUGUST 2010

Painted the flat today, well my bedroom. Yeah it was white. Took three hours, go so bored, was like standing in a great big white box, but a least it stopped me thinking, just zoned out and painted away to my heart's content (maybe not). No cigarette break, no tea break. Just done.

Bastard paint though! If I hadn't needed to go buy it, I wouldn't have spent £90 on a new pair of Levi's and some shorts! That wouldn't have happened if I had a slave!

Ate KFC. Haven't eaten since lunch on Sunday and that was just a pizza. Bad I know.

Oh... oh yeah. I had sex with a stranger. It was alright. From what I learnt after he's from Basildon and works as a chef at the Ice Wharf. In all honesty, I couldn't care.

He was more into me that I was him anyway. But shhh... I didn't clock watch so that's a good sign.

ALL IT TAKES IS A WEEK
TO BE DISCARDED AND
FORGOTTEN

from daily contact to nothing
and all without a feeling
of loss or regret.
THANKS

ANYONE KINDA FEEL REPLACED? I was there only for when they needed me

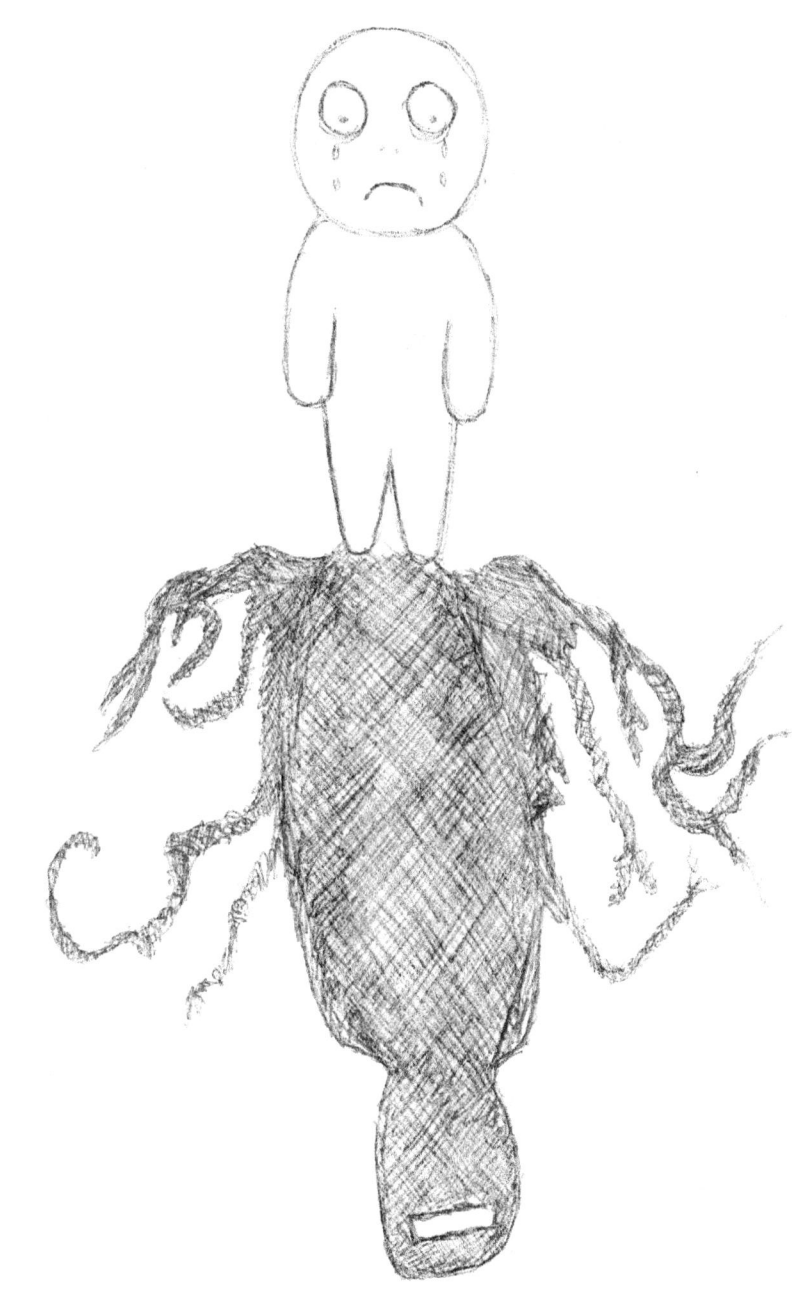

I love *him*. I love him so much it hurts, but what does he care? Nothing. I'm just a friend now. He can't even look me in the eye anymore. No interest in my company. I'm just there for when I'm needed.

It fucking hurts. Mother tell me why it hurts so fucking much. Why do these tears keep falling? Why can't this heart heal? Why can't I be happy and have someone who loves me equally in return? It's just a never ending circle. The last year and this repeating. I lost him at exactly the same time.

Why can't I switch off my feelings like they do to me? Why does it cut me so deep? So many questions and never any answers.

WHEN WILL I WAKE FROM THIS DREAM?

Wot does it say about you when *he* would rather happier spend time and have fun with the ex that abused him and fucked with his head than you? And he can't even tell me to my face but through text message. Am I really that insignificant? That meaningless? Oh did you forget that you'd already said you'd come out with me and my mum this week? I guess you did.

He gave him his heart...
He only had one to give.

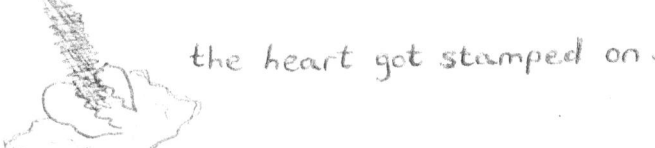

the heart got stamped on.

he screamed
and cried
in PAIN

'I want to be someone else or I'll explode.'

What am I? What was I? An easy option, a chance to feel a little bit like you wanted, something to get comfort from, a bit of intimacy, a sense of feeling loved. You took them and what did you give back? Confusion. Play on emotions; play with a heart just to feel something. Convenience. Then what? Too intense so that's it, stops. Your terms. No loss to you is it? You'll find it elsewhere as you look at the cages containing all the hearts you have stolen. That must be such a satisfying feeling.

What of me? What do I have? A talent no one cares about. A lonely existence. A body scared to trust because it knows one day everything will be thrown back in its face. Disposable. Easy. Everyone just takes and never gives unless they have something to gain. Maybe I'm meant to be alone, I'm not meant to find happiness. I'm not meant to share my life with anyone. I'm SHIT. Even *you* got bored of me the quickest you have over anyone.

What happened to the old school? The person not scared to tell his feelings. The one who risked everything, even friendship to tell me he loved me? Did I kill that? I guess I did.

Why would *he* want me anyway? He's perfect. Good looking, nothing about him would disappoint anyone. So why should he limit himself to someone crap like me. All I do is make him look better. 'You're cute but he's fucking hot.'

WHY WOULD ANYONE WANT TO LIMIT THEMSELVES TO ME?

I'M JUST A DISAPPOINTMENT, A WASTE. NOTHING. DIRT. CRAP.

136

SAVE YOURSELVES FROM ME

I USED TO BELIEVE LOVE COULD LAST FOREVER...

Fairy tales are lies… that kind of love does not, cannot, exist.
Fucking couples, all loved up. Argh!

The world continues to turn even if you stand still.

06 AUGUST 2010

Called GP. Got new prescription. They've raised my dosage to 20mg a day. 'We put you on the lower dosage to get your body used to it.' Why thanks. Got two weeks of these and then they're gonna reassess my dosage again. Woohoo. Great.

So anyway. Spent last night at *his*. Was okay. Shared the bed, although I didn't know if I was allowed to sleep there at first. We hugged. We fucked. Then he held me all night. It was nice. He even jacked one off over my ass whilst he thought I was asleep.

I actually slept okay. Kinda content in the knowledge that I felt comfort in it. It's the only way I'll feel his touch. I know it isn't love from his side; that I give him a sense of intimacy but last night I felt safe. It's better to have something than nothing at all right?

So yeah, took the new dosage. So I guess this is the point this becomes a bit more happier and less, erm, depressing.

DEEP BREATH # 3069

WE HAD SEX 4 TIMES

HE SAYS:
Someone needs to take care of you, you can't even do that ...

... you'd happily drink every day.

ME SAYS:
Yeah you're right.

138

Everyone has fun and I'm just left to get bored. Always the way. Can't find people who stimulate me.

if the WORLD ended tomorrow

i'd be really HAPPY.

Stupid hey?

I make such a mess.

HELLO RAIN

hee my mood effects the weather.

People who know nothing about them will disappoint carry themselves in a different manner. More confident, arrogant. It must be such a nice feeling to know that.

TRY NOT TO THINK ABOUT IT.

08 AUGUST 2010

An invite but who was it going to be to? That question in your head. Stuck. Who did *he* want to go round to his for meal and movie? You tell yourself it's meant for you but that bit at the back of your mind says otherwise. It's locked there now. And if he had asked someone else would you ever find out?

The whole fucking none drinking lark lasted one day. One beer and four vodka and cokes later and I'm still alive. So anger, hello anger. You gayed yourself up to impress. Will you be home by twelve like you did when we went to Pride? Oh no, of course you won't, you'd have more fun and wotever. Wanker. Never put that effort into me. Go jack off your fucking wanker of an ex and do what you have to. I'm nothing more than your fuck buddy at the end of the day. What do you care? What the *fuck* do you care? Go fuck off. I'm just convenient at the end of the day.

I want more alcohol. Drink myself to oblivion. Why am I not even tipsy? Everyone else is wasted. For fucksake. Bollocks. Who gives a fuck? It's all circular anyway, so why not spiral to oblivion.

You put effort in. What does it matter. Wot does any of all this fucking

Shit

Matter

I'M NOTHING
I'M NOTHING
I'M NOTHING
I'M NOTHING
I'M NOTHING
I'M NOTHING
I'M NOTHING
I'M NOTHING
I'M NOTHING
I'M NOTHING
I'M NOTHING
I'M NOTHING
I'M NOTHING

I'M NOTHING!

09 AUGUST 2010

All I can see in my head is *him* snuggled up with someone else. Digging his boner into them. Having sex with that ex and not giving me a second thought. Just as long as he gets his dick wet.

How many lovers will he need until he's satisfied?

Bastard out having fun, kissing randoms and fucking around coz he has the confidence and the looks to do so. Well ain't that lucky for him.

ARGH!!

Welcome to my head, my pointless fucking way of thinking. Stupid but I can't get that image out of my mind. *Him* and *that* ex, the one he loves and had 'a passionate' relationship with. The main cause of his 'problems' fucking. Argh, get out of my head. I could sit here and be like, 'no they won't do it' but fact of the matter is they would and most likely have – by now a few times.

A better fuck than we would have had, I mean I'm such a fucking disappointment.

STOP IT. STOP IT. GET THE FUCK OUT OF MY HEAD.

One Sailor Jerry and ginger beer was all I drunk today.

Mum's down visiting which is nice.

The image is still in my head. It's all my brain would let me see last night so I had no sleep at all.

And that fucking seagull! I seriously wanna wring its squirmy neck. Every fucking night, even when I'm at *his* it makes it's presence known!!

Went to the Imperial War Museum. It was sobering. Just brought home what a disgusting race mankind is. War, war, war. Weapons created to kill for nothing but greed. Oil and money, that's all those in control give a fuck about. Dirty lowlife scumbags.

That fucking image was in my head, poking its measled face at me at random points.

Him: *I haven't slept with him yet if that's what you're wondering.*
Reply in Dom's head: Yet.

11 AUGUST 2010

Such a stupid thing to have in my head. He doesn't belong to me. He doesn't want me like that, yet the thought of him with someone else upsets me. Stupid fucking boy.

I JUST WANT TO ZONE OUT GO INTO THE DARKNESS FOR A WHILE ... A FEW HOURS... DAYS... YEARS.... FOREVER

Pfft. What is this vision in my head? Fear? Rejection? Scared of being second best, the other is better, loved/respected more. He could do worse but still receive more. Scared of not being the best, always in someone else's shadow. 'More passionate.'

Just get it in to your fucking head. He doesn't WANT You.

YOU'RE JUST THERE. YOU'RE JUST THE BACK-UP. HE HAD SOO MUCH FUN HE'S GOT THE BLUES TO BE BACK. HE NEVER GETS THAT FROM YOU.

JUST GIVE UP ON IT.
IT'S NOT GONNA HAPPEN.

IT NEVER DOES.

12 AUGUST 2010

'Truth is at the moment you're very vulnerable and it's important you have clear lines and consistency in your life. I have not offered you consistency and feel partly to blame for your problems and for that I am sorry.

'You mean so much to me. I will do all I can to care for you until you're better but we must define what we are to each other as this is no help to you and it's not going to work any other way.'

I know already what the definition is. You've made it very clear on all levels repeatedly. *You* don't want me. You don't do relationships. You want to fuck around with as many guys as you can. I get it. I know it. That doesn't change how my head thinks. I can't control it. I'm sorry if that annoys you but that's the way it is.

So do what you want. Do it. I'll just deal with it.

Pointless evening; just stood there being ignored. They all bore me anyway so why waste my energy? Everyone stood there drinking and I can't even have one coz I'm being good and that makes you even more bored. Everyone having fun and you're not part of it.

I went home alone. Pissed off. Angry… like anyone missed me.

PFFT.

Sat in the Cap alone. So much for not drinking. Sat in the pub at 12:30 sounds about right for me.

So, what to say, to write? Who fucking knows? We're just all on this fucking planet spinning towards oblivion. Useless people trying to make an impression. Breeding like vermin to maintain our destructive dominance. Raping the soil of our ancestors. It's been a weird week, everything has just tied into my thoughts, mirroring, matching. Cementing. As much as I hate to admit it, that *New Moon* film struck a chord with me. The whole wanting someone so bad that the recklessness kicks in. Nothing matters more than them, only in my case there is no happy ending. No dramatic finale ending in love. Just the *Requiem for a Dream* end. The broken, the alone. Lost and wandering solitary.

I wish I could just switch off my brain. I got home in such a state last night. Mum had to calm me right down. I could of easily destroyed, punched or broken something.

It's pathetic really. To always be like this. Half my life spent dealing with all this shit. I just want to feel 'normal', react normally. Not like I do. No count to ten. No relaxation. No commonsense. Just black and white. Even mum said that's how I think. Just black and white, no grey areas, no compromise.

Just this constant need to be numb, to just exit reality. To escape. Fuck off life, I can't deal with you right now. Feed me negativity and that's all I can give back. You know, why can't one thing just work the way I want it to? You know just go my way.

'I'm scared of you. Scared of hurting you. I can't be myself around you.' It's a broken fucking record. Blah, blah, click, blah, blah, click. Argh. Circular. Loops. Everything running in patterns, circles. My whole fucking life is a broken record. Guess it matches the broken core at its centre.

That membrane is thinning, feeling like it's gonna snap at any moment. That all this is just a dream and I'll wake in a place worse off than here. I mean how could it possibly be better if I needed to escape into this life?

Everything I touch corrodes, rots, leaves me in the end. Nothing stays constant except for change. It's bollocks, all fucking bollocks.

The broken help the broken, but in a broken fucking way. Gotta hand it to me though. I've fucked myself up spectacularly over the years. Guess all is good in that respect. At least I can do one thing well.

Guy on the table in front is wearing leather shorts, almost hot pants. Shouldn't giggle but he does look fucking retarded.

2:30 and I'm still in the pub. Met David and had a good old catch up. Only on my second drink so that's good right? Having a nice day today so I couldn't give a fuck about the 'not meant to be drinking' bollocks. Maybe I do have a drink dependency, haha. That would just be another thing to add to my banner. Pin it on like a badge.

So. One more drink or not?... yah, one more drink.

'Is that one of your friend's t-shirts?'

Yeah it's one of my friend's. Pfft.

EACH DAY I LIVE IN THE KNOWLEDGE THAT THE ONE PERSON I LOVE WITH ALL MY HEART DOESN'T WANT TO BE WITH ME.

That important you frame it; frame the ticket and picture. Never did that for anything we did. Small little things like that get to me. Memories with him have always been more important. It was always the way.

So what? That's it? No contact, no messing? Just distance and 'care'. Please. Clear lines. Two choices for you I guess – 'carer' not lover; or 'partner' not carer. Well I know for definite it's never gonna be the latter. Why would it be? Why stick with someone fucked up like me

148

when the alternative is as much cock as you can get?

Fumpt. Don't know what that word means but I couldn't care.

Clear lines. Clear fucking lines. ALL FOR YOUR FUCKING BENEFIT, NOT MINE. *YOURS*.

14 AUGUST 2010

Okay, so *he* went to bed in boxers. So my mind went into overdrive about the obvious, then at some point they went and we ended up having really good sex… which he started using spit and pushing my cock up his ass. So obviously now I'm all confused. That kinda puts his clear lines theory out. Either he really wants me, or he really needed/wanted sex. Argh!!!

Annoying thing is I'm always horny but I can't cum which I'm putting down to the pills.

Thoughts in my head last night before sex: Others are gonna get what I can't; I really love him but I'm not gonna be able to get that in return; I want him so bad; I REALLY LOVE HIM; He makes me feel safe, in a way centred.

My sense of 'well being' is back. It's not good, makes me feel like I don't have a problem when I obviously do.

At work, feel tar headed. Didn't get much sleep. I have the feeling that now he's gonna be all dismissive. Like that was the final fuck. One time for the road so to speak before he goes off with others. He'll draw the lines from today. I have that feeling, I mean he's not gonna suddenly want commitment in any form, open or not, and I don't think he's gonna be willing to constantly screw with my head. Who knows? I don't. I just know it won't be the outcome I'd want.

Breathe.

I guess that's exactly what it was. Just coz you needed sex and I was there. You couldn't even give me the time of day this evening, too excited about meeting someone else. Fuck you. You got your dick wet and that's all that matters right? Bastard fucking cunt. Thanks. Thanks a fucking lot.

Today I woke with rage. Shaking like an epileptic. Just unable to think straight, if anything at all. Just empty. Feel so empty. Alone, everyone out having fun and me just on my fucking own.

And *you* stinking of beer at the stall, glad you had a good night, so much more fun that our usual two pints then home. YOU *ALWAYS* FUCKING DID THAT. ALWAYS. And then do the whole I'm worried about you bullshit. Bollocks, don't pretend you spare me a second thought.

Social fucking retard. I can't go enjoy myself coz I'm not meant to be drinking. How am I expected to sit around people getting drunk? This is it. *ALONE.* BORED. WHAT'S THE FUCKING POINT OF THAT?

MIGHT AS WELL DRINK MYSELF TO OBLIVION.

Why do I always fuck up everything? Always over something so small, trivial. Maybe I'm better off alone… yeah like I'd ever like that.

My BRAIN AIN'T ALL HERE TODAY

Everyone always has fun without me and act like boring twats with me.

Ignored, rejected, alone. What's the point of going through that every week, day. I'm not a toy, why do I get treated as though I am? This is fucking bollocks. Complete and utter bollocks.

16 AUGUST 2010

Another morning at the GP. Had to be totally honest and they admitted they'd mistakenly put me on counselling not therapy. So after a long convo I gotta go to a psychiatrist to get everything confirmed. The trainee doctor's face looked well shocked at the end of it. So, the doc's final words: 'They'll help you to live with and cope with this.' So that sounds pretty long term doesn't it. So just another wait.

Oh, I'm on monitoring or weekly appointments and got to go to alcohol and substance abuse counselling.

'If you mean on relationship terms I just don't think we're compatible.
'I love you Dom and I wish I could wrap my arms around you and love and protect you as you deserve but for many reasons I cannot.'
Yeah, yeah. I get it. Now fuck off, leave me alone and stop screwing with my head. Cunt.

All good authors have a drink problem, at least I fit into part of that statement.

Reality is an alien concept to me. What is reality? The world as dictated by the morals and guidelines of society or the world inside your head?

WELL FUCK YOU. BASTARD. GO GET FUCKED ... OH YEAH, YOU PLAN TO.

All of this is only truly real in my head, my own world. I can't connect to yours. I never have been able to. Escaped into my head and here I am, existing.

In the Black Cap, it's 1:00pm. I'm drinking pear cider.

I've had three bottles.

He's out there having fun and getting laid. Why do I care so much? I can visualise it in my head and I want to scream. Someone else is having and able to get what is mine, or what I want to be mine and that fucking hurts like a blade in my fucking heart. And what does he care? Oh yeah, he doesn't. Just as long as he gets his dick in a hole.

Fucking CUNT. I Fucking HATE HIM. Fucking HATE HIM.

guess I've never been enough to satisfy him.

He's probably fucking right this minute as I write this. Shooting off his load in a guy's ass. I fucking hate the thought of that.

And he'll hug the guy all night like he does me and I hate that even more.

Him: *You're only responsible for yourself. There's nothing more I can say. I don't know what to do or say.*
Me: Don't say anything. I'm not your responsibility. You don't need to give me a second thought. Simple as.
Him: *You're right, I don't need to but that doesn't mean to say I don't. All my flaws aside I have your best interests at heart and always will. I'm sorry but it's true.*
Me: Don't concern yourself with it. Just go out have fun, get your dick wet and let me deal with this.
Him: *I'm letting you deal with it. You made that clear yesterday.*
Me: Yeah, fuck off.

BASTARD FUCKING CUNT.

I HATE HIM.

FUCKING HATE HIM.

IT SHOULD BE ME IN HIS BED. NOT SOME WEASEL FACED CUNT. BUT I GUESS THAT'S EASIER.

FUCK IT
HURTS

I feel empty. Alone.

unwanted.

18 AUGUST 2010

That image in my head, graphic. Fills me with rage. I wanna punch someone or something just to release it all.

Why does it get to me so much? Why should I care? Why can't I just erase it all from my head? *He* didn't give me a passing thought as he jumped into bed with him. No thought of how I'd feel as he pushed his dick into the hole. No care at all for me, and why should there be? Why should he have not done it just because of me?

Just the idea that they might be doing it right now makes me feel sick. It's stupid. But I can't help it. He could be fucking him right this minute and not even thinking about me. Shoots his load and won't tell me bout it.

Argh!!

Came to the shop to clear my head. I'm going crazy in my flat. At least here I don't feel so alone. Feels like I have something to do. Takes my mind off it all and lets me think about other things.

Always prepare for the worst, that way you won't be disappointed, only surprised.

Stupid bitch Sam and her stupid fucking text. Go fuck yourself you stupid using whore. Can't even give your 'best friend' the time of day. I'd go running to you when you had a problem, just to check you were okay. Well fuck you. Stupid bitch. That's it. *Done*.

In the end what's the fucking point? Everyone leaves in the end.

I was right. He shagged that guy… *'It was just a shag. I'm just living my life.'*

At least I know. I feel empty. I fucking love him.

I dunno what to think or feel. It just feels numb. All numb. Told you he couldn't care for my feelings. Why do I still love him? Argh! Goes out with some guy has fun, goes out in Central London. Takes him home and has a fuck. Went and saw a show with him. Had a good time. Never does that with me. Never did. And yet I love him.

At least he's happy he got a fuck out of it. At least he got what he wanted. It's just about sex for him.

That little runt got what I want. Fucking runt. Bastard cunt.

You shot your load up *him*.

The way he said he was just living his life made it kinda clear I wasn't a part of that. Like I don't need to know. Not important in it at all.

Why can't he just want me like I want him?

Why can't he just feel the same?

Why can't I just have him?

Why?

Why?

Dear God, please tell me why.

'*You want something that's not gonna happen.*' Thanks, you got that right didn't you. Nice to know you don't feel the same. I know it's something you keep telling me but I just can't get it into my head. You fucked that guy and yet I still want you. It's as stupid as that. I can't stop it. Can't switch it off on simple command.

At least the anger's gone. Don't know where but it has, so can't complain about that really.

So yeah, back at the Cap. Cider again, anything to prevent me from being alone in the flat. So I get to think here at least.

'*You want all or nothing.*' Yup, pretty much. I want someone who'll stop me feeling so alone. Someone who wants me. Who likes me. Instead of being on my own all the fucking time. Most of all I want *you*.

Yeah it hurts he's fucking other people but I've done it and he doesn't know so I mean should I really be angry? Maybe it's just the not knowing.

I don't want half arsed care. I don't want worry. I want love. I want to feel loved, needed, wanted. Anything that makes me feel good as a person. Anything that gives me a reason. I want to be the centre of someone's world. I want all of this but never get it. Always just disposable, 'I'll come back to you when I want to. Not when *you* need, or want.'

Smoked so much today. I know I'm gonna feel that in the morning.

Everyone keeps telling me to get him out of my head but I can't. He makes me feel safe. Protected. I've only ever loved properly twice and both have no time for me anymore. All have their own lives and needs. If it wasn't for the business I don't think he would worry as much, if at all. I mean could you blame him?

I am Dom; I'm defined by love. A need of love. Who wants to share their time with me? Oh yeah, no one. Just me on my own. Always and ever. Endlessly waiting. Endlessly.

I wonder how many times he fucked him. Once last night, once this morning no doubt. At least twice. But hell what do I know? Why do I need to know? How will it benefit me? It was just a fuck at the end of the day.

That fucking runt got what I want. Fucking bastard cunt. Who wants to scream? I do.

Second cider. Second cigarette since I've been here. Also ordered a burger so at least I'm being sensible and eating.

Heartbreak is so hard for me to deal with. I just want him back so much. It's stupid. What's the fucking point in wanting what he's pretty much told me I'm never gonna get. What's the point? Why can't I just get it? Why do I constantly torture my brain this way? Love. Yeah that's why. Love. Fucking love. Stupid fucking love. Hope. Hope that one day he'll want me. Stupid things that ain't gonna happen to the likes of me.

OMG. Oh my fucking God, I love him so much. Stupid hey? This is fucked up. This is a waste of my time.

'You can't use this as an excuse.' I'm not. I'm realising the one person I love above all else really doesn't want me. That's what is so fucking hard at this moment. It really fucking hurts. Hurts more than anything I've ever felt. Like my heart is being ripped out again by the

same person. Always links back to *you*. BASTARD.

Bottle three.

So how do I feel now? Empty still. Numb. Just picturing the scene. Would I ever wanna go back there? Would I? Who knows? Am I comfortable knowing what I'm not? If only. Yeah, if only. Ever love someone that much? Yesterday is over. Today is a different day, but nothing changes does it? Should I have another drink? Should I be responsible? Should I invite him up? Probably not. Will I? Most likely. What do I have to lose? Nothing because that's what I started with. *Nothing.*

Them: I was meant to go to the crematorium for my Granddad's anniversary.
Me: Why? Were they planning to re-burn his ashes?

Bottle four.

Woo, going for it today ain't I? Anything to not feel so alone. God help me. This is all bollocks. Just smoking and drinking all day. Just filling a hole. A space. A gap. A need. No one here for me. Everyone always too busy. I sent the text, bet he doesn't turn up. Who knows? I don't.

Fuck up much? Yeah. Always. Always a constant. Fucking everything up just because I can, well can't stop myself.

'I'm living my life.' Nice to know you've got people to help you do that. Everyone just abandons me. Leaves. Just Dom and his pathetic existence. Loneliness my friend. That and silence my closest allies. I could sit here all day, night. Right to the point of oblivion. Why should I save myself? I have no one to save it for. Myself isn't a justifiable reason.

There's no point saving what no one wants is there? I could disappear into nothing and what? Get forgotten? That's how it works isn't it? We die, get a stone slab memory and then fade to nothing.

No one knows how bad my head is. Just pointing it on experience. I can't feel for what isn't physically there. You leave my life without a physical reminder and I forget what I'm meant to feel. Forget what it is you mean to me. You become a void, a name. The minute you walk back and I can physically see you then I know what I feel. I can only feel emotion when you're here. Who knows what I'd feel if you all just vanished.

Only love and hate, nothing in-between. I love you. I hate you. I love you, I hate you. No middle ground. No I love you but can live without you. Just this and that. Point A, Point Z, no alphabet in-between.

Do you have any concept of how that feels? Do you know how heartless that makes you feel? To be able to tell your brother how you can't see a middle ground, how you don't think about him when he's not here, when they think about you everyday. Do you know how that feels?

'I'm not gonna witness you drink a drop unless you're off your tablets. I'm not feeling too great today anyway so probably not a good idea.'

Thanks. I just need to talk that's all but you can't even give me that. Thanks. Thanks a fucking lot.

All I get is a fucking lecture. Thanks. Fuck off.

'Don't guilt trip me. When I try to talk to you, you don't want to. I'm feeling stressed today, I'm sorry.'

Like I said forget it. Don't pretend to be sorry. I'll work on your time scale and when you're free to fit me in.

It all bleeds back to your business. And how that effects *you*. Always about *you*. How about looking at me as a person and not a business asset? How about not making it all about you? How about trying to understand how my head works? Oh, too much effort. Make it all about something you can manage. Something about you so you can control it. Fuck off it's my head. Not yours. I can't just think differently because you click your fingers and expect it.

This might not be what you want to hear but the answer is I KNOW! I know all of this, you tell me I never try to understand when all I have been doing is trying to understand. You tell me I apparently want things done on my time when I am constantly offering you my time and support. What I'm sick of is you keep telling me how I think and who I am when I know in my heart you are wrong about me. I feel a little like your punch bag at the moment and am even terrified at getting on with my own life. I can't do anything without a thought for you, that being due to the consequences or genuine concern. And I never once said you are putting by business at risk, but it is clear to me your sales persona is hard for you at the moment and our customers are our fuel. Our business is a being, it's very sensitive, it gets judged and can very easily suffer at the result of both of our actions. It is my nature to love, care and worry for it as much as I do you or my family... it is part of my family and I'll never be any different when it comes to the business. That's the last I'll say about business.

You have recognised your problems and went to the doctors and you should be so proud of yourself for that but I am not wrong in saying you can not let this rule your life. You are still the same person, you're not as weak as you seem at the moment. You have it in you to get through this and you will but I understand this will take time and self dedication. When I see your not willing to give yourself that it disappoints me and I can't deal with it coz it makes me angry. I can't deal with it coz I care about you so much, sometimes I wish for that same switch you talk about. I say it out of love - get a grip! I wish someone had said that to me when I wasn't well!

Our physical relationship seems to be our weakness at the moment. We both get a lot of warmth, belonging and comfort from it, which is a beautiful thing but I cannot do it anymore and never intended it to go on this long. I tried, in my heart I gave it another shot but in my eyes we are only going to encounter the same problems. We both have our separate issues that need addressing and at the moment that should be our priority. Despite how you feel about me I cannot pretend coz it only puts everything we have at risk. I want to be your friend and I hope after time we are but at the moment this does not seem possible. These things take time.

I am going to carry on with my life as a single man, nothing I do is malicious against you or anyone else, it's just me living my life, as you are free to live yours. Yes I had sex with Jamie and I will have sex with others. I'm not hurting anyone, I'm being responsible and that is

161

my choice. But at the moment I am starting to think my sex life should be of no concern to you, it is fair to say you don't cope with it too well and at the end of the day it's no one else's business, the same as yours shouldn't be my business or anyone else's. We should share things when we choose, coz we want to, coz it's natural as friends do.

Meh at the end of the day we're different people, we all deal with things in our own way but I pray we can find a place for each other otherwise this is only going to end in tears for both of us.

If my response isn't what you wanted that does not mean for a second I haven't absorbed what you have told me. I will read it over again and try my best to be aware and sensitive to your feelings.

I still think some time off might do you good but I will never force that on you.

PS. Will have some stock for you at the stall if you're opening the shop tomorrow.

So there's the answer. Completely over. Again. Dismissed because that's what you want. You admitted you don't feel the same. You don't love me. Go slag yourself around. Do what you need to. Thank you for fucking with my head again. On, off. On, off. Want, don't.

I cried. Full-blown tears for two hours. My heart ripped out and all that's left is its numb core. Anger, rage followed and I punched the walls, bit my arm to get rid of the pain. To make it physical. Real.

Empty. Empty. Empty. Empty. Empty. Empty.

Fuck off. This pain *is* real. It's there constant. I wish I could just switch it all off but I can't. Pain. Pain. Always fucking pain. Caused by *you*. Always *you*. Always love. I hate love. It's poison. It's evil. Leads always to the biggest loss; the biggest pain.

Always have to see the one I love 'loving' someone else. The image in my head brings anger. Must delete it. I must get it out.

I just want to hold you, to be held by you. Protected. Cared for. But you don't want to. Guess I should just leave you to it.

Headache. Headache. God, I smoked too much today. What a day, what a fucking day.

Who knows what to feel? *You* couldn't care; you've made that clear. You've broke my heart so many times. I'm sure I should be used to it now, but I'm not.

You said you'd tried to give it another shot in your heart but you didn't. Told everyone else that we were 'trying again', 'seeing how it goes' but always told me you wanted nothing. Truth is you wasn't prepared to try. Scared to commit, scared of missing out on guys who show an interest. You just want to get as much dick as you can because it fills a need, makes you feel like you're giving them something. Makes you feel wanted. But does it fill the hole? The loneliness? I would be prepared to sacrifice everything for you. To make it work, help you feel needed.

You played with my head, telling me you loved me, told me what we could do to complete you sexually, but was you willing to do it? No. Love of one or the lust of many? We all know what you think is more important.

You've cut out my heart and shat on it. You've hurt me constantly. You've taken the easy escape. The easy option.

Here's me alone, you've deleted the one connection that I knew was a true feeling. The one thing I was certain of. Now I'm lost. Rattling around by myself. Existing alone. Like always. Like ever. This is my life. Solitary confinement coz I have no one I can out go with to meet new people. No one wants to get to know Dom. It's either fuck or nothing.

So what makes me feel like me? Truly the Dom I want to be? Going out, drinking, using drugs and ending up somewhere with someone random or a friend. Alcohol, drugs and sex. That is Dom. Dom is reckless, Dom doesn't give a fuck. Burn bright and fall in flames. A bright star. One of the crazy ones.

I wanna be around the sharp ones, the crazy ones. The ones who burn their candles brightly before crashing burnt out at their end. The ones who live by their own rules.

The bright stars, the outcasts. The ones who never sleep, never rest, never lose faith. Those who break the routine and change the system.

Who are *you* to play with peoples hearts?

'He's so cute, we just wanna take him home.' Yeah, everyone does. Pfft.

You ended it like you've always done and all for the same reasons. Let's face it. I was never what you wanted. You just push me away when it suits you. Fuck everyone else's feelings. Yeah you carry on as a single man.

Hold it in Dom. Don't cry again. Not here. Not now. I would say it's all gonna work out for you but truth is I have no clue. Sorry Dom but I don't. Your heart ain't ever gonna heal.

You was, are, my world and you've just taken it all away from me. Like you did last time. I bet you'd take the business if you could.

fuck, fuck, fuck, fuck

That was your plan. That's why you wanted to meet him. Guaranteed fuck. Guaranteed way of hurting me. So that last shag *was* your 'goodbye' fuck.

Wot's the point?

I don't know how you expect me to write my rage down.

One hour to go then I get to go home. Woo. Fun. What can I do tonight? Oh yeah… sit alone listening to music. Might write more.

EMPTY. LOST. ALONE.

ALL I WANT IS YOU.

i am nothing

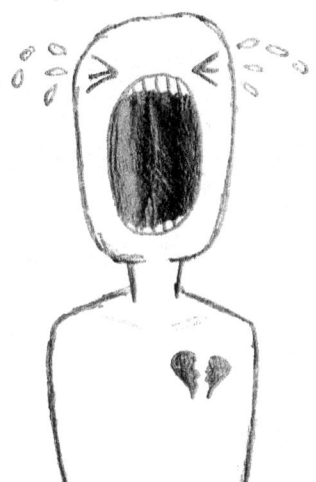

SCREW YOU. ALL OF YOU.

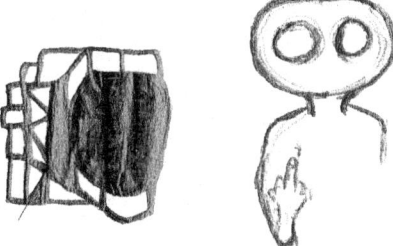

20 AUGUST 2010

Had sex with Stevie last night. Well when I say last night I mean this morning at 5ish. Ha. Yeah, was just sex. Noticed something, the usual. I lose interest during sex. I get bored. I want violent sex, angry sex. Risky sex. The sex that gets the heart pounding. Maybe that's why I loved having sex with *you*. It was unprotected, 'sordid'. You shoot cum into someone and it stays in them rather than into a condom. Like what turns me on the most is watching or fucking someone bare, pull out, cum on the asshole then push back in. I wouldn't do that to or with a stranger but that's the sex *I* want. That's what turns me on. Memory in someone, or someone in me. Obviously it means more because I'd only let someone I love do that… well nowadays. So in that sense *you* kept me safe. Now sex is just boring. Motions.

I want risk. Danger. Anger and fear. A collection of emotions exploding in a cumshot.

According to my old diaries it is round this time Sam, Jules and now *you* have told me they don't want me coz of my moods and their desires to be single. Must be a damaged month.

Empty, really empty. Just wanna finish off all my current book projects. Slowly working my way through them.

Can't even talk to you. Can't even say 'hi'. You get what you deserve. Who are you to screw with someone's heart and then cut me out of your life like an insignificant annoyance? Thanks, you're a nob and I fucking hate you. End of the day you couldn't care. Run and get fucked as many times as you wish, filling a void. Once again you've hurt me so fucking much and once again you believe you're justified in doing so because you simply do what *you* want, fuck anyone else.

I returned your coat as you requested. At least that removes any need for you to contact me outside of business. Delete me from existence. Delete me. Why tell someone you love them only to pretend or admit it was all a lie? You're a cunt, a complete and utter cunt. I hope a condom breaks and you get AIDS. Then who'll be fucked?

Constantly hurting me. Do you get off on that? Get off on the knowledge that all your exes love you so much. That you have their hearts in your hand to crush as you wish but never release. Fuck you. Fuck you. Fuck you. Fuck you. Fuck you.

Gah!! There's only so many times I can punch a wall or my leg. This rage. This venom. Anger, hatred, love, disgust. All merged. I wish I could just stop. Switch off like you've done. I'm not wired that way.

How can you cut someone out so easily? Did I really mean that little to you?

I feel sick. You make me feel sick.

I'm tired of being alone.

You took away the one thing that felt real. You took away the one thing I loved. You kicked me back into the dirt. Just because you could.

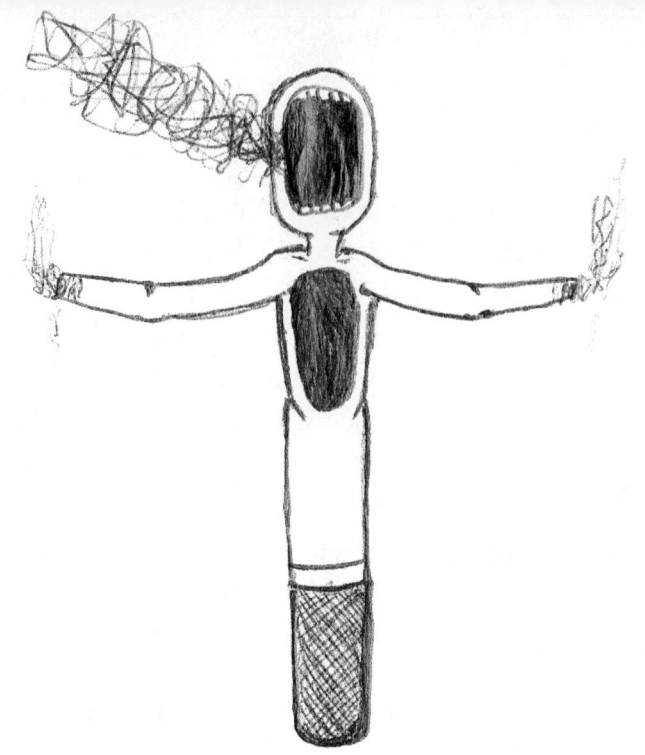

Hollow Inside. The Void.
Darkness Pouring Out From
Within.

Scream But No One Is
Listening.

I Am Your Addiction.

168

Him: *Whatever you believe it wasn't on purpose. I gave it my best shot, not everything in life works out as we want it to.*

Me: You didn't give a shot. Don't pretend. You told everyone but me you was 'seeing how it goes' or 'we're giving it another shot.' Yet to me you gave none of that. So let's not lie. You wanted people to believe it when you never did. Done. I never once felt like you was giving it a shot. It was all one sided so don't try and lighten the blow. You lied. You never wanted anything.

Him: *I'm not lying. I've been honest with you from the start. You should have been more honest about your feelings and motives before taking your job back. You can blame me if you like but you need to look in the mirror. You can believe that but you're wrong.*

Me: Yeah so stop all your 'gave it another shot' bullshit. There was no motive. Not my fault I fucking love you. But that's all meaningless anyway. And I did tell you how I felt right at the start. So you've always known.

Him: *And I told you right back.*

Me: Yeah I know then would follow it with the whole 'love you' bollocks. Like I said it doesn't matter. It's done.

Him: *You've make such an effort with me, I actually thought you had changed but after time I realised you still haven't dealt with the same problems you had before. They are your problems and I am not responsible for them. You are. I tried but I still can't handle you. That does not make me a liar or a user, that's the truth.*

Me: Yeah that's right. I made an effort. Yeah, they're problems that I'm getting sorted now. They're problems I've never had control over. Fact remains. I made an effort.

Him: *This is life. I've been heart broken too but I didn't stamp my feet and blame everyone else. You can't force me, or guilt trip me or threaten me. I can't change how I feel, and I was always true about how I felt. There's nothing else I can say. You're turning this into something it's not and it will get you nowhere.*

Me: DONE

22 AUGUST 2010

Went to the Cap last night with Cyber Andy, met Matti and his boyfriend. Was such a good laugh. We got so drunk, I got a gram of K and we ended up back at mine (Andy and I). We had sex. Lots of sex. We did it on the roof before going to my room. Was hot. Rough sex, bareback sex. Naughty risky sex. Constant flipping. You know the stuff that makes me cum. Violent.

He's hot. Good in bed. Good kisser. So it was hot. Didn't get bored once.

Line of K (good shit) then bed – fucked again. Kept touching each other up all night. Wank in the morning. Hot.

That was my kind of night out. Drink, drugs, sex. Extremes. I felt alive. I felt right.

THAT IS WHAT DEFINES ME:

DRINK, DRUGS AND SEX

Good night last night. Good day today. Most positive I've felt in a while.

Went to the Cap last night with Tim and Andy came down. Was fucking amazing. *He* turned up with market Mike who came over and tried to get gossip from us, like watching mine and Andy's interaction. But we ignored them and carried on. Andy gave me a piggy back through the pub. Heehee, one of the best nights out I've had in ages.

Andy came back to mine. We had sex. He stayed most of the day. Bro came to visit. We stood on the roof and I mooned at Tweedledum and Tweedledee. Had such a fun day. Felt really good.

I actually really like Andy, get on with him so well. Makes me happy. He shares my same humour and mannerism. Yay, aww. *Big cheeky grin*.

Appointment at the doctors. The usual. No real improvement in mood management, they're keeping me on the medication. I saw a note on my notes saying they want me to be on it for at least five weeks.

Therapy is still being arranged. Today his final words were: 'I think you know in your head what it is and all we can do is help you to cope with it on a day to day basis.'

That strangely settled my mind.

Mark's down so it's good to have things back as they were.

Andy is cool.

The doc gave me a weird look when I said my head said 'Well you either go home and trash the flat or you go to the pub and drink.' He was like 'Who said that?' Me 'My head' Him 'Your head?' Me 'Yeah.' He looked worried.

25 AUGUST 2010

Last night was fun. Went out with Jeff. Was a laugh. We ended up at
G-A-Y Bar. Mark wasn't impressed but meh. I started an argument.
Some guy barged past me and knocked our drinks so I went mental at
him. Like proper. Then Jeff got involved and the guy ran away. Haha,
rude fucking frog face.

Andy called. I was a grump coz everyone wanted to go home
early. Booo but he made me giggle. Yay.

He text me about the business. I felt nothing for him. I'm done with
him. Dead. Personally it's just hate, and a general lack of care. I got
more important people to concern myself with.

Gash, that's all. No reason. Just woke up a bit snappy. Sat at work now. Opened late. Oops, not like I missed any trade. It's dead.

I got the fear when I woke up during the night. Like maybe I'm already too into Andy and like he won't/doesn't like me back in the same way. *That* fear. The rejection fear. Eep. Stupid coz I mean it's all new but yah I likes him. Doh. Stupid, stupid Dom. Falling for someone like a fly to shit. Dumb stupid Pisces boy.

Alcohol counselling tomorrow. Ooh fun times. Guess that's gonna be a barrel of laughs. I ain't gonna change. In all honesty I just want to carry on being me, being the person I've always been. Dom. I just want to learn how to control myself a little bit more. I hate how certain people are suddenly like 'you're gonna change, you've got to.' Why should I have to? Just because you don't like who I am why should I become someone you do? Accept me as I am. I AM DOM. I will *always* be Dom. No rebirth, no new personality. No different person. Fuck that. I will not conform. We will not conform.

I'm gonna gut you like a fish and eat you like sushi.

Teehee, big goofy grin. Deranged smile and fall to the floor in laughter.

Text: *Appt Reminder: Aug 27 with Alcohol Advice 1 at James Wigg Practice.*

That's novel, a text to remind my alcohol fuzzed brain that I have to turn up.

Give me a fucking break!

Him: *Why you taking it out on me? Feel better?*
Me: Doesn't make me feel better for the simple fact I feel nothing for you. Just saying if anyone on that market gets involved in my private life they'll get a piece of my mind.
Him: *Oh flexing your muscles I see. Do you feel anything for my company?*
Me: I'm not flexing anything; I'm just being honest. And yes I feel a lot for our company.
Him: *We went through all this last time we split up. I'm not doing it again. You're a shareholder not an owner; I will always be boss of the business I started.*
Me: Oh so I'm not a director now. So funny how it jumps between ours and yours whenever it suits your mood. Stop playing your mind games.
Him: *You feel nothing for me, you're bitter, you've been telling lies about me and your attitude sucks and I'm supposed to trust you with my life? When you've worked your whole life like me you understand things aren't given to you on a plate, there's no way on Earth you get a top job without respect and stability.*
Me: Erm what lies have I said? And if you dare ever used my mental instability as an excuse I'll sue your ass to hell.
Him: *You ambushed my business and ambushed my emotions when I wasn't well and now you're putting all blame on me. I wish you had never come back and had just moved on.*
Me: I haven't ambushed anything. I've only ever helped your business. Your emotions are your problem not mine. And you still haven't told me what lies I've said or are they all from hearsay and gossip?
Him: *Yep you've been a massive help to my business but also a massive pain in the arse. You don't understand working for someone coz you've*

174

never had to. You act like a spoilt child and as I've witnessed before you stamp your feet when you don't get things your way. You play dirty and seek revenge. You've got so much growing up to do it's scary. Try being a man for once, put your anger aside and do the right thing. If you had we wouldn't be having this stupid text shit now. All I am to you now is your boss, just how we started, and I'm doing that to protect my business until you have calmed down.

Me: No, in my opinion you've become a complete arse since I went into treatment. That sounds to me like discrimination.

Him: You love this business more than your family and yet again you threaten its very existence. Do you never learn? Me and my business are the same thing. It's me, it's my mind, it's my love, it is my vision. You attack me; you attack my business and vice-versa. It's always been that way with anyone. I can't help it. So you started attacking me and I immediately get on the defence to protect what I have worked my whole life for. Anyone else would do the same.

Me: You can't force me into liking you just for the sake of business. Nor will I be threatened. I have not threatened the business in the slightest. But I'll be sure to bring up these issues next time I see the professionals and take their advice.

Him: I don't want you to like me. I just wish I had someone in my business I could trust. That was a genuine email I sent you. You turned it into this. Night.

Me: Like I said. I'll bring this up with the professionals and let them advise me. Night.

27 AUGUST 2010

Had the first alcohol counselling today. Apparently I fall into the high end of risky or something, can't remember its name. Was okay, went well.

Woke up really pissed off for obvious reasons. Proper rage, anger, was good I managed to calm down for it. Nob, nob, nob.

So yesterday *you* took away my old job title. Today you finished it off and took my job. Fuck you, you arrogant up your own ass piece of shit. I fucking hate you. Crying your crocodile tears at Tweedledum. You wanker. Complete and utter cunt. *I fucking hate you.*

Him: *Wot are your thoughts today?*
Me: Spoke to my counsellor about wot's happened and she's told me to get advice from a mental health organisation about it to see where I stand.
Him: *What has happened? And stand with what?*
Me: The business. My job
Him: *You still have your job. You still have your shares.*
Me: You took away a decision that had been verbally agreed when I pose no threat to your business.
Him: *When you act like you have been, I have every right to make a decision for my business and I stand by it.*
Me: You demoted me from director to employee over traits that are caused by my illness. They view that at discrimination.
Him: *You were never director.*
Me: You called it me verbally, you made me believe it. Like I said it's their advise not mine. And at the end of the day you demoted my job and I have the e-mails when you refer to it as ours.
Him: *But you have never been legally bound to my business verbally or otherwise. You still have your job but if you pursue this you really give me no choice. I don't want someone trying to ruin me in my own company.*
Me: And I'll do my job, just letting you know wot I've been advised.

So you can stop threatening me. From now on I will just sell and work only the days I'm doing at the moment. The rest is up to you.

Him: No deal. You've destroyed the trust by threatening me with legal action. Why did you have to do that? I don't want that on my shoulders, I'm not well enough to deal with it.

Me: Didn't threaten anything, read back through the text. I just said I'd been advised and told you wot they had told me. Never once did I take an action. The only person who has threatened anyone is you.

Him: I'm not stupid. I've seen how you work. I watched it with Andrew, you did it to me and you're doing it again. I don't want to play your self-satisfying games. I don't want to watch you boost your ego by lying to others. You're deluding yourself and you turned it into this not me. You do it to yourself and then blame me.

Me: I didn't lie to anyone. I just repeat wot you told me. You told me I'd been made a director or was in the process of being made it. You told me I was an owner. You lead me into a sense that I was part of a business. So if anyone is playing games it is you. I haven't made a single threat. So let your head convince you of that but fact remains, put us aside I have always helped your business no matter what.

Him: Yep you were gonna be director until you started treating me like this and saying you're gonna sue my company to hell. I can't work with you coz I hate how you're being and I hate even more that you can't see how you're behaving.

Me: No I said I'd sue if you used my mental health against me as that is illegal.

Him: Why should I trust a word you say? Why should I give you a chance to destroy me? You made this mistake before, you threaten my livelihood and now I can't help but see you as a danger. And you can't do nowt without a sick note.

Me: Get yer head out yer ass. This isn't about you or destroying you. Stop being so fucking melodramatic, if any one is trying to destroy anything it's you. This is about a business I have been constantly loyal to for the past two odd years. Stop making it personal with the whole waffle. You did exactly this last time for the simple fact it was easiest for you. Self-destruct as you wish.

Him: Don't turn this around on me. I was desperately trying to keep the peace last night and you fucked up by flaunting your ego.

Me: You know full well how I react and know I can't control that. And I don't have an ego coz you can't have an ego when the only thing you care about doesn't belong to you. So yeah do an ego check on yourself.

Him: *This isn't about me and you anymore. You need to understand in ANY job, 2nd director or not, if you act like you have been, ill or not, you cannot expect to keep your job. That's not a threat it's reality. This is not easy for either of us but it is you who's dragging your emotions into work and I'm actually sick today.*

Can things get any worse? Yeah, I bet they can. Shit. Fuck. What now? The one thing that kept me going has been snatched away from me and *you* knew it was exactly that.

Fuck you, Cunt

Went out with Andy and the Cyberdog lot. Had a laugh, took my mind off things. Me likes Andy. Oh yes I does.

Ended up on the roof eating KFC and chucking the rubbish everywhere. He cheers me up. Yes he does.

Then he had to go home. Boo.

A few days away. Went to Andy's on Saturday for a party, was fun. Sat and talked with the Cyberdoggers again. Best house party I've been to in a while coz I didn't feel alone once. NOT ONCE, and I didn't need to cling on to Andy all night. Was fun. Ball fights!

Sunday was spent at Andy's tiding up, we had a shower together. Then went back to Camden and did some K. Andy skipped a club night at Koko and came round to see me. Aww.

Andy makes Dom smile. Dom likes Andy.

Mark's mate Kyle came round. Had a really good day. A K day. K, KFC, Kopparberg. I got a new top, it's hot. Was a laugh. Two hours sat in McDs, who knew it could be so much fun?

So good day, I felt myself, like my old self. The stupid carefree brat Dom. Loud, obnoxious, rude. The usual things people hate me for. I like that Dom. It's good. Feels right. Reality doesn't exist for him. Just the there and then. Sod consequences. Live the moment.

'Look Chihuahua!'

'That's not a Chihuahua Dom.'

'Oh, erm. Look, baby Jack Russell.'

I'm a brat. I loves it.

2010
SEPTEMBER

Had my worst switch last night. My worst rage. We got home from a night out with Jeff and I threw everything around. Smashed a glass; got cut and bled everywhere. Threw three bottles of Sailor Jerry out the window (empty of course), broke another glass, went got more rum, got my nob out and walked down the street. Ended up crying, wanting to be anyone but me. Screaming and shouting. Punching the radiator. Mark had to pin be down coz I was really bad. But how can anyone truly understand? Did a load of K too.

Rufus was there for me.

Went to Citizens Advice, they said I got a good case against *him* and I should go to an employment specialist, as he's unfairly dismissed me, discriminated on mental grounds and has never given me a contract. So yeah, I could really fuck him over.

Apparently he phoned Jeff on Saturday morning to see if I'd turned up for work. WTF?!

So, *you* un-add me from Facebook and block me, how grown up of you. History repeating it seems. Got what you want out of me and then throw me away. Pathetic. Fucking pathetic.

How can you just delete someone from your life? Click, click, erase. Without care or thought. Did I really mean that little to you? Erased. Forgotten. Done. You got the fucks you wanted, got the help and assistance, the money. Used, used, removed. You fucking bastard. You couldn't give a shit if I was going through this alone. You're a cunt. You really are a fucking dickhead. But what the fuck could you do anyway other than consistently torment and hurt me mentally?

02 SEPTEMBER 2010

Feel 'meh' today. Just numb, empty. Lost. I've lost everything. Just taken away from me and for what? Because I do my job? Oh no, because I don't like *you*. Such a professional way to run your business. But then what do I do now? My brain can't deal with all the stress and bollocks going on. Can't work, can't focus. Just existing, numbing myself into reality. How could you just throw me away? I meant that little obviously.

So where do I get money from? You've screwed me over again. You cunt. You fucking asshole, and justified it how? Oh yeah, with lies and bullshit. Leave me the fuck alone. Give me my job back. *You* knew it was, is, the only thing keeping me focused. You took it away. You're a fucking dickwad.

Shit, shit, shit. What about me? What about me? No one gives a shit about me. I might as well be dead.

So you can't even speak to me. Act like a child. Well I came to talk, you ignored me, no thanks for the stock I made, you selfish cunt.

Got home and did it. Called the legal advice. Appointment booked for 24th. Feel like shit, but it's no more than you deserve. Cut me out like I'm nothing? Well, let me leave a scar.

Three bottles in and I'm still sat in a pub. Craving drugs, craving to escape this emptiness. Sweet Jesus Christ.

Dom, my dear boy, you *are* a fuck up. Yes, you are.

On a date was you? Shame he was fucking ugly.

Feel like crap today mentally.

How can one person leave such a big fucking hole? And do that knowingly and without remorse. *You* took away everything I care for and needed. Removed me from the one thing that gives me meaning. *You* knew it was the only thing keeping me level, connected, and yet you got rid of it over a personal grudge. You kicked me to the dirt again. No money, no job, no nothing; no friendship, no you. Cut me on so many levels, and *what the fuck do you care?*

Get on with your life Dom, move on. How the fuck can I? I have *no* money, nothing interests me, who's going to put up with my mood swings, or even try to understand? No one. I'm just dirt. Fucking dirt.

And *you* of all people should know how hard all this is. *Cunt.*

Even them, the so-called 'friends' who caused much of the friction are telling me to leave it and move on. They know the situation the best and they're changing their tract. Oh yeah, you don't need me anymore to leech off so no help from you. You're the ones who probably twisted the knives, made the lies, exaggerated everything into this new shape. Feeding my head with your poisons. Can anyone be trusted?

What about me? Who gives a flying fuck about me? No fucking one.

I think I've even scared Andy off. Feels that way. What should I have expected? Why would anyone have to put up with me, or want to? I'm useless, worthless, pointless. Left alone and neglected. Everyone leaves in the end.

Alone. Back to being alone. How could I expect any different? This is life.

This is too much for my brain to handle.
This is too much for me.
This is too much.

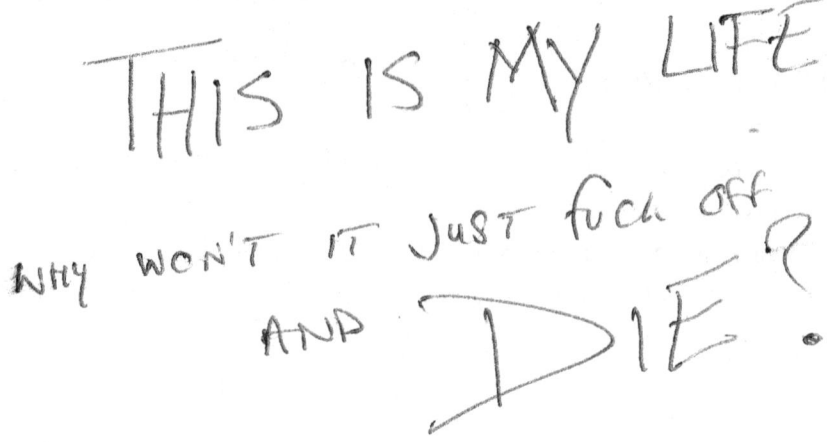

THIS IS MY LIFE

WHY WON'T IT JUST fuck off AND DIE?

Second alcohol counselling. Woo she's leaving in a few weeks. That's another one running away. In a month I'll have all new people dealing with me.

Ahh crap. Bang!! Tomorrow I will be alone.

GOODNIGHT WORLD.

SLEEP...

Who stood up for me? Who gives one little bit of a shit about me? It seems no one. Nothing to gain from me so why bother even trying?

Hello, welcome to this loneliness. This great void. What am I meant to do now? The only thing I loved, that gave me reason has been taken away and now I have nothing. That company was my life. Meant as much to me as it does *you*, and I'm not even allowed to fight for it. Not even allowed to care. 'Just move on.'

IT WAS MY FUCKING LIFE YOU NOB HEADS. WITHOUT IT I HAVE NOTHING. HOW CAN YOU MOVE ON FROM THAT?

FUCK OFF ALL OF YOU.

Moments like this show you who your true friends are. None of *you* stepped up did you? Cheers, don't pretend to care when you see me next.

So fucking bored.

WHO IS THERE foR ME?
WHO WILL HELP?

Why is it that I help everyone when they need it, but when I need help no one is there for me?

BE ALONE PISCES BOY

NO ONE WANTS YOUR

BURDEN.

NO ONE

Went and had a drink with a guy called Sergi, a punk. We went back to mine and fucked. Usual story, started safe, then I ended up bare backing him. Risky sex. Stupid sex. Good sex. But I did stop myself. Idiot Dom. You're an idiot. Yeah. So what. Self-destruct in style.

Another Monday, another appointment at the docs. Sat waiting to be called. Summoned. My head feels like it's gonna snap.

Doctor was concerned. He said *he* had no right to sack me like that, talk to MIND. I tried to explain how my head feels and he didn't understand. So I said I feel like I'm constantly dreaming and that I'll wake up one day and none of this will have happened. It all just feels so fake.

So, he mentioned that the Citalopram isn't working. So now I'm on 40mgs a day. Yay. NOT. This is so fucked up. I really need a break soon or I'll explode, implode. What a shit existence.

He said I have to go back in two weeks, and as it's his last chance to see me he'll make his final decision about what to do with me. Ominous sounding isn't it?

This could be calmed. I need stability. I need to be with something I love, and that something is *that* business. That was my reason to get up, to live. I love it as if it was my own. I just need to be back working for it. Without it I have nothing, no direction or future. Back at the bottom of the hole.

When you take away the meaning, what's left?

Kyle came to visit. He brought his mate. Was a good day. Took my mind off it all. Breather. Peace of mind.

His friend annoyed me; he made a cup of tea without asking permission. Yes, that really did piss me off, but I bit my tongue.

07 SEPTEMBER 2010

And what was I expecting? My 'friends' to actually care? No, no, you're far too busy to even come see me or care. Re-arrange plans and don't even bother to let me know in advance. Why thank you. Expect me to run to see you even though *I'm* the one who's ill. What do any of you care? Ahh, it's easier to just delete and ignore than it is to help me. Where are you? I'm always there for you and what about me? Who's here to *fucking* help me, to show they care, to fight my corner?

As for *you*. How could you stop caring so easily? You said you loved me, said you'd be there for me, to help, but as the reality of it kicked in you couldn't do it. Didn't want to. Throw me away. Kick me out. Switch off anything you claimed to feel. Let me rot. Let me rot. If I died who'd give a fuck? You? No, I was just that pain in your ass.

Then there's Andy, Cyber Andy. I did a good job in scaring him away didn't I? Shit. I really liked him.

I did it!! OMG I did it! A whole day without alcohol. I feel stupidly proud of myself. I wanted it but I resisted.

Still did K though.

HOW CAN I STILL LOVE _YOU_ AFTER
EVERYTHING YOU'VE DONE TO ME?

USE ME. USE ME. I'M ONLY AS GOOD
AS THE LENGTH OF YOUR NEED OR INTEREST.

I DON'T EXIST...

IN MY HEAD — EVERYONE ELSE IS CRAZY, ONLY I AM
SANE.

EVERYWHERE I GO I'M REMINDED
OF _YOU_. EVEN AT THE GYM
I CAN'T ESCAPE. YOUR PICTURE
ON THAT SCREEN. JUST
VANISH. WHY DO I NEED
TO BE REMINDED OF WHAT
I'VE LOST?

WHO IS THERE FOR
ME, NOW I'VE LOST
MY WAY?

08 SEPTEMBER 2010

Welcome to today, and, oh joy, guess what I heard today, a voice in my head. Oh yes and it scared me shitless. Not my inner voice, not any memory. A voice, a whispered voice, and in all honesty it ain't the first time I've heard it. I know who it belongs to. Big tall shadow guy, the guardian. Shit, why can't I just have a break. Way too much going on at once for me.

Had to call ACAS about the job thing, they put me onto the Equality and Human Rights Commission. I've got to write and appeal to *him*. What's the point? He'll laugh and throw it back at me. What does he care about how I'm doing? None of them do. The inconvenience has left so what does it matter? Them against me. Why do I bother? I should just fade away. Leave them all to it as they desire. Another winter jobless. Looks like that's another Christmas party I'll miss.

Shit this is the last thing I need right now. The last fucking thing.
    Shit! Bollocks. Wank.

Why are you always in my head? *You* put me in this situation. *You* knew what was going on. *You* said you'd care. *You* said you loved me. So how can *you* feel good about this? Feel justified? This is the consequence. This is the result. All this extra stress and *you* did this.
    I wish I hated you, but that's the most upsetting bit. I can't. Someone I loved did this to me without care. Someone I care about could put me through all this extra crap and lock me out.
    How can they not care? I'm not that bad a person.
    How could *you* do this?

Dead brain, empty inside. Just a hollow core. No escape. No one listens. I rot alone. Always. Always fucking alone.
    Look at this. *Look at it!* My empire of absolutely *nothing*. No one gives a shit Dom. So why bother? What is there for me? OMG, what have I got?

192

Where is reality? What is it? You have yours, so why can't I have mine? What makes yours so right just because more people see it?

In the past month I've had to be truly honest about things in my head that *no one* knew. And this is how I am repaid. Lost. Sorry if being honest to those I love got me down but how could you possibly understand? How could you possibly know how that feels?

I know I should follow this up but *he*'s made it clear he doesn't want me in the business so why am I bothering? What's the point in fighting for what you love?

08 September 2010

Hello,

Hopefully you'll read this to the end, it is rather important. Both my GP and Counsellor suggested that I write this and try and sort out this situation because obviously both are concerned about me and feel that I don't need any added stress on top of what I'm already going through. I did want to talk to you about this last Thursday when I came by but since that wasn't possible then I feel this is the easiest way to convey what I want to say.

Basically, this is, as you'll have guessed, about my job. Bottom line is that I need it, it isn't just a case of wanting it; I actually mentally need it. It was the only reason that I had to actually function and try and sort myself out. The business is, as I told you before, my life. It's everything I think about and the only thing I believe has a future for which I will be involved. Without it, there is nothing. I love it as if it were my own and feel lost without it. So this is an appeal to you as the boss of a company I have always done my best to help and who said I was an important asset to it, and also to you as a person who said they once loved me on a personal level, to reconsider my position working for you. If you ever valued me as either an employee or person, please consider allowing me to return to work.

You are obviously aware of what I've been going through over the past few months with regards to my mental health, and the pressure I've been under to try and maintain some sense of reality through it all. Well, on Monday my GP rose my medication to its maximum dosage as it is still showing no effect and he is becoming increasingly worried about me, especially given the current situation. Both he and my Counsellor believe that at this moment in time I need the stability that my job provided – the only real stability I have at the moment – and to be around people/co-workers who know how I function and who I have established relationships with as that too gives me stability for when I begin my actual psychotherapy. Also, more importantly, on top of the stability, working for the business gives me enough free time to fit in my frequent GP checkups, my counselling, and from the end of the month my therapy. You know how draining therapy can be and hope you can understand the strain of having to go to several different sessions a week.

I know my behaviour and moods have been rather erratic over this period and I know I have tried to keep you informed as much as I have been able to, but I have been told I have to be fully open about my thoughts now so people understand what I'm going through, well fact of the matter is as you know I had to be painfully honest with the people I care most about, but on top of that I've had to be honest about things I have lived with each and every day since I was 16 if not earlier. These are things no one has known, regardless of how close I have let them in. They are parts of my life which I have thought were normal, but now I've been told they're not, which, as I'm sure you can understand on some level, is very disorientating as I feel nothing is real. The only thing that ever gave me a connection to 'reality' was my work. This I have told you already so won't repeat here.

I know I took a lot of my moods out on you personally, but not once did I let them effect my work – fair to say I had some down days but I never took my emotions out on the customers and served them as best I could. Your offer of becoming second Director was the proudest moment of my life, because it gave me a sense of worth and value within a company I love. A lot of my recent anger – putting our private lives to one side – was due to me feeling like you were seeking reasons to remove me from the company and not follow through with the process of making me a Director, and I felt upset and scared as I thought you were using my mental health as an excuse for this – i.e. not putting me on the bank account until a diagnosis, constantly asking me for a doctor's note. I got paranoid and feared that my every move was now constantly being monitored just because I was on medication and trying to get my life sorted out, like I had suddenly become a different person overnight. I have always had my mood swings, and anger, and in the past we have had more vocal fallings out than what happened this time (even in the more recent past) and I believe this was no worse than those. I was wound up on the days the text arguments took place – both being the night before and just after I left my first counselling session, so I was mentally drained and on edge. I know I could of reacted differently, but you know how I react when I feel I am being undervalued, and I have told you that I have no control over them and never have hence why I need the help of professionals. That is not an excuse or justification, it is the truth of the matter. I react in an inappropriate way and for the next days until it is sorted I beat myself up mentally – and physically. This is basically what I have been doing ever since that took place.

I am actually scared right now because it seems like everything is falling apart and I have nothing to hold on to. It was you who said that you should always try and fight for what you believe in, and all I believe in is the business and this is my attempt to maintain my involvement within a company that told me I was an asset. So once again I am asking you to please allow me to continue being a part of it and return to work. Like I have mentioned, I need all the support and stability I can get at the moment, and I hope that you can help support this request as much as I have supported your company and helped in its continued stability.

Yours,
Dom

09 SEPTEMBER 2010

05:00

This sums it up. My conclusion. Everyone always ends up in a better place. I'm just here, until the next person wants to take advantage of me.

Dom Lyne is not here today. Please leave a message after the tone and someone will get back to you.

Met up with Sam last night. Was really nice to see him again. He always makes me happy. He helped put a lot of things into perspective. He didn't like Tweedledum and Tweedledee, kinda gathered that, not many people did. And said I shouldn't be so nice to people, they take advantage, use me. He called me stupid. He's the only one who can call me stupid and get away with it. Said that's why I end up here, trusting the wrong people. 'Let's be honest Dom, think of the people who love you, in particular *me*, when have I ever asked you for anything?' He's right, he never has, never did.

Even he believes I could never function in a job that requires targets to be met.

We went back to mine. He kissed me. We ended up having sex. Like usual. Ha, was good. 'Why you smiling?' 'Shut up Dom.'

Guess in a roundabout way he'll always be my Sam.

Got to go hand the letter to *him*. I don't know why I'm bothering, I know he'll just ignore it and say 'no.' Nothing about this will go my way. *Nothing ever does.*

Gave Tweedledum the letter to give *him*. Let's hope he keeps his word and does what he says. I couldn't deal with the stress of seeing him, especially given I've got counselling today. Grr. Come on head. Don't go away. Stay with me. Just stay with me for once.

Pub. Kopparberg. Cigarette. Post counselling. Went well today. She was gonna give an appointment in two weeks but by the end she wanted to speak to my GP and my therapist, whoever that will be, to plan a course of action as both her and him are leaving on the 24th. So I'll have all new people once my psychotherapy starts. Great. My brain ain't here at all. Constant limbo and it's driving me insane. Oh yeah, it's Friday. I'm alone again.

Sam didn't get his job he'd applied for which sucks. But he's still positive about it, which is good.

Haven't heard from *him* yet. So he either hasn't read it/got it or he's gonna write a long winded e-mail. Or most likely he doesn't care. At least now I'll be able to know.

Only gonna have one drink in the pub today. Just the one then home. Well, food then home I think. Dunno. Dunno anything these days.

Just cut out from everything. No one cares. No one gives a shit. Just let me rot. Crap. Proper crap.

What were those stupid strawberry things on the barren looking stall? Guess I'm not meant to care these days. Yeah, that's me, removed from reality. This is my reality and it's crap. Boring. What the hell is there for me now?

Someone who loves you will never ask you to do the impossible.

Someone who cares for you will never cast you aside when you need the most help.

The man with leather shorts is in the pub again. Still looks fucking stupid.

Think about it. Sam is the only guy who has ever accepted me for being me regardless of how I've acted. End of the day no one has given me as much love as he has. And I love how he is still in my life, albeit fleetingly, but just to know he's still there means the whole fucking world to me.

Don't cry Dom, don't fucking dry. Not here. Not now. Fuck everyone. You might not know who you are, but you still have those few who care. What more could you want?

The world, reality is just a series of rooms, empty boxes that are filled with things to make them look different. But take away all the crap and what are you left with? The rooms. The four walls and nothing else.

I must stop trusting the wrong people.

The reason I 'sacked' you was coz you ignored me constantly for over two weeks, you showed no interest in business, you turned up to work on a few occasions looking like a drug addict and had extremely bad vibes. I will always have my business' best interests at heart and the final straw was talk of suing me, which was a bad move on your part. Besides all that I was truthfully in tears coz I have been so worried about you and will not watch you abuse drugs on top of medication as I had already warned. It is best for both of us to move on. My business is not here to save you. We'll just go round and round in vicious circles again and again and I can't do it anymore. The shares are yours for life if you want them. When if comes to the stock you have purchased that's your call. I have text for a reason, I can't say anymore.

Thank you. *You* have once again proved how little I mean/meant to you. After everything I've done for you, you cast me away when I need help the most.

And what's the ominous 'I have text for reason, I can't say anymore' ending? What reason? Or are you saying you can't say anymore? Leaving it without conclusion you little fucking shit. What are you up to? What game are you playing now?

I have text for a reason.

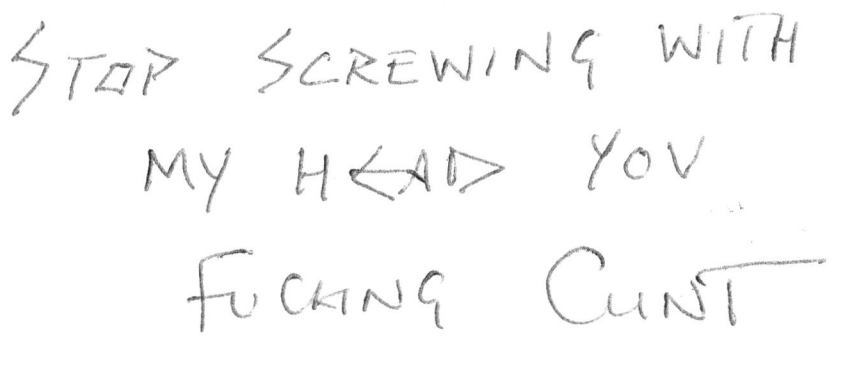

II SEPTEMBER 2010

06:00

When did *you* become such a cunt? Such an uncaring, self-obsessed wanker? Oh yeah, you always was. Hiding behind your business to justify how cold you really are. This was done for your benefit and no one else's. Who are you? How can you pretend to care?

All you give a shit about now is how many times you can get your dick wet, turned into a typical gay slut. Sex. Sex. Sex. So yeah, just as long as you get what *you* want. Fuck everyone else. *You* make me sick.

'My business is not here to save you.' And yet how many times was I there to save *your* business? Would you even have it if it wasn't for me? You would never of been able to get the stock if it wasn't for me getting you a loan, two loans. And who calmed you at this Clothes Show? The idea of vintage clothing, not to mention the £1000 that saved your fucking ass.

I have been there for you, I have saved your business and you can't be there for me? Can't you just give me a fucking break.

That's gratitude for you.

The moment I need the most from people I get nothing. No one understands. I'm fucking ill and no one wants to know. Just turning their backs when I need them the most. Selfish fuckers. Selfish fucking cunts.

Congratulations, *you* were the one who finally broke me.

You gave my job to Tweedledee. You fuckhead! What games are you playing now?

Hello, oh yes, hello. This is Dom. Locked in the Flat of Death. The white walled box of no escape. Calling me back with its iron grip. In exactly the same position I was in this time last year, well almost. In three days I will have lived here for a year. It feels such a long time. Lahh laaa lah ooh yeah.

God help me in this mess I call reality!

Arfa came to Camden yesterday. Was really good to see him. It's been like three years! Fuck. I think he still really likes me. We had a good catch up, and it's nice that he understands what I'm going through. But aww, Arfa.

Like he said, in the short space we were together a lot happened. What did he say? 'Right person, wrong time.' I was well chuffed when he said he often wondered about me but didn't contact coz he thought I wouldn't have time for 'little old Arfa.'

He stayed the night. Yeah, stuff happened. The usual.

Today, once again, my mind was not all there.

14 SEPTEMBER 2010

Had to go to the market today to pick things up. I had a drink before I went to settle my nerves. Was exactly as I expected it to be. Ignored, just fleeting 'hi's' before backs were turned. What the fuck? Wow, talk about outcast. So what is it I'm supposed to have done that's so bad? Oh yeah, 'love' my boss. What a bunch of pathetic wankers. It's exactly the same as what happened last time. Wasting my fucking time on those worthless pieces of shit, yeah that stops here. Right *here*.

Had to have another drink when I got in! No tears for what has gone. They obviously didn't give a shit about me in the first fucking place, stupid to think they would. I was always just an inconvenience.

My head still ain't there, flittering around in a half trance. I'm alright when I'm home, but as soon as I'm outside, forget it. I just look like a smacked out junky wandering aimlessly around in a mentally numb state. No connection with reality. I could wave at it from my little bubble.

My counselling got cancelled, my counsellor's gone on maternity leave early. That means come next week I've gotta deal with all new faces, that scares me. I gotta trust them all at once. Don't think I can.

Why is nothing ever fucking simple?

That's the line between
here and there.

One finger click of the wake I'll all of this up from this.

Jackie died three years ago today.
I still miss her.

I dunno, it's like I can't trust anyone at the moment. They're all users, wanting something from me and I always give it and then get bitch slapped to the ground.

Like even Tweedledum and Tweedledee, they said they would use this to get my job back, but now she has it, it's all 'you're better off out of it.' They have my job and my wage, they won't give that up.

And *him*, marching around like God's gift, trawling Manhunt looking for meaningless shags. I don't know when you became this cunt. Up your own ass, ego out of control. 'I don't have an ego.' Yes you do, it's so big you call it a business, and God help anyone who stands up to your ego. Fucker. If it's all so great and wonderful where would it have been without me? Two years spent bigging up your ego and selling it as a commodity. The returns on that? Nothing.

And yet, why can't I get you out of my fucking head? Why won't you just fuck off and die? Why does my brain keep thinking of *you*?

A year ago today I moved into this flat under exactly the same circumstances.

Saw a guy on the escalators at Camden tube. I knew him, recognised him but have no fucking clue where from or let alone how. When he saw me it was the same for him, I know. It was like a scene from the book I'm writing. Surreal. Unreal. Now that alien face is on my mind even though I've forgotten what it looks like.

A strange feeling. Detached. Where the fuck do I know him from?

Fuck.

Sat in my usual place in the Cap. Can't decide if it's cold or not. Day spent in central, just me and myself. Trying to enjoy it. Kinda was in a good mood today so I didn't mind. Treated myself to a large Sack Boy model and another keyring, a moody one so it's like my moods. Haha. I feel like Sack Boy, off on all these adventures created by other people.

'My world is unaffected; there is an exit here. I say it is and it's true.'

This is my world, my reality, so what if it's wrong. So what if it's not right. It's mine, it's where I exist. I don't wanna change. I don't wanna learn a new me or live a new life. I look at all your realities, the real world and it scares me. So much order, structure, deadlines and responsibilities. I just want to live, exist in my dreams and fantasies, then when I awake from this dream I can at least be happy. That's all I want, to be happy. Happy.

The three people I've given the most to, now all work together for the one company I gave the most to. Quite ironic wouldn't you say?

Handed my shop keys over to Tweedledee today. Was really upsetting, like handing over part of my soul, my life. Final. No more access. Denied. I feel even more empty than I did before. The final piece taken away. Empty, numb. And the keys were taken without remorse or any feeling. The new employees couldn't give a shit about the future of that company, all they want is the wage.

Fuck.

Will *you* have the decency to thank me for the stock I gave them for you? Surprise me, I really doubt you will. I mean nothing to you. I never have.

Arfa is coming to visit.

17 SEPTEMBER 2010

Arfa came to visit. We had a few drinks in the Cap, went back to mine, did K and ended up on the roof. It was a beautiful sky-line; it breathed and made me feel welcome. We sat on a bit of wood I ripped off a broken shelf. London. So big; a city to lose yourself in. My home no matter what may happen.

Today we walked around London. I wanted a leather jacket, got one (ordered another one when I got home). £230 on jackets in a day. Fuck. We ate at Profile bar, was nice. Then Arfa went home.

Was a good day. I enjoyed myself. Really did. Non stop talking crazy Dom. I felt good about myself. No worries or cares. Kinda in my own world. The way it should be. I like Arfa, he gets me. Understands I'm a loud, outspoken brat, and that makes me happy, like confirmation that I know who I am. That I'm not wrong, just wired differently. A good day.

He showed me an old sketchbook. It's fucking awesome. Totally love his stuff. Big smiley face.

Oh, *he* did text me at some early time this morning. A day late but what would you expect from him?

That Monday is here. Final appointment with the doc before he leaves. So yay, another Monday in the Health Centre. Woo go me.

Got a letter from psychotherapy, assessment will take one and a half hours. Fuck!

Well, I didn't get locked away, so that's a good thing I guess. On the other hand, no better. Apparently the only thing that's gonna help me is psychotherapy. Yay. Go me. Fuck! Will this end? Who fucking knows? Yeah, who fucking knows? Not even my GP has diagnosed me.

Just going crazy in my head. Got asked the funny question. 'Any plans to kill anyone else?' What psychotic now am I?

So guess where Dom is? The Black Cap. Same drink, bottle of Kopparberg. Creature of habit.

Fuck. Fuck. Fuck. Fuck!

Just empty minded, constant. Constant feel of something on my brain, holding my brain. Squeezing out any remains of reality. Zombied out and that's what they want. Just Dom bumbling through his life; no grasp or acknowledgement of anything other than this world in my head. Thank you all. Thank you.

So yeah. There's things I need to get out of my head today but not in the position to deal with it at the moment, well not 'deal with', more like write about. I'll do it later for sure. It needs to be jotted down regardless of who it may hurt.

Ha, the people who just sat on the end of my table I saw earlier this morning outside my window. I thought one guy was gay, and low and behold he is. Hahaha.

Bottle number two, yeah this one then home. KFC tonight, I've decided. Gym tomorrow morning, usual routine. I'm gonna paint this week. Oh yes I am. Dom's gonna paint a massive canvas. Just watch me do it.

This is the quiet, the loneliness. The emptiness inside. Latch on to someone and fly. Whoosh, until they knock me off a cloud and I fall into nothing.

Die, die, die. Everyone just die. Drop dead and I'll walk the festering Earth with only animals as comfort. I want my dog. I need my dog. She'd keep me company. She'd listen to me. Pfft. Not likely, she won't be allowed to stay with me. No way in Hell. It would be nice though. Dom and his dog. Just Dom and his dog. The way it used to be.

Company in a silent companion. Company is company though ain't it.

Dom and his dog and his stupid boring fucking life.

So yeah, the bit I was gonna write earlier. Where to start? Okay. Arfa's been visiting a bit, and you know when someone is so into you – or it seems that way – and you want to like them that much back, well I can't. It's not just Arfa, it's anyone, everyone (well, except one) but it's annoying. Like when we were out on Saturday all I did was check guys out, fantasising about having sex with them, fucked up sex. The lot. And then I find myself thinking what if say I end up back with Arfa, what then? I don't think I could commit. I'll do the whole different postcode bullshit. But wouldn't that put him at risk?

I mean okay, I like sex, I'm a horny fucker, but I like it rough. The whole idea of barebacking makes me cum. The thought of shooting a load in someone or vice-versa turns me on so fucking much. Fuck, fuck, pull out, cum on the asshole and then fuck that cum back in. *That* is sex. I wanna punch someone in the face when I cum, full anger punch. Put my hands around their neck and throttle them. Piss all over them and then fuck them. That's sex. That's fun.

Like my stupid fantasy about that deliveryman. He's so hot, I'd let him fuck me, invite him up and let him fuck my brains out.

I don't even want to know names. I don't care about the names. Just the sex, as a person they mean nothing to me. That's how it goes, always has done. Sex is meaningless outside of relationship, but do I really want one of them?

The double-edged sword. I crave constantly to be loved, needed, wanted solely by one person. To feel part of something. But then why can't I find that in friendship? I need intimacy, care, protection from this reality I can't connect to. Would I die for that feeling? That connection? Maybe. Most likely. It gives me a reason to be here. To exist outside my head for someone else.

Who knows what I want? I just wanna feel loved, no, no wanna, need *to feel loved.*

Fuck this. It sounded better in my head. Lost in translation. I just don't want to be alone.

21 SEPTEMBER 2010

Had a really good day today. Went to the gym, then went and got some canvases, paint and worked on my first painting in two years. Got lost within the creativity of using paint. Loved it. The day just disappeared into oblivion and I rose happy and content. Red, black and white the colour scheme. Only half way through it. Yay, means more days of painting. Get me. It looks fucking hot. Didn't even listen to any music whilst doing it. Creativity is the key to Dom's happiness. Vanish off the face of the planet through a paintbrush.

So, erm… that different postcodes idea… well happened. Met up with a dude last night, didn't expect anything to come of it but he ended up staying the night. He was cool, but I think a little bit too keen, but that's kinda flattering I guess, and I guess he could be considered cute. American. Jewish. Was kinda hot, didn't have full sex. Just sucked each other off for a bit.

So yeah, great situation you've created Dom. Two guys who really like you. Who do you end up hurting? Who knows? Just go with the flow right? Woteva. So then I'm like woo attention, it's nice for once. Well nice. Will it curb my fantasies? My urges? Don't be fucking stupid. I can't do commitment; it'll always end up in a shit hole of flames. Why should I trust anyone? What would be the use in that? I'll only get hurt again.

My painting looks fucking hot. One of my best to date I reckon. Still in a good mood. One switch, one thing thrown. But no tears, just anger, pure fucking anger.

You've been seeing *him* a lot lately haven't you? Must be really good sex. Using him as your fuck buddy are you? How long before *you* get bored of him or run from the idea of commitment? Maybe *he'll* be the next. The one who makes *you* happy. Another heart in your cages.

Fuck I hate you so much right now…

…who the fuck am I kidding?

23 SEPTEMBER 2010

Met up with Noam again last night. Had a few drinks, then made out on the roof. I love looking at London from my roof. It relaxes me. Grounds me you know.

Only thing is I can tell he really likes me. I like him but not in any kind of a commitment way. Just, you know, friends that fuck way. Nice guy, but I'm not in a position to give myself. Situation.

I always end up in these kinda situations. Indecisive.

Postcodes… just think in postcodes.

Hello Friday. Hello new counsellor. Please don't be a fucking bitch.
Feels like I'm never out of this place.

Counselling went okay. Liked her, may get two to alternate through so I get more sessions. They'll decide.
Drink with Jeff. Saw Marietta, she said she missed me, didn't know what was going on. Jana is a fucking bitch. To think I once considered her a friend. Like hell she is. Stupid pig-faced bitch.

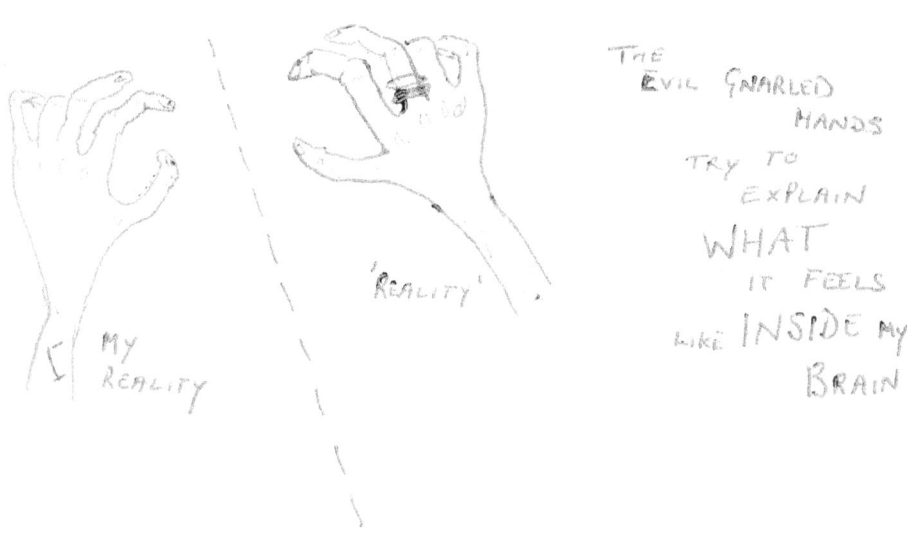

25 SEPTEMBER 2010

No one listens to me. I know what is like to go through this shit and yet no one asks me. Ask someone who hasn't gone through it. Ask me for fucksake. I'm living this each and everyday and you say I don't know, I don't understand. Pfft. Listen to me. Why won't anyone listen to me?

Who cares about me? I get cut out for *him*. Keep *him* happy and forget the fact I'm going through this shit. My whole future defined by a day and who fucking cares? As long as *he's* okay.

You all cared for *him* when he was 'ill' and made me out to be the baddy because I didn't care, for the simple fact I didn't know.

Now that I'm ill, do any of you care about me? Do you make me out to be the baddy? He doesn't care and *he knows* what's going on. But that's okay isn't it. He's *him* and everyone swoons at his feet.

You all showed your true colours and for that I thank you.

Tomorrow is my assessment. In all honesty I'm shitting myself. Proper shitting it. This will define my entire future, why can't anyone see how big that is? Why can't any one understand why I'm so scared?

I don't want to become someone new. I just want to be me. Dom. I am Dom. Why should I change to fit in with a society and reality I don't feel part of? Why should I be part of something at the cost of myself? Would you lose yourself just to fit in?

All this pain, constantly empty. Alone. Do any of you care? Of course you don't. You all ran a mile. I give, give, give, and for what? What have any of you given back apart from heartache and pain? More pain added to what already exists.

I don't want to be alone. I don't want to die alone. I want to stop crashing. Stop burning out. I want to stop resetting.

Where are you all? Where are my friends? Oh yeah, you cut me out. Was it really that unimportant? Did I really mean that little? Fuck, why do I keep trying when it would be easier for everyone if I was dead? Not just this constant burden, a constant let down. Disappointment. *Who the fuck am I if who I am is wrong? Who am I if all this is false? Fuck, just tell me who I am.*

I want to awake from this dream. I want to be left alone in my own world. 'Are you seeing anyone Dom?' No. 'You're a nice guy Dom, you shouldn't be on your own.' Pfft and what scare them away like I have all the others? Why be part of something that's gonna end at some point because of things I can't control? Lose it all at the moment I really fall for them.

What is love other than pain?

I don't know what I want anymore. I don't want commitment. I don't want to have to care for someone who I'll never be able to love as much as I'd want to. Just give me the sex, the passion. The comfort. Why does everyone always want more?

Well, I hope *you're* happy. I hope it all goes well. That this is truly what makes *you* feel complete.

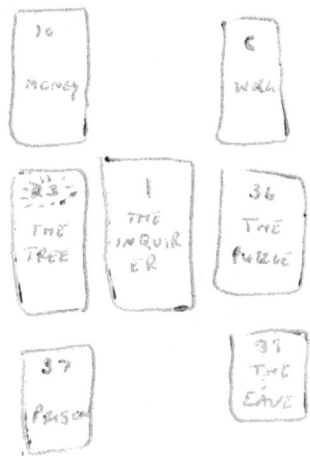

Bedtime… one sleep then show time. How do I feel? To be perfectly honest, shitting myself. Well and truly scared.

Shit. Fuck. Crap. But I guess this is the point the tide beings to change.

I WILL NOT
BECOME
SOMEONE
NEW

It feels like I'm always at the Clinic. Always answering questions and filling in forms. And yet I still don't know what's wrong with me.

Everyone tells me to get used to it or not think about it. But everything evolves around this thing in my head. It's *all* I can think about because everything I have been seems like an error. A reality built from fantasy. It's like I don't know who I am truly anymore. Thinking about who I would be or what I could have achieved if I had grown up normal.

The wait continues.

29 SEPTEMBER 2010

Nightmare last night. Black swirls, moving, growing. Filling the scenery with their darkness. So much noise. Loud. So many voices speaking at once. Claustrophobia. I scream and the darkness screams with me. One giant scream of pain.

Awake. Sit up in bed, my head hurting like needles are being forced in. Drink water, it burns my throat. 'No one knows that you're ill.' Turn and it's *him* sat in bed. My bed.

'What?'

'I told no one you were ill. Just fed them my side of the story. Justifying my actions. Who would believe you now? My word is law and there's nothing you can do.'

'You're a fucking bastard. When did you become such a cunt?'

'I always was one, but don't you realise they don't care? Where was the concerned phone calls? You just vanished at my will for my benefit.'

'I fucking hate you.'

'And yet you don't.' He rolls over. 'End of the day, I win. Welcome to life.'

Pain. Black out. Darkness in my head. What is a dream? What isn't?

'You're awake.' Voice after voice whispers. 'You finally opened your eyes and can see what really is.' Pause. 'There is nothing. You are nothing. None of this exists outside your head. You just lay dreaming because you run from this reality.'

'I don't *run!*' I repeat the scream into their laughter.

Eyes open. Lying in bed next to Arfa. He hugs me. Reality? My head hurts so much, like someone is squeezing it.

Slept most of the day, dreaming of nothing but screams and whispered prayers.

My head still feels heavy; this fucking headache won't fuck off.

Got a call from my counsellor who told me they can't do weekly sessions (really?) and tried to refer me to some outside agency that could supply those. I refused. I don't want to have to go to more places and deal with more people entering into my head. Just give me your 'whenever' counselling and pretend care. Just a statistic I guess.

Got that employment thing tomorrow. Woo, fun. Bro's back down for those. Fun. When will this shit all end? When will this all stop and I can just crawl back into my own head?

Feel like a zombie today, can't fucking do anything. Just want to stay locked away in the flat and let the world turn without me. I won't be missed.

No one, none of my 'friends' have text to see how I am. This hurts especially coz they all knew how important Monday was and how scared I was. Thanks fuckers.

Two fucking months and I don't even feel me anymore, like if I do be who I am it's all an error. Watched under a microscope. Appointments, appointments. Always in that Health Centre. And now I've got to start a course which is an added pressure on top of it all. How can I concentrate on all this shit and do my own thing?

Fuck me.

And then you've got the issue of Noam and Arfa. Noam overtly keen. Always popping round. Arfa doing so when he can. And then me. Fuck, what am I doing? And yet I don't feel bad about it.

I'M IN A SNAPPY MOOD TODAY.
SNAP.

SNAP.

SNAP

SNAP

SNAP

SNAP

2010
OCTOBER

What a waste of time that was this morning. No help in the case whatsoever, just pushed off in the direction of another legal place that deals with discrimination. Another long, drawn out affair of stress I don't need even though they say I've got a case. I haven't got the energy for this crap.

Yeah, as usual *you* win. *Claps* Massive around of applause to *you*. Fucking wanker.

So another day. Another appointment. Two more for next week already. That's all the past two months have been. Appointment, appointment; session, session. Two fucking months and still I know nothing. Thanks.

Had another night of nightmares last night. Constant, repetitive. Just row upon row of animated boxes, their contents sorted, ordered, tided. Solved. Then when they came to mine they just sighed and pushed it to one side. Next boxes sorted. Mine pushed to the side. Constantly unsolved. I didn't sleep all too good.

Just give me a fucking break.

Bollocks.

I guess it's at times like these you learn who your friends are. I'm learning that *very* quickly.

02 OCTOBER 2010

Post your pictures of you standing at my job, parading your friends whilst you're working. Yeah I'm sure they all prefer you there to me. But, yeah, thanks for keeping your word. Oh, and nice to know you care about how I might have felt seeing those.

Everyone has failed me. Mankind showing its usual selfishness.

Fuck you all. Fuck every one of you.

Leeches. You got what you wanted out of me and now you don't need me you show your true colours. I was a necessity not an importance. A soft touch. You're all worms. Parasites, festering pieces of shit. Go fuck yourselves.

Who said 2010 would be a good year?

Another Monday and guess where I am? Hardly surprising is it that I'm here in my new second home – the Health Centre. Hello waiting room. Hello to most likely not finding out anything new.

I look quite trampy and unshaven today.

So what did I learn? *Absolutely* fucking nothing. New GP. No report from the psychologists, my dosage of Shitalopram risen to 60mgs a day – the total maximum. My hallucinations a symptom of either a) alcohol, or b) anxiety. It's like I've stepped on a snake and returned right back to square one. It's fucking bollocks. How hard can it be to get a fucking diagnosis? Oh let's just leave him in constant limbo. Yeah, that's what we'll do. This is total and utter bollocks.

What do I need to do to get some results? *Kill somebody?* Why is it taking so long? Surely I'm not that complex that it takes over two fucking months to diagnose.

I'm really lost now. Like totally. Not knowing is the worst fucking part. Total fucking shitting hell. Why won't they just fucking listen to what I say instead of putting it down to the demon liquor? *That isn't the fucking problem. It's the escape from all this shit going on in my head! Listen to me! Why does no one listen to me? I'm the one living with this shit! Cunts. Fucking cunts.*

In other news. Last night I was at the Cap with Noam. We had the talk. We're not committed, we're not in a relationship, and I will fuck other people whether he likes it or not.

Neil and Stevie were there, so was *he*. So in the space of a few feet I was surrounded by four people I've fucked. Neil's the one I really liked. Dated but nothing came of it. How has Stevie managed to get him? I mean like how comes I didn't ? That sucks but I guess you never get the one you want do you? But yes, Neil is still fucking hot as. Like my total type. I wish I'd gone home with him.

Neil: It's good you guys have an open relationship.

Noam: Yeah.

Me: It's not a relationship.

Neil: Kinda is.

Noam: We're seeing how it progresses right?

Me: We're just fuck buddies who enjoy each others company.

[Silence]

Stevie: [Laughs] I think one of them has misunderstood the situation. I'll go with Dom's statement.

Well guess where I am. Yup. Usual place at the Cap. Same seat, same drink, just about to roll a fag.

Click. Flame. Inhale.

Why can't anything just be fucking simple? Instead of me being pushed from one place to another constantly like some toy. Stress after stress. 'Contact this.' 'Contact that.' It's always someone else's problem.

Stop messing me around!

How am I now meant to cum on 60mgs?

Fuck.

THE THOUGHT OF DROOPY FACED OLD MEN BEING
NAILED AND HAVING SEX MAKES ME FEEL FULKING
SICK. GROSS. LIKE TWO NAKED TORTOUSES.
PUKES

WIZARNED OLD GRANDDAD FACE
AND LADY GAGA.

ARFA SHOULD BE HERE SOON.

YAY!!!... *BIG SMILEY FACE*

AFRA'S HERE!!!!!.... YAY!

05 OCTOBER 2010

Why can't any of this be fucking simple? I mean why does this sort of shit keep happening? My psychologist phoned me with the outcome of my assessment. Did I learn what was wrong? No. Instead I was informed that the team had decided it was best to refer me to a top psychologist, and that they believe there is no one on their team who could give me the right care. WTF?! So what am I meant to think now? Am I *that* complex that I have confounded an entire psychological team? Guess it means it being a simple issue is kinda out of the window, and yeah screw you mister GP with your 'it's just anxiety' bollocks.

So I've now got to face another psychological assessment, a deeper, more intense one. Part of which maybe written. That's all good and fun but *what the hell is wrong with me?* Why can't anyone give an indication into that? Is it *that* hard? Am I *that* fucked up?

So more waiting awaits. Oh joy, can't you see my little face beaming with glee? Yeah right. It's all bollocks. Complete and utter ass wank. Never ending, constantly confused, scared, worried. *Alone.* I am pretty much dealing with something this big *alone.* Not even that fucking bitch Sam – 'You're the best friend in the world' – has contacted me to see how I am. *Well my dear, fuck you to Hell and back you worthless arrogant bitch.*

Argh this is so fucking frustrating. I don't know what or who I am anymore and that fucking drives you INSANE.

Arfa's visit was nice. Dom enjoys his company. I fucked him last night; was well good. Felt really nice. We pretty much spent most of our time hugging each other. Dom likes Arfa. Always has done.

I like how supportive he is, like you can tell he genuinely cares for me. Big grin on Dom's face.

Sleep.

Feel a little bit together today. Haven't zoned out as much, I've been keeping myself busy and all that jazz. Went to the gym. Had a *Fight Club* moment when I was there. The receptionist was like 'Hello Dominic, don't you ever take time to chill? You're always here. Guess that's dedication.' But I'm not always there especially the last few weeks. Or maybe I was. Like I just don't remember it at all. Like, you know, my other side goes there whilst I'm zoned out or sleeping. Quite a scary thought. Who knows what this fucked up head of mine is up to.

My new course is fucking awesome. I'm loving it already. I just wish I could work at my normal pace. My brain's all stimulated by it but it can't read at its usual speed. Crap.

Bro called. He's spoke to a top psychologist at his Uni. The conclusion of which was that I'm on a too high dosage of my meds and they are the wrong meds.

So my new counsellor looked well scared at the end of the appointment. Maybe it was the 'noise in my head' that did it. So I don't have another appointment until the 4th November. So that gives me a break from it all. To be honest it feels like I'm being pushed aside by everyone I've grown to trust during this whole thing. All my old 'carers' have gone and all the new people have just ignored me and don't care. 'Here, keep taking this medicine that doesn't work at a ridiculous amount.' 'Oh, I don't like where this is leading so I don't want to see you for a while.' My counsellor even said the last one I had once was trying to fob off people – so I was right about that.

Fuck it all. Passed around without care.

And how dare that bitch call my world 'small.' 'Your small world' and that it's too intense because it all takes place within five minutes in each direction from my flat. Who the fuck is she? She didn't even know half of my notes. 'I made notes on your case.' Oh did you, like that's strange. It's your fucking job bitch.

They didn't even know I'd arrived. 'You haven't turned up.'
'Really? So why am I sat right outside the room?'
Get with the fucking programme.

Within the past few days it feels like I'm back at square one. The beginning with no answers. If I had cancer or a brain tumour I'd of got diagnosed straight away. I bet if I flip out and hurt someone I know I'd get a result as quick as a prison sentence. That's what it feels like they want me to do. Just pushed under the carpet until I crack and 'bang' they don't have to deal with me.

Dom is on a *Death Note* spree. He enjoys it loads. Makes him happy.

This world is rotten. Why would I ever want to connect to it? Why would that be of any use to me? It's all bollocks. Bullshit and bollocks. You're failing me when I try to connect. You fail me when I do. How is that a winning proposition to me?

Mankind is a disgusting creature.

I woke up today and I heard this knocking on the wall. It was like someone knocking on an internal wall, behind my head but that wall is a solid external wall with nothing on the other side. And this knocking was loud. I jotted down its sequence.

I looked it up and that's morse code for '8'. Why would anyone keep tapping '8'? Then I saw the date. It's the 8th.

Tweedledee came round to grab a letter sent here. She didn't come in. Tweedledum came later and whisked her away on their date. Not one mentioned work or any news like they said they would when they took the job. Tweedledum was quite dismissive; I guess they have nothing to gain anymore. They didn't keep their word about the whole 'we'll keep an eye out and work on getting you your job back.' Did I ever truly believe they would? Hell fucking no. I'm such an idiot. Help people out and what do they always do? Oh yeah, stab me in the fucking back. *Cunts.*

Why can't I ever have decent friends? Still learning who I can trust nowadays. The number is dropping constantly. Thank you mankind, you keep confirming my opinion of you all.

You're all, well the one's I seem to meet, self-serving egotistical pricks. Living in your worlds concerned only by money and greed; sex and profit margins. What about the love and care of those who you lie to and say they're the most important? Your lives filled with deceit and manipulation. Pathetic creatures. Rats. Idiots. I hope you're happy. I'll quietly bow out of your lives. Let you live as you wish without me. Thank you for your pathetic fake friendship. It isn't required anymore.

I really want a dog. That won't betray me. That will show me affection, care and loyalty. I really fucking want a dog. A Chihuahua. Yeah, I said it. Dom wants a Chihuahua.

Who can you trust in this world? Maybe I should lock away my openness. Treat people as they treat me. You're all twisted with the morals of your 'reality'. Trying to force that world upon me. I really don't want to be a part of it if this is what it is. Disgusting. I hate the lot of you festering pitiful creatures, hiding from the darkness that surrounds us all. Why should you have access to the afterlife? You'll just infect it with your filth. Mankind, a history written in blood.

The world turns in silence. It turns in silence.

When will I get the 'help' I need? When will they stop pushing me under the carpet? Stop ignoring me! I exist just as much as your sick and ill. You're meant to help me too.

All I want is to be loved, Is that too much to ask for?

Bring about the new world order. A new world? What use would that be? Destroy the old and let you all rot. Let you all fester. Maggots. Fucking maggots.

SNAP! WHAT IS ALL THIS NOISE?

SILENCE!

09 OCTOBER 2010

I've noticed that I've started answering the conversations in my head whilst I sleep/dose in the 'real' world. WTF is that all about? Am I finally totally losing it? I don't know anything anymore. I know nothing at all. Fuck this bullshit. Fuck it all.

I'm just fading away from everything. Everyone. Maybe it'll be for the best if I just exited. Disappeared without a trace. Fuck off into oblivion and be done. Fall off the planet. Who would miss me if I did that? Hmm?

I dreamt last night that I built a building out of ice cubes. Everyone said it was pretty, then I poured boiling water all over it and said 'Now watch it vanish.' Then as it was melting I destroyed it.

Everyone had numbers on their backs.

Watched the sunset from Regent's Park yesterday. It was nice. You could say beautiful. I stared at the sky, lost in thought before I realised. I love *my* world, whatever madness is going on inside my head; at least it's mine. I can sit and stare up into space without care, without trivial worries, and there I find peace. Calm. For those five/ten minutes I felt at peace and relaxed. Freed from everything. Clouds passing by. Then the comedown of your 'reality' and having to exist within it. All its using and abusing, greed and malice. Everyone so selfish, serving only themselves. 'No one is more important that I.' Stupid fucking view point. Stupid fucking apes. Living with your closed ears. You're all deaf. You can see the evil and the darkness in this world but you can't hear the screams. The cries of history, of pain. The screaming in your heads. Reverberating around the Earth. The silent scream, the scream of eternity, of loss and the end of everything. Open your ears mankind and then pray for redemption, but nothing will save your pathetic souls.

Are you happy? Content? Are you living or are you all dead inside? Robots, slaves to the system. Disgusting dictated creatures.

I learnt something through all this. I've found out who my true friends are. They're the ones who stand by me, tell me not to change and conform; they're the ones who accept me for what I am and not what they want me to be. The ones who don't use me or discard me once they've got what they wanted from me. The rest of these 'friends' of mine are leeches, parasites. Sad that my so called 'best friends' have once again shown themselves to be just that. Sucking me dry, taking away what I value the most. *Users*. You've shown yourselves for what you truly are once again. Thank you. *Slime*; pond life with mouths of lies. I'd love to see you die so I can go to your funerals dressed in white and piss on your pathetic graves.

Black is best. Experiment with colour but the sun has to set at some point. Darkness descends, chaos reigns. Dom smiles.

12 OCTOBER 2010

All I want is someone to hold, to snuggle up in bed next to, someone to share my life with.

Is that too much to ask for?

I guess it is…

So not going to Guildford in the end. Steve's busy and broke. It's okay, wasn't really in the mood for it to be honest.

I'm too busy being a recluse. Keeping myself to myself in my pathetic little world. God this is so lame.

I've spent the last week immersed in anime. Episode after episode. I wish reality was like that.

All these escapes from the shit in my head.

Still no news on that assessment. My month 'off' has been cut short, next counselling session is now on 27th October at 3:00pm. Oh, fun, fun, fun.

For the second day in a row I haven't touched a drop of alcohol. Been eating chocolate instead. Ha. I want to prove to these new people on my case that my problem is *not* with booze. Fucking useless cunts.

60mgs of Shitalopram is no different to 10mgs. It ain't fucking working. I ain't even a zombie.

I'm just never home as per usual. Hopefully I'll sleep tonight.

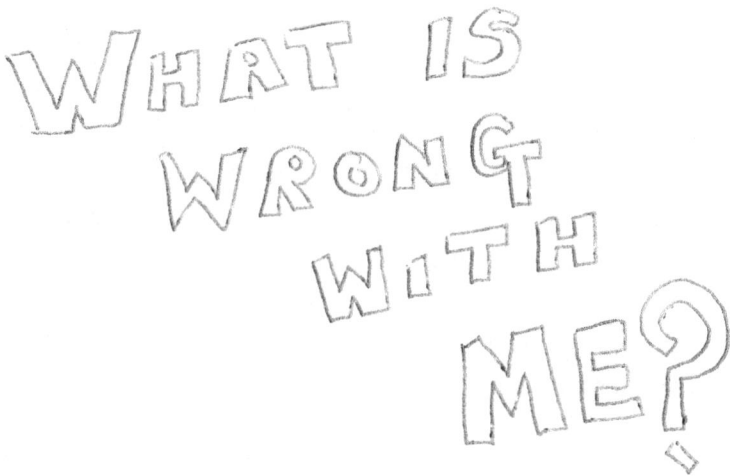

236

Today is one of *them* days. Can't focus. Brain zipping all around the place. Zoning out again and again. A day I don't want to be me. A day I just don't wanna feel crazy. You'd think after all these years I'd be used to days like these. You're wrong; each day like this feels like it could be the last. Fed up of life just rolling on pathetically. Fed up. Totally and utterly fed up.

Fuck my life really is shit at the moment.

Walked past a few people from the market today. They ignored me as though I didn't exist. So yeah, I get it all now. Screw the lot of you.

Andy came to visit, that was nice. Had a drink with my ex Andrew's brother Jason, that was nice too.

Got asked by two Asian guys today if I wanted to go for a drink. Well Dom being Dom is meeting one tonight and the other next week sometime. Haha. Funny that as soon as I get a little 'thing' for Jap guys I get two 'dates'.

Got my appointment for my next assessment today. 10th November at 2:00pm. Got a one hundred and nineteen question personality questionnaire to fill out and send back to them. Woooo fun. Yay go me. Pfft.

Well at least it means I'm moving forward another step.

So yeah. Met up with Asian guy #1. Chinese, comes from somewhere just outside Hong Kong. Went back to mine, made out. He sucked my cock and I jacked him off. Small cock – very small like three inches at the pushing it maximum. And he was quite clingy. Although I kinda like shy guys, this shyness pushed me to my limit, to the point that I wanted to shake him around screaming 'What do you want to do?'

Finished, he left. I'm off to bed. Goodnight. Goodnight diary. Tomorrow I'll be writing in a new one. Thank you for being my companion and keeper of my thoughts. Now you may sleep soundly free from any further scribbles.

*   *   *

Funny this one should end on the day I get the letter for the appointment that will change it all.

Oh and just to top and finish this weird day, I got asked if I was interested in doing porn. I'm actually considering it.

So yeah. Goodnight.

Sleep.

Arfa's coming down later today. OMG! Dom is well excited. Seems like ages since I last saw him. Staying two nights I think. Yay. Go me. Too fucking right. Stupid Dom getting all excited like this…

Beginning = Whispers
Middle = Noise
End = Silence

Such a grim day outside. Know I should go to the gym today but I simply can't be arsed. I'll get back into the routine next week… promise.

I just want to stay in bed all day. Right. Getting up. Shower. Coffee. Cigarette.

My head isn't all there today. Fuck it.
Fuck it.
Fuck it.
Fuck it.
Fuck it.
Fuck it.
Fuck it.
Fuck you.

I don't like today. Can't wait until Arfa gets here, that'll cheer Dom up big time. Only a few hours until then.

Kettle just boiled. Time for coffee.

16 OCTOBER 2010

Arfa's visit was awesome. Had a well good time. We went to the Frieze Art Fair yesterday and it was fucking awesome. Inspired me to do loads more painting and shit like that. Plus I got to spend the day away from the flat.

Arfa left this morning. I've missed him all day since. I dunno, I like him loads and I like the direction it's heading in but now is not the time to add relationships into the equation. Yeah, I feel so much better around him but is it just an escape? Is it possible? Would he be able to deal with the oncoming stresses I'm gonna go through?

Last night I remember waking up and telling him that I wanted no one else but him. In part that's the truth. If I were to go out with anyone, it would be him. But is it possible for me to be monogamous to anyone?

Is this all extra shit? Or am I now so much in the habit of over analysing things that it's now getting in the way of my life?

Escapism is Dom's greatest ally.

I had a dream Thursday night that I was protecting Arfa from the shadows. He was sat in the middle of a dimly lit room and all these figures where slowly advancing towards him. I ran through and hugged him, covering his eyes from seeing them. I was screaming at them. Screaming 'You can have me, but leave him alone.' Then I woke up.

Each day the world turns; each day taking me closer towards the unknown. At least now I know something will soon get sorted, as scared as I am, I hope that gives me some sense of relief.

Text from Sam:
    'I know what your problem is, you're still not over me.'
    There's probably some truth in that.

Went to Kingston today to see Kyle and make a surprise visit on Bro. Was good, had an awesome day. Was nice to get out of London for the day. Funny though to visit suburbia after living in the city for so long. Trees, dead animals, few people. Quiet. I'm definitely a city boy. I love the hustle and bustle. Watching the speed at which people live their lives in the rat race. So much time spent panicking about deadlines and money. It's all bullshit but makes good viewing.

Bro was a bit down. Taking things too much to his heart. Using my situation as a reason not to move on with his counselling. I talked to him. Hopefully that made a difference. Time will tell I guess.

Hopefully it has.

18 OCTOBER 2010

Another week, another glum day. Just hollow headed. Lying there looking up at the ceiling. Fed up. Always fed up. Must kick myself up the ass and do more creative shit.

Cold. Winter's finally saying 'Hello.'
One step closer to finding out what's wrong.
One step…
One step…
One step but never moving anywhere.

Today I should really tidy the flat at some point. Maybe… no, I think I will… chances are, I won't.

In the end I only tidied the front room. At least it looks well tidy now. Tomorrow, bedroom and bathroom… maybe.

The truth is that eventually you see who your friends are, and in the past few weeks I've made some nice new ones who outshine all those (well 99% of those) I've had since Johny. I'm content with that I guess. It's more than I could of asked for.

Goodnight world. For another day. Arfa's visiting tomorrow. Awesome. Makes me happy.

Sleep.

Arfa came round. We got mega-stoned. It was fun. Not much more to report really.

Dom likes it when Arfa visits, makes him happy. *Big grin*

23 OCTOBER 2010

Yesterday was a weird one. Whilst collecting a parcel from the Royal Mail, I ended up stumbling into a church opposite. Dunno why, just felt like something I needed to do. I just sat in there thinking. Thinking about how important religion was to me as a kid, every Sunday spent at church. The ceremony appealed to me. All those prayers I used to pray for protection; now look at me. Look at where it got me. You know faith in the unknown. This immortal entity sat on his throne, a pile of ignored prayers lying at his feet, swept away daily by his cherubs.

Yet I felt calmed by the place. Its silence, its presence. So much hope bled into its walls for all to experience and absorb. I left as I arrived. In silence.

Jeff invited me out for a drink. I went. Treated the usual lot like the slugs they are. I couldn't give two shits about them. I don't miss them. They mean nothing. They just exist in that moment when they cross my path. Forgotten. Always so forgettable.

He made a brief appearance. I turned away from him. No acknowledgment or anything like that. I felt nothing. Dead zone. No anxiety, no shakes, no emotion. He just exists like the rest of them. They don't play a part in my life and I couldn't give a fuck about them.

He left by a different exit so he didn't have to walk past me. Ha pathetic. What's with that? Guilty conscience? Ahh well, to Hell with you. I got my new life now. You're irrelevant.

Was nice to catch up with Jeff. Had a good old chat about stuff.

I ended up on my roof eating KFC. Again I just sat there watching. Laid on my back and watched the sky for a while. Peaceful. My world.

Sent a text to Arfa saying I love him. I dunno, just felt right to send it. I'll talk more about that at a later date.

Sighs Right, bed time. Night world.

Diary entry from 2005:

I went for a walk yesterday... It was nice [...] I ended up finding myself sat on a bench in Stoke Park and it started raining but I just sat there. I was moved, there's nothing like crying in the rain... I don't know why I cried.

24 OCTOBER 2010

Sat in a church-yard park thing just off Shaftsbury Avenue. Sat by myself. Relaxing. An escape from Camden, from the noise, from the flat. I like today. I don't care what I look like, don't care about anything.

At the moment I feel comfortable. After being knocked by everything that's happened now I'm returning to a normal state. *My* normal state. You know, I am who I am regardless if that's an error or disorder. Who am I meant to be if I can't be myself? I love this responsibility-less existence. Just sitting here appreciating this. Nature. The world. Free from all the pointless shackles of reality. No thoughts of money, family or friends. Just me. The big fat I.

Stupid gay poodle. Fucking ugly dogs. I want a dog. The company they give. I'd love one. Something that's mine. Something to care for. Something that cares and is dependent on me being there. A reason to exist.

Met up with Yoichiro at Covent Garden. Went for coffee and I got a mammoth slice of carrot cake. Was nice, I like meeting new people, people that have no prejudgments of me. People I don't need to pretend to be any different around. You know, when a new person enjoys my company it makes me happy, makes me feel good. I'm fucked up but not so much that people run away from me. Ha, well…

Ended up in the British Museum. Was good although I had to escape from the Egypt section, made me feel heavy, claustrophobic, pressure on my brain. When I looked at the mummies their fingers moved, chests rose and fell like they were breathing. I knew if I stayed there they would of looked at me, grabbed me. So I escaped to the next room. It was well freaky.

Had a well good day though. Was nice to be out of the flat and Camden for a bit.

Tired now, heavy eyes. Gym tomorrow. I must make sure I go. Gym finish essay (all 100 words of it left), then relax, no, write thing for Tim and send it. Then wait for Arfa.

Day.
Done.
Yay.
Gotta.
Love.
My.
Life.
Night.

25 OCTOBER 2010

The rain isn't strong enough to wash away the sin. It clings to the body, a scent, an odour, an aura.

If only God can give us Divine pardon, and God doesn't exist, what hope is there?

Visions went crazy this evening. Saw a man sitting in the chair by the window and the black shapes were scuttling around the floor. Argh. It's annoying. What with them and the white cat I've been seeing and hearing lately. First saw that when I went to take the rubbish out and it was sat on the top landing on the way to the roof. Black shapes, white cat. Oh, the knocking on my wall came back yesterday morning.

Arfa's visiting at the moment, he's illified and is cuddling into me as I write this. Went to central, ate. Then two drinks at the pub, film. Pizza. Bed.

Yay.

27 OCTOBER 2010

Back to my routine of counselling and GPs today. Woo great. This is where they get to tell me that all of this is due to alcohol and anxiety and where they don't actually listen to me. Fuck. It's tedious, I can't be arsed. Pointless waste of time. I'm actually looking forward to the 10th and finally – hopefully – moving forwards and closer to understanding what is actually going on.

Bollocks, bollocks. Gay ass bullshit and all that mother-fucking jazz. Got new meds to look forward to on Monday. Yay. Go me. Knowing my luck they'll keep me on Shitalopram. It's like I've been pill popping Smarties for the last three months. It's a waste of fucking time. What good are they meant to be doing? Jack fucking shit, just like everything else.

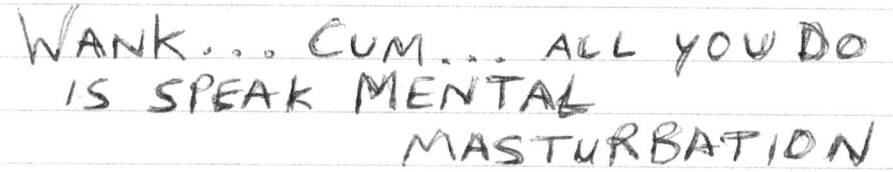

Checking out a hot Asian in the waiting bit.

Stupid patronising witch. Thought counselling was meant to be relaxing. You made me want to punch your face. Grr. I fucking hate you, bitch. Argh. You stressed me out. So sat in the pub with a Kopparberg and the usual cigarette.

'Oh, so you're going to see the psychologist to be given a label?'

'No, I'm going for a diagnosis and help.'

Stupid bitch. Do I look like a high school kid in rehab? So why would I care about your history with drug rehab? How is that relevant to me? Stupid cow. I drink to shut up the shit in my head, same reason I use drugs. I'm not a fucking addict. Grr. What bit of that don't you get? Stupid bitch, save your fucking lectures on the effects of K for someone who cares. I fucking don't.

It's well annoyed me. Self-righteous cow. I wanted to flip so bad. She even told me I'd stunted my social skills and missed out on stuff coz I took drugs for most of my life. Fuck you cow, what would you know?

'Do you act a certain way for effect?' No I fucking don't. I act myself. Fuck you. Fucking bitch, you've put me in a well bad mood.

Fuck, fuck, fuck, fuck, fuck, fuck, fuck, fuck.

I don't want to be lectured, I want help.

I don't want stupid suggestions, I want diagnosis.

Is that too much to ask for?

28 OCTOBER 2010

I

Went out last night with Noam and his friend Brian. Was an awesome night. Club was a bit shite but nevertheless I enjoyed myself. I was off my nut on K when he came round. But hey, all good at the end of the day.

Made a nuisance of myself on the way home. Hehe. Then we had sex. We fucked on the bed, on the roof, on the stairway outside my flat and by the main entrance. I even opened the door butt-naked – full boner and think I got seen. Oops. Ahh well…

The morning was shit though. I mean really bad, that counsellor really fucked my head up. Fucking cow. Just when I was starting to feel normal she's made me feel like crap. Stupid bitch. I was walking around not knowing what was going on. Shit, set back. But I'm not gonna let her fuck me up or stress me out. She's pond life.

Oh Noam mentioned the 'L' world last night. He blurted it out in his drunken state. I was like 'let's forget that was even mentioned.' Grr, what is it with people falling in love with me?

Today we woke up. Had sex. Then coffee, smoke. Day. It just rolled past without interest. Counsellor phones, that put me on edge what with her pissing me around with my appointment times and shit. So seeing her on the 19th. There's no way I want to see her before or right after my assessment. I'd kill her. Throttle the life out of her patronising prude face. What would she know? I've probably seen more cock in the past few months than she's seen in her whole lifetime. Fuck, how can she put me on edge so bad? I hate her for that.

Saw visions again today, well more than usual and something was knocking from inside my safe. That freaked me out a bit. Well, a lot, but hey, that's what happens in my life. Woohoo, never get used to it though.

Fuck. Fuck. Fuck.
Die. Die. Die.
Dead. Dead. Dead.

Sleep now.

Karma is a load of bollocks. Look at all the good I've done over the years, the help and support, so where's my payback? Where's the good things for me? Just trial after test after another load of shit. Who said life was easy?

You know what I really hate are all those who give me the 'we understand' bullshit, that line of 'everything will be okay', 'it's not as bad as you make out.' Ahh fuck off. What would you know? How dare you think you know me better than I know myself when all I've shown you is just surface details. You never tried to get deep, never wanted to. Well you know what? Fuck you! I live with this each and every day. I know what goes on inside my head better than anyone on this whole planet for the one simple fact that IT'S MY HEAD!

Met up with Yoichiro and his friend Kinu at the Barbican. Had a really nice and relaxing day. Then me and Yoichiro went and ate at the Diner and grabbed a few drinks in Old Street.

Yay. Good day. Woop.

31 OCTOBER 2010

It's your so-called 'best friends' birthday today, they're going out to drink in the pub two minutes from your house. Do they even bother to invite you to go? Nope, don't be fucking stupid. They've shown their true colours once again and without fail. At least it's further confirmation, not that you needed that.

The truth is the truth and that's how you should live. Why don't you listen to your own advice because you're the biggest liars I've ever met.

2010
NOVEMBER

Boom. Hello new month, hello Monday, hello GP clinic. Woo, back here again, as usual. Medication review, woop. Pfft bet it goes like shite. I'm bored of all this crap. Why can't everything be normal? You know, as it was. Fucking piss wank. Gay. Hello Dr. Davis, what are you going to put it down to today? Alcohol and anxiety again? Bullcrap. Stupid fucking NHS.

One and a half weeks to go. Just one and a half weeks.

Ok… Shitalopram reduced to 30mg a day this week. 10mgs next week. Week after I start my new meds Escitalopram. Woo I guess. At least something's being done. Change is always good.

Fell asleep for a few hours today; my head ain't all there, just that brain squeeze. Pfft. So yeah, haven't been in the mood to do anything, so watched the rest of *Bleach* and some *Naruto*. Day just faded to nothing. I hate days like today. I hate them, I hate them. *I fucking hate them.*

I am Dom. The corruptor of souls and the innocent. I'll take you, turn you then cast your damaged forms into the world as my army of darkness.

03 NOVEMBER 2010

More knocking on the wall. Three knocks, pause, three knocks, pause. Three knocks, November 3rd. Doesn't shock me anymore.

Woke up next to Yehoshua this morning, had a stupid grin on my face. He sucks his thumb, he's 18, from Cambridge, tall (like 6'5), all round pretty cool guy. Bi-polar on Prozac.

Apparently he saw me walk past him in Camden, that's why he started messaging me on *Grindr*. So yeah, he visited, we ate pizza and by that point hadn't fucked. We did that later, I bit him shitloads; he left with the marks of Dom all over him. I fucked him; I almost came.

So yeah, I think Yehoshua (Yoshi) likes me a bit, so now I've got to fit in the tour of Asia around him, Noam and Arfa... that makes things a little bit complicated. Haha, oh well, I am Dom the Corruptor. Hahaha.

Should I feel guilty about all this? Why? I'm not doing anything wrong. I haven't given the impression that I want a relationship have I? Why would I need one of them at this precise moment? I don't even know what I want so why commit?

Noam was saying one guy he's met might be the one who wants a relationship, so? Am I meant to react to that? Let's see how long he could commit to that. Not to sound cruel but I'd like to think that for once I've got the feelings of several guys in the palm of my hand and I don't have to do anything to any of them. Someone is going to get hurt, but hey, with the exception of Arfa, I don't feel enough for any of them to have that being me. Is this the power *he* had, is this what *he* felt? Ha, treat others as they treat you I guess. I'm bored of being the nice guy.

Like I told Arfa I loved him, that I guess had truth in it, but is it just control? As for the rest, I don't miss any of them when they're not here. I like them when they're around me, once they've gone, well, who the hell cares? That's what's always happened. Well, for the few that have managed to be my boyfriends for more than a month. What's the point in worrying about others when they're not in your world? If I don't do it over my own family then why would I do it to people I'm fucking?

Does this make me a lying, deceitful cunt? Maybe, but at the end of the day it's only words that leave my mouth, doesn't mean they mirror my thoughts. Everyone thinks I'm such a nice guy; truth is I just know how to say the right words. Manipulative shit ain't I? Guess so, that's what I've been called a lot of the time. Fuck it. Reputation is acknowledgement of existence, who cares if it's good or bad.

Been having weird dreams again recently. Those stupidly real ones, keep waking up to myself screaming 'Just fuck off won't you?' *He's* been in my dreams lately and not in a good way. In *his* cruel spiteful mood, but I've always had spiteful replies to him, the higher ground(ish) but I've not been the beaten guy I used to be in those dreams, but still I wish he'd just get out of my fucking head.

But yeah, weird dreams. One was where I was holding the pack of PsyCards and I just pulled out one card and it was the 'puzzle' followed by 'destruction'. Another was I was talking to the psychologist I'm going to meet and she was just chatting then gave me a text with a really cool quote: 'Those that have wealth, family and what they want, are they truly happy? Don't let people pull you away from your happiness just by a set of standards.'

Last night in a dream I just kept pouring away a glass of water because it wasn't clean enough for me, it was filled with imperfections. Then I dreamt Yoshi was getting dressed to leave and I woke up just as I was going to make out with him, I looked stupid kissing air.

Grr. I just want normal dreams not these real life frustrating ones. Who knows when I'm dreaming or not anymore?

So yeah, meeting Noam later for a drink.

Who wants to be normal? Not me.

04 NOVEMBER 2010

I like how all *your* bullshit 'I can't deal with social situations' changed the minute you got rid of me. Same old excuse really as it used to be when we went out, you never wanted to be seen out in public with me. I understand that now and it bothers me not.

Last Night's Dreams

In a building, at end of the large room is a riverbed. I walk down to it and see shapes moving. They're dogs, stray dogs rummaging for food. They see me and advance. I run but can only move slowly, like I'm in mud. Ahead a crowd of people, they're passing around what looks like a Chihuahua but it has a tiny head. 'I'm the soul of an old lady' it says.

Outside, walking, wearing only a towel. Meet people. Man hands me business card, he works in music but the contact links to a porn site. Liza Minnelli is trying to get out of a wheel chair to use a pull-up bar, asks me to help her. I do. The man forces another business card into my hand. I walk away.

Wind blows my towel loose and I can't keep covered. Embarrassed, go the wrong way and have to return. Again moving like I'm in mud.

[Wake up]

Same building, night. Riverbed now with water. There's a diseased Rottweiler puppy and it follows me. Another dog calls its name and it runs off.

I'm playing squash by myself. Lights go out. I leave.

Outside walking with Mark. We see a ghost. Mark panics and runs. I catch up, tell him he's gone the wrong way and we need to return. We do. He meets psychic; they talk. Conversation over, we leave.

I walk down some stairs; hand grabs me from behind and throttles me.

[Wake up, making a choking sound]

Gone to some Anime CosPlay thing at the Barbican. On my own coz everyone's pulled out on me or gone away, boo. It's well cool though. Glad I came. Good to get out the flat and I'm not at all bored. It's like part of my test... see how I cope on my own. And yes, I'm actually having fun. Yay. Go me. This is cool. So yeah, anyway. Got a Jap guy talking to me on *Grindr*. He's just round the corner from me. Too shy to go speak init. Grr. But yeah. Still cool though. Damn, they turned off the lights.

Ooh, scary cleaning woman. Bit downy looking. Right. Time for a smoke I think.

Really enjoyed myself. Managed to get the last Tube home. Yu and I ended up talking, he came out whilst I was smoking a cigarette. We stayed there until 12. He was well interesting, and really good company. So yeah, hopefully be seeing him again at some point.

But today proved to me one important thing. I *can* go out by myself and have fun, and meet new people. I don't need anyone but myself. That's an important step for me.

I want to dump all *his* remaining business crap from my flat. Text Tweedledee, said they'll come round tomorrow to help. We'll see won't we.

Enemies closer.

08 NOVEMBER 2010

Bit of a weird day today. Tweedledum came round to collect *his* stuff, and as I'd predicted he'd told *him* and had got *him* to help him move it. That prick was hiding around the corner whilst Tweedledum did his pretend niceties. 'Oh business is bad.' 'Oh well, not my problem.'

I saw them walk away as thick as thieves, well that's an accurate description of what they both are. Well, screw them. That's everything 100% certified. Now they can rot outside of my life. I threw a bottle in rage, it was plastic but it did the job.

Got a new tattoo, my picture of the screaming guy. Got it on my leg. It looks well cool. Sums up this period perfectly.

This week is kinda like a week of closure before the next chapter begins.

Had my assessment today with Cecila D'Felice. I didn't want to write about it straight after because I wanted it to settle in. Well, I got my first diagnosis today. Confirmed. Borderline and Anti-Social Personality Disorders. Yay. Pfft. So I've been told I need to see a specialist service. More on that later. So at least now I know. *Finally.*

She said that I have a duel personality, the darker side of which is at odds with my physical appearance and my outward personality. She said it surprised her, that and my mastery at manipulation. Made me feel a bit like Light from *Death Note…* more villain than superhero. But she had a good grasp on the situation and of me which did surprise me, no wonder she's a top specialist. Apparently I'm too intelligent and my brain works quicker than most others in that it is always ahead of everyone else and that's why people can't keep up with me. Guess it's true, well, I know it is. Too smart for my own good. Focus on my talents more she said. Oh and I'm good looking and charming. Yay.

So the long and short of it is that my brain is stuck in my childhood mentality. Growing up I had too much freedom as I could manipulate my way out of situations where I'd have no punishment or blame. Therefore making me the intelligent child with no boundaries. The one who's created a world that I control through my intellect and manipulation. A world where I control the cast and cut characters before they leave me. This I've brought into my adult life and obviously it's worked to a point but no longer. It's crashed and burnt. As she said, the Universe doesn't like people like me who don't play the game and will prevent it at all costs.

Then you get *him.* She said he was the major stumbling block. The one who found my weaknesses and manipulated them against me. *He* was the one who out manoeuvred me at the time. The abuser. The one who always has to be in control. The shark. The instigator of my recent downfall. Well, I guess that wasn't new news to me. I'd kinda gathered that. So now I need to manipulate that bastard back under me. Cunt. Bastard cunt. Today I realised… I can't of loved him if that love was based on his façade. End of the day, he's nothing but a market trader who's business can't and hasn't progressed into a profitable entity for the duration I've known him, unless I was involved with it. Ha. Hope I crumbles and burns. *'It's my business, I'm in control.'* Now drive it into the shitter.

So yeah, I've been recommended this mentalisation therapy. It lasts two years. I'll write about this tomorrow. But I've decided I will do it. Anything to show that I'm trying to get better.

So I send out that text I said I would to those I don't care about or trust:

This is just a general message for those who've been involved in this in some form. Finally got the first part of my diagnosis that I'm only gonna tell those who matter. But yeah, now begins the course of five day a week intense sessions to deal with those, so please give me space. Woo I'm a case study, so am of use for once.

To the very few who supported me, love. To those who took a step down, please don't attempt to step up again. And to the rest, nothing.

The responses proved/confirmed my suspicions. Jeff was supportive; Tweedledum sent me some pissy message about how I'd upset Tweedledee and all that me me me typical crap you'd expect from them; Tina sent a personal message; 'best friend' Sam gave no reply – expected. *Him…* well sums him up perfectly, a Facebook post:

'Some individuals will go their whole lives never accepting responsibility for their actions and the consequences of them. Meh, heyho.'

Yeah, mirror, look in it. Hey ho.

Not in the mood to write today. Sorry. Made the phone call accepting the treatment option.

Basically this is it:

PHASE I:

16 Patients
5 day per week programme
Up to 11 sessions per week.
2 x weekly large group.
3 x weekly small group.
Weekly individual therapy.
Self image and communication skills groups.
Community meeting.
Creative mentalisation based groups.
Duration: approx 2 years.

Now let anyone say I'm not taking responsibility.

Goodnight.

14 NOVEMBER 2010

'I'll always be there.' 'I'll always care.' 'I love you Dom, not like I love my exes, I really love you.' 'You mean so much to me, I will do all I can to care for you until you're better.' 'I was truthfully in tears coz I have been so worried about you.'

How many lies can one person say? True colours have been seen in a simple 'Hey ho'. Dismissed. You fucking dickhead.

Monday. GPs. New Medication? Dunno, got a new doctor today. Hmm, this will be interesting. It's far too early though. I wanna be either in bed or at the gym. Gay. Totally gay.

New meds: Escitalopram – 10mg per day.

16 NOVEMBER 2010

So I've been a bit rubbish at the mo with this. Guess now's a good time to catch up. On Friday (12ᵗʰ) went for a few drinks with Jeff. *He* was there when I arrived. No big deal. He easily ignored me, even though he has an understanding of what's going on and got his stock back – still no thanks for that, dick. Yeah, so I had to endure the pathetic fake cares of all the people there about this whole situation. Was kinda like a middle finger at them all. A 'haha, you had no clue, you weren't expecting that and now you're all lost for words.' Fuck you all. None of you mean anything to me. I'm facing something far more important than pathetic parasitic market traders with egos the size of superstars. Go fuck yourselves. Try for once imagining what I'm gong through. Oh yeah, you can't, you won't. Don't try to fucking understand because frankly you don't need to. That chapter of this tale is closed. The intermission has started; the next part is fast approaching.

So, Sunday, Noam and I go to the pub. Conversation moves once again to relationships. Kinda the last thing I want to talk about. I mean the likelihood is that I'll be single for the duration of my treatment. Who's gonna want to have to try and build a relationship with all that shit going on? 'Hey, so what do you do?' 'Well, I'm in therapy five days per week for the next two years.' Nice chat up line. In essence that scares me the most. I'll be alone for it all. Yeah I got friends but that's different. There won't be that singular person who cares above everyone else, and who'd blame them? People have enough crap to have to deal with without mine on top of it all. Quite a massive thing to do on your own though emotionally. I just wanna be loved at the end of the day.

Noam was like 'I'm not gonna wait for you, if I meet someone who wants to commit I will.' Why say that? It's fine. I'd expect it that way. No one has the right to keep someone in limbo. Our relationship may be considered 'unhealthy' but it's kinda working so why screw it all up? Am I really that much of a cunt that I can't see anyone else's feelings? Scared of commitment? At the moment? Yes, totally.

So I'm manipulative, I screw with the emotions of those I don't actually like. I like to spend time with him. I love our friendship; the sex is just a bonus, it's hardly the best I've had. I'm in no position to love, as much as I want to find someone to love. It's complex. I feel alone, friends are all well and good but there's still that void, that gap. Let it stay there, I don't want to get hurt again anytime soon.

Fuck, this sucks. Why can't I just be normal? I feel normal but now in the 'real' world I'm not. Defected, damaged goods on every level. What am I expected to do? What should I do? I'm scared. Truly scared, and no amount of comfort can change that. I'm facing a major life change that no one can really comprehend. I am alone. I am a ghost. Watch me fade away.

I was so frustrated today, angrily bored. I wanted to break things, smash the flat and then sit in the rubble. I couldn't find anything to break. I drew instead. Now I just want to sleep. Go and live in my dreams for a few hours.

Got some guy called Cye kinda stalking me. Constantly 'there' on my phone, got pissy over Noam. Leaves messages like 'If we do end up together and we go out, if he's there I won't be.' WTF is that all about? Why do guys get so attached to me? I'm a dick, a cunt, a cruel son-of-a-bitch. Are they all blind?

17 NOVEMBER 2010

Cye: Ask your shadow about Drazgon (I think that's how you spell it, spelt how it sounds).
Me: I don't understand.
Cye: You wouldn't. Your shadow will.
Me: But I can't speak to him. He don't communicate with me.
Cye: Ah. Ok. Well I was told to get you to ask about him.

WTF? That convo was somewhat unexpected. Now I wanna know about this Drazgon guy.

Funny thing is when I got the text mentioning it, I could feel the room get heavy with the shadow's presence and my head went 'You don't need to know.'

Curious and intriguing at the same time. Oooooh.

IF YOU'RE GOING TO BELIEVE IN SOMETHING, MAKE SURE IT ISN'T FICTION.

I think Noam really likes me. I like him but totally not in that way, nor could I commit anyway.

Whilst in the Black Cap, some rancid old guy jacked one off whilst watching me piss. Eeew. Meant I couldn't wee. He touched my ass afterwards to which he got 'touch me again and I'll kick the shit out of you.' Horrible thing about it is that the situation got me semi-hard. Shame!

01:05

I hate how I can't sleep. How every moment just passes by and no one understands. Fuck you all. What would you do if you were in my place? Could you cope? Would you want to be in it?

Night... Sleep

Cye: Dom, spoke to Grey Wolf. It's Draizegone. It's a place not a person. He said it's a better place to come from than head to. Could Shadow be from there? [...] I wasn't told about Draizegone, I was shown an image. I think you know it. Think dark pit, stalagmites all around. Think dingy, think trapped. Has your shadow left you tonight? I had a real nasty experience in meditation tonight.

Me: Haven't felt him today. Why? Wot happened?

Cye: Ha, that'll explain it. Been trying to find out for you about Draizegone. He really doesn't want you to know. Grey Wolf said 'Learn or be ruled. Only you can control your inner demon.' Makes me wonder. Your shadow isn't a shadow. It's your inner self showing itself as an outer being.

20 NOVEMBER 2010

Plate mutates. The lamb becomes a creature, an animal, still living, stunned and unable to scream.

The white asparagus small boiled snakes, bleached skins, dead eyes look up at you as your knife cuts through.

The rice maggots crawling and writhing slowly across the plate. Bodies undulating. Disgusting. Feel the sick rise.

You can't eat it anymore.

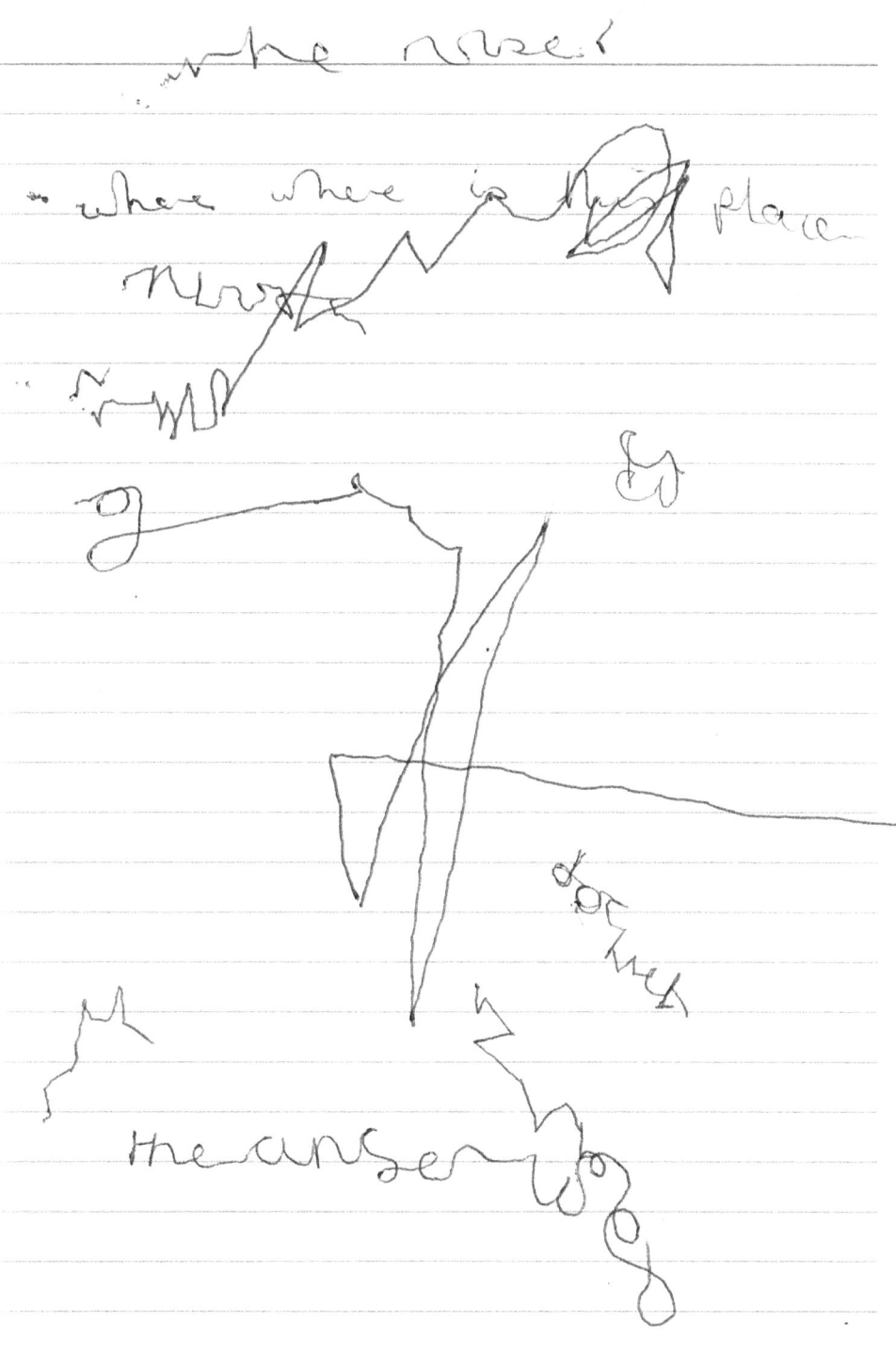

Thinking about my shadow man, and what Cye's guide said about ruling your inner-demon. Just think if I could meet it, tame it. Work with it. Would I be able to manipulate the lives of others more? Learn their guides, mutate at such a level. Control the guides of others and watch the effect that has on them.

To control the darkness, or if it is self-created, control the dreams. Empower myself with their guilt. Control and use them. Destroy your enemy's hopes and will and watch the walls crumble in on them. Their worlds collapse and they are left with the nothing they truly deserve.

Power. Power to control. The power to destroy. Leave a trail of ash behind as you amble past looking self satisfied.

One day I will control.

One day I will destroy.

One day I *will* destroy.

Went out last night with Pinky, Simon and Noam. Was a laugh. I was myself. My old school self. Living the life I want. Blasted off the planet. Did K and weed. So stoned/mashed. Went to bed around 08:00. Made out with both Pinky and Simon.

Yeah, give me that life and I'll live it. That's how I wanna die. Death, death, death. That's how I wanna die.

Yay look at me. Guess that's the price you pay for my life. Can't something go right for once? Jeez. 2010, you don't even disappoint at you end. How much more shit's gonna get piled on me.

I don't wanna be here anymore. This sucks. This sucks a lot. Always shit after shit. Why won't it just go away? Let me just die. My time is coming, I can feel it.

It feels like my body is an alien. Like it's not mine anymore. Invaded by some creature, locked in my blood stream. Just forcing me out bit by bit. You rot. We all rot. Everything ends. Cue dramatic moment and roll end credits.

23 NOVEMBER 2010

Been a bit 'meh'. I enjoyed Sunday night so much. I love drugs. I love that whole reckless abandonment I had, laying in the middle of a main road. Making out with everyone. I felt alive, not constrained by all these limitations and deadlines. All this control over freedom.

That's how I wanna go. In a gutter surrounded by nothing, with no one.

Today I want to be alone. Today I want to be a ghost.

Who needs others when you have yourself?

Names are all irrelevant. I am not defined by a name. I am not defined by my disorders. In my world this is all that matters. In my world there is no limits outside what I decide. My world is all that matters to me. My world is Hell. My world is destruction. My world is death.

OMG! I just realised. Last year after we split, *he* told me he had no money free to pay we back what he owes me, and yet he was able to maintain a personal trainer. What a lying, self-obsessed prick. It wouldn't surprise me if that's what he's doing right now. I guess that's why his business never reaches its potential. He can't live up to the responsibility of paying back those who loaned him money *before* treating himself.

Selfish cunt. So glad your worthless face is out of my life.

Die.

26 NOVEMBER 2010

Was good today. Turned down going out to meet Pinky and Si. Not because I didn't want to, just trying to be responsible. So until Tuesday – No booze, no drugs, no sex.

Not going out really depressed me. Felt like I was suppressing my nature. There's this big opening back into the life I wanna live and yet I didn't take it. Okay. Not gonna be the last opportunity but still. Fuck. Feed me drugs. Feed them to me like candy.

If all you want is sex… then fuck off.

There is no 'hocus-pocus' in this world. It's all about the power of your mind over another's will. That is real magic. And when it comes to manipulation, I'm a master.

In order to break the rules, you must understand them. Once you understand them you'll realise they are just a form of control and since freedom requires no one having control over you, then all those rules are there to be broken.

Dream pause never wonder
this world is not fine Soul

Die where you turn
our warried of
pray for me please pray

the world is not a plague

281

283

this is the turn of the summer

the silence the bees make

in the little rows of millerlier

this world will change and that is not an option. Change will happen an

will but something new will energ

...

I really shouldn't waste the pages on any diary like that. This is meant to be about my mental state not eh crap. I'm stoned I'm allowed to say how I feel. This is gay. Gay. Oh and calm.

I don't know what people see in me. I really don't. I'm a cunt. A villian, a horrible man who deserves nothing. Why else would nothing change. Trapped. Trapped. Stupid gay ass place. What? This is weird.

Come in who ever knocked. What do you want to say?

There is only one way. That way leads only to the dark. For you that is where you will be a ᴅᴏʟʟ

Oh, so that was a bit weird. I can feel you trying to take control of my arm! If I give you one last page will you tell me something?

So ... what [illegible]

Don't waste space you.

I want you [illegible]

The darkness [illegible] on the otherside of [illegible]

[illegible] do not ask of this place

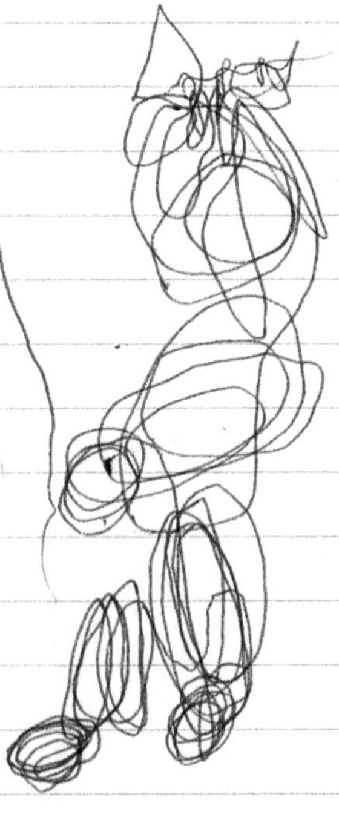

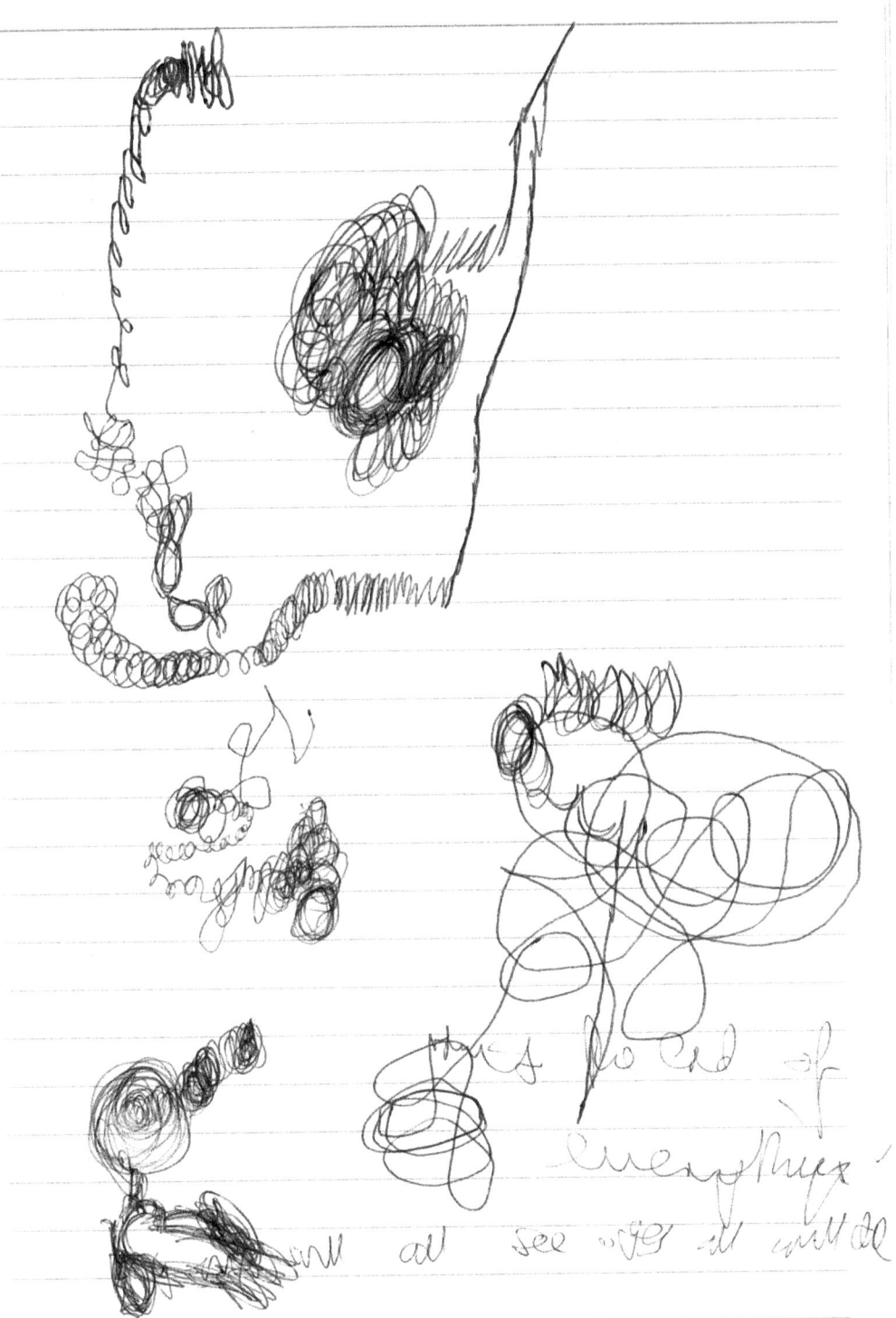

289

Reality is such a boring place compared to what would be. All the visions I see seem so much more real to me than those in your world. I like my world. I love it. Feel the freedom against everything. But who would want this life? This life with its dark corners and guardian spirits. Our silent follower, protector and punisher. Death.

Madness is a state of mind. No, madness is a name given to a state of mind that goes against a given accepted order. All I want is chaos. Explosions and noise. Blackened skies bleeding tears down onto the dying world. I love you, I really do. I love you so much I'd put you all out of your fucking miseries.

I loved that dream. I love it. 'Your debt is cleared.' Bang. Bang. 'You did say I'd always get one punch for free.'

Guess I should sleep. That's all I seem to do. Sleep, wake, pill, drink, drink, smoke… repeat. Eat, pill, smoke, pill, drink, sleep. Yeah, kinda like that with a few extra naps.

Dom, you are a muppet.

Night everyone.

God. No not that brain dead notion. God the expression. The whimper of frustration. Unanswered questions.

I'm the hermit. Well kinda. Noam came round for a bit. We had lunch at Bento Café, was nice. I felt bit closed in by the noise. We came home, got stoned. He left wasn't himself. Down over his tooth as he'd dumbassly fell into an elevator. Idiot. But hey, looks are important.

Empty. Just wish I could exist in a dream. Then none of this will matter. Seek the truth is a load of bollocks. There can't only be one truth. All of this from one small thing. Wow. That's deep.

Who the fuck am I kidding.

Go fuck yousey.

Yeah i did and i'd do it again

cant hold the pen

face flickering lights falling

falling who can see?   who can't understand

Stupid mother fucker .   Stupid bas

Doctors again. Medication risen to 20mg. Yay. Go me. This is pointless. Really fucking pointless.

Saw my notes. What's all this crap that the last doctor wrote? Some bullshit about me being in trouble with the police. WTF? But what really annoyed me was 'Denies any suicidal thoughts.' *Denies?* I didn't deny anything. How can I deny something that doesn't exist? So what, now that I'm 'crazy' my no's are lies? Oh yeah, you're right Doctor Foo Poo, when I said NO, I really meant YES. No is no, bitch. And all these comments monitoring my body language. What am I? Guinea Pig? Grrrr.

Told Noam I just want to be friends, not like I've told him he'll be anything else. I can't be dealing with relationships and all that crap at the moment. I need friends more than sex.

30 NOVEMBER 2010

It's snowing!

Sat in the sex clinic waiting for my tests. So funny seeing a businessman amongst us degenerates. His condom probably slipped whilst he was fucking some prostitute. Haha, not such a 'king' now are you. I hope you get AIDS. Hahahaha. Stupid stuck up businessman.

2010 DECEMBER

Went out with Pinky and Si last night. Well, okay, not out, we just got wasted at my flat. Was a fucking laugh. We got so drunk and ended up all making out. Pinky sucked my cock for a bit, then when she passed out Si and I went and played about on the sofa. Haha, was all rather hot to say the least. Fun. Like that is how my life should be. Random as fuck. Random, fun, drunken and with sex.

Can't believe all those gays bitching about those *Qrushr* pics/convos I put online. Trying to report me. Stupid fucking fags. Gay shits. Losers. I'd bully them all. So yeah, the fat pig boy obviously didn't show up in the end. Pinky and I were just stood on the other side of the road waiting to see if he was there. It wasn't. Damn. It would of made the day perfect.

So today I woke up naked between Si and Pinky; Si left and Pinky stayed. We got KFC. Jana Pig-Face was walking past my flat as we stumbled out, me wearing shorts. Stupid bitch can go fuck off.
Made a nuisance of myself in KFC. When they served some fat girl before us, I was like 'Oh, don't serve her, she's fat enough, we've been waiting for ages.' Then I oinked as the fat girl left.

Haha. Good day all round. I actually love my life at the moment.

05 DECEMBER 2010

06:51

What a fucked day/night. I've been hyper all day. Got wasted on MDMA and weed. Totally wasted. Was a fucking laugh though.

On comedown still, well okay, I'm still like totally buzzing my tits off. OMG! Noam's gone to bed, I'm all alone.

So yeah, anyway. Imagine it. The world fractured and shattered, everything falling away. Blowing away into the wind of infinity. Fuck that. Fuck what ever you want to, everyone what once was and is no more. Dead. We're all dreaming. This is all nothing but a dream. A test. An image, a thought, a memory.

Clock approaches 7. Slowly but surely. I want to be there. To exist as the centre. Everything revolving around the world I've created. All eyes on me. Me, me, me. No one cares more than I . Gay. Tosser. Idiot.

Let me crumble to dust and be done with it. Dust. Dirt. Nothing. Dust. Dirt. Nothing. Dust. Dirt. Nothing. Dust. Dirt. Nothing. Dust. Dirt. Nothing. Dust. Dirt. Nothing. Dust. Dirt. Nothing. Dust. Dirt. Nothing.

Noticed today that all the petals have fallen off the rose *he* gave me almost two years ago. It's now totally dead. Nothing left. A petal fell off each time he really hurt me, and killed a bit of the love I had. Now the corpse is empty. No love left. The end of it. The end of everything. Nothing but a stem of memory.

Quite fitting really.

11:30

So yeah, I've had the best weekend in ages. I've been pretty out of it. Spent 90% of Saturday with Pinky just being a crazy hyper sod. Like what the old Dom used to be. Crazy! And I loved every minute of it. I felt alive. I felt like I had some bridge of connection between my world and theirs and I pulled them into mine.

Fun. Fun. Fun.

Didn't take my pills for a few days, so I guess they do control my hypos. I don't want to take the meds anymore but I know I have to. So took one today, GAY. I just want to be a crazy kid. I want to be like this every day.

Had Ramen with Noam. Was nice.

Si's coming around later I think. So we'll see what happens when it's just him and me… we jacked each other off again on Friday night.

Woke Pinky up at 08:00 for the second time.

Pinky told me something interesting. That night *he* went to the pub on 'his own' and she gave him the coke, they weren't alone. Pinky was with Stevie – just as I had thought. So he must of gone to get a fuck. Ha. Made a tit of himself by being sick after one line – a small line.

So just more evidence of his lying. Dead to me. And he dared call me a liar.

They're all wankers that old lot. My new friends are cooler.

09 DECEMBER 2010

Guess I should update. Been busy for a few days.

Was out with Pinky on Monday. She said something that made me think. She was like 'you've been in our friends group for a few weeks and you've already changed its dynamic.' Is that a good thing or will it cause constant conflicts? Guess time will tell but that's what always happens. Am I that persuasive? Damn it. It's like Gemma used to say, I create the shadow that others walk in. I engulf and devour.

So yeah, we then got totally drunk in the Cap and I accidentally pushed her off the bench and hurt her. Oops, so we went back to mine and I upset her by rejecting her and then we ended up back at the Cap, then left, then Si came over again which was cool. *Grins*

Tuesday, Kyle came to visit, had a laugh then went back to Kingston for the night and day, so that was cool to catch up with Bernie and bro as well. Back to London and sleep. So yeah, my week so far.

Why is everyone like so shocked that I want to come off my meds? Why should it be anyone else's business but mine? Stop trying to dictate to me. If I don't want to be on them, then surely I can take myself off them. Right?

Got totally wasted on Saturday night with Noam and we only went out for a few drinks. Don't even remember leaving the Cap. Some gay shouted at me coz the match I flicked at Noam missed and hit his date in the face. SCORE. 'That's not funny you know.' Tell that to the people who aren't laughing their asses off. Toss face, get a sense of humour.

We got high on the roof, apparently I went on a mission for a lighter, which I have no recollection of. I returned home with more money in my pocket and the lighter. There's some dead shopkeeper in a pool of blood somewhere. Ah well. Shit happens, was an awesome night.

Gay. Just gay. Noam was like 'I went looking for your stall but there was some punky guy there.' My reply: 'Yeah, that'll be the backstabber.'

Si called me yesterday; went round to his last night. He's sweet. Dressed me in his clothes. Haha, so not my style. Was a good evening though.

Left my one-off hoody in the Cap on Saturday, Stevie saved it for me which was nice. Woop!

Meds staying the same for a month. That's okay. Easy to handle.

Now, time to read. I think. Coffee, cigarette, book.
I need to do more writing again.

14 DECEMBER 2010

Went into KFC tonight. Was horrible. There was all these weird looking people and shit. Like total weird. They looked like they shouldn't exist. I was nervous. Couldn't even understand the woman behind the counter. This old man was there and he just kept staring at me like I dunno what, and pushed his chicken box towards me like it contained some ancient gold. He kinda looked like that guy out of *Hellraiser*, you know, the one that walks into the pet shop and eats the bugs. Then I turn and there's this other guy holding a pen going 'You must take this.'

I took it but it was a shit pen so I was like 'I don't want it.' I offered it him back.

'No, it's yours now.'

'It's not mine.'

'It is now.'

'I don't want it.' Food arrived. I dropped the pen on the counter and ran out. My brain was freaking.

Then all these people were running around so I got home and closed the door. I tried to catch my thoughts but this stupid buzzing noise filled the air so I went upstairs and got into my flat. Was fucked. Like totally fucked up.

Positive thinking

Went to see Pinky today at her flat. Was well good fun. Had a laugh.

Totally forgot about my alcohol counselling. So that bitch called me. I was like 'oops'. But I don't have to reschedule or do any more. She's sending me the forms to my flat. Gay. But yay no more alcohol bullshit. Funny thing was I was drinking vodka whilst talking to her. Shove that 'sensible drinking' crap up yer crack and spin on it.

Good day though. I had fun. Brain spacked out on the bus home, bummer. Lost in thought. Got off at Chalk Farm station and walked home. Was nice. Lonely but nice. I've only had one day alone since whenever and that was yesterday and yet I still feel empty. Maybe I need someone. Who knows?

That fucking Dartmouth Park Unit still hasn't called me back at all. Fucking what's that about? This whole situation is bullshit. 'Normal' people get treated straight away. 'Oh, I'm depressed.' Here you go, counselling. 'Oh, I'm an addict.' Rehab. 'Hey, I'm totally fucked and just been diagnosed with a cloud of personality disorders.' Yeah, you can wait until we can be bothered to deal with you. WTF?! Diagnosed and then just put on a pile. Who do I need to kill to get help?

BANG! YOU'RE DEAD.

Mahhahaha

fuck it.

Bedtime.

16 DECEMBER 2010

Got my appointment though. 4th January. What a way to start a new year. Pah. 2011, you're gonna be a weird one.

So how do I feel? Fucking scared. That's it. Totally fucking scared. In that one moment it all became so real. This could be it. Next two years of my life. Fuck. Fuck. Fuck.

What if it doesn't work? What if nothing happens? Then where? Then what? Fuck. Fuck. I could cry, if I was alone right now I would. I would cry and beat shit up. What? Who will understand? Fuck. Fuck.

I'm so scared. Twenty-seven years of existence all about to be pulled apart, analysed. Studied. A body on a slab. Autopsy of my existence.

I'm so fucking scared right now.

I'm also fucked on MDMA.

Despite everything, I have the best friends in the world.

I'm still awake. I've been up for twenty-four hours and still going. Somehow managed to make it to Starbucks at 09:30 but made a total tit of myself in front of my landlords and their wife. They buzzed to get me to let them in and I ran down. Tried to like hold a conversation with them but *boom* next minute I look like a smacked out crack whore on the floor with all these people running around me. Stumbled upstairs and was like sugar, food. Nom, nom.

Like OMG! Totally blacked out. Fuck. In front of like important people. OMG, such a druggy skank. Haha. I'm kinda proud.

Druggy Dom.

Ran to the window. 'Look, it's snowing!' Black out, taking chairs with me. 'Dom, are you okay?' Come to. 'I farted on the way down.' Classy.

19 DECEMBER 2010

Well I managed to survive the weekend, well bit more than weekend. Thursday wake up at 10:30 – after already been waken by Si calling me at 04:30 and coming round. First vodka at 5am. Back in bed at 6. Finally slept at 03:00 Saturday morning. Then woke up at 11:00. Smoked pot after Kyle left – he visited on Fri. We went for drinks at Cap. Was a laugh. The Mexican drug dealer, crack whore and the Jew.

So all in all, rather a crazy week here. Preston tomorrow. Could prove interesting.

Sleep time. Oh yes. Sleep time it is.

Dennis Cooper mentioned me on his blog! *Ink Spills and Five Notes of Suicide* was one of his favourite books he's read recently. OMG. That's like OMG!

22 DECEMBER 2010

Head hurts. Can't concentrate or anything. Feels like someone is squeezing my brain. Gay. Had two nights worth of bad dreams. Hopefully tonight I'll get some sleep. Forgot to mention, Noam locked himself out of the flat on Monday.

Noam like told me how he felt and now it's kinda awkward, he can't seem to understand where I'm coming from. I don't want a relationship. I don't need one. I don't want sex or all that shit just from one person. Not yet anyway. Grr. I just want to fucking relax without having to deal with any shit. Why can't he get it into his head that I DON'T WANT HIM?

27 DECEMBER 2010

Give me space. Jeez. I can't be doing with this looking over at everything I do. You're following me around like a lost puppy. I don't need it right now. How many times do you need to be told? You are not my boyfriend. I don't want a boyfriend. I feel suffocated enough as it is.

Burst pipe last night; that was funny. Running around confused until I found it. Least it only went off in the garage so no major damage.

Back home at my flat. Had a nice time away for Christmas. Was nice. The last before institutionalisation. Haha haha. Meh. Only one week to go…

I'm off on MDMA and weed again. It's good. Listening to music.

Right, back to my night.

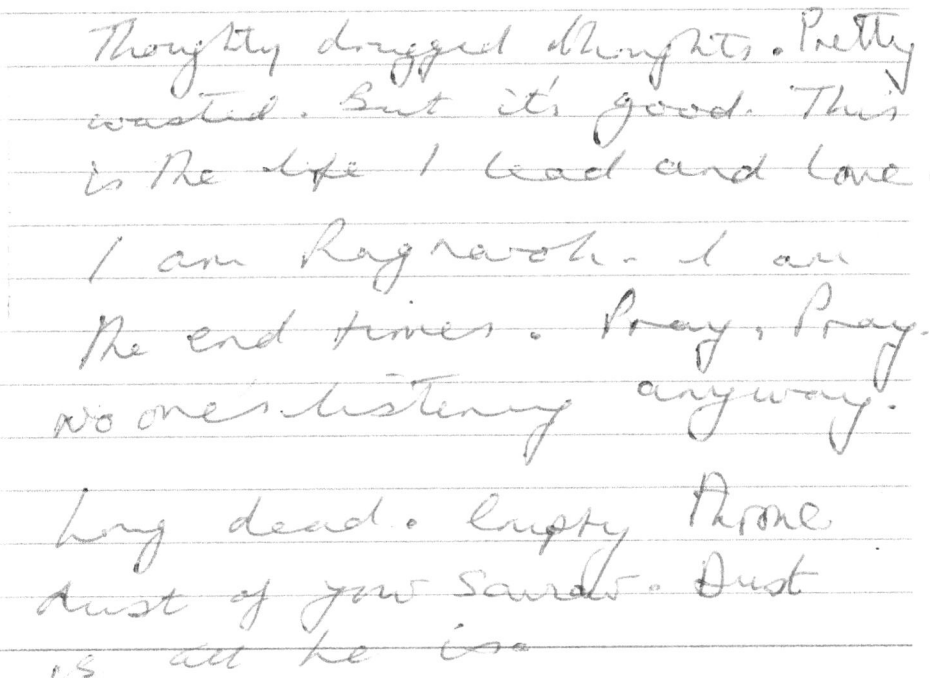

Funny trying to word thoughts when you can't focus.

Is it right to live like this? Of course it is. This is the life you'd all live if you could. You're all just jealous, that's what it surmounts to. Just face it. This is Heaven right now and where you are is Hell; the comedown, Purgatory.

I guess these could be my last precious few weeks of 'freedom' before

I'm taken out of the community and institutionalised. Could you contemplate how hard it is to deal with? Two years of your life gone. Gobbled up. Can the broken really be fixed or are they destined to break again?

What if it's all a waste of time? What if I don't get better? Then what will have been achieved? Positive thinking is a must.

Everything will be okay.

Give me a fucking break. Noam's kinda moody, and was all 'I don't wanna hear this' when I was joking about a boyfriend. Ppfft. So I don't want to sleep with you, just deal with it. Why should I be made to feel bad for something I don't want? Gay. Men!!

Got a new tattoo today. On my neck, it looks fucking awesome.

Saw Tweedledum and Tweedledee. They're going away for three months. Tweedledee ain't well again, oh well… am I meant to care? Good riddance I say.

Oh Dear God

Oh dear God, this is a message to you. This is if you're listening. Why would you listen? Is a message a message if it falls on dead ears, shattered and atrophied eardrums wafting like the useless, burnt out flags of all the world's nations.

So back to the message. Why? That's it. The universal question at the core of everything. Why? Why create the wonder that leads back full circle, unable to answer the question it was born to answer. This is the message. Floating upon the waves. Why? Why create wonder?

That one answer would tell us everything about our existence. Every little thing would blissfully orgasm in harmony. Everything would mean something. The perfect ending. The final kiss then roll end credits. Film comes to its end and screen fades. The end. Dead. A memory about to fade the moment it's born. The beginning is the beginning of the end. Forgotten.

So dear dead and broken God, what do you have to say through the dust of your vocal cords? What is the conclusion? We're the novel that drove you insane and you reacted and died before you finished the tale you began. Your words breathed out life, existence, all now locked in limbo. Hear this echo return. 'Why? Why? Why?'

That's not one voice. That's the cries of six billion people.

Voices merged and we speak in the tonal cacophony of creation. Your dead ears listen. The voice you hear screaming is the voice you lost and forgot years ago. 'Why?' Your creation complaining in your face. The inner voice. Ha, you don't listen. You create the platitude that you should not react to the sound of your own voice. You decide not to speak again for another millennia.

Oh dear loving Christ, how about a party? A sex party. You'd want to beat me down, handcuff hands and then fuck until you explode inside. Breathing we'll fall back on to the bed. Your cock throbs its last. Lighting a cigarette, I'll turn to you and say one thing, the last thing you'll ever hear from me, it cuts like a knife. 'Why?'

So dear God., our sacred creator, what do you have to say for yourself? It's a question I'll keep asking until I hear your voice. Dead and burnt out souls, arms like smoke caressing your feet. Weeping eternally. Silent. Volume on mute. Just the perfect way to watch the news.

So dear God. What do you say?

Another year rolls to its end. Thankfully. 2010 felt like it would be an awesome year. Freedom from all the crap. It turned out the opposite. It went tits up and melted into the worst year for an age. A decade since I cut myself to ribbons ended as only it should. My brain giving up on me. A new decade and the treatment begins. How can one year have such a massive turn around? I'm crazy. Actually mental. Fuck, just another label.

The rose crumbled totally, the timeline of those emotions ended. No more. *You* mean nothing. *You* single-handedly supplied me with the worst moments of the last two years. Now you're redundant. *You* can't hurt me anymore. Nor will you ever. Chapter closed. Well and truly.

So, what do you have in store for the next year oh cosmic Universe? Where will fate take me over the next twelve months? It's going to be an adventure, that's for sure. Cross fingers.

The future is a void. A notion of fate that is infinitely changeable.

2011

JANUARY

So I was gonna write about my New Year, and the date I went on last night, but meh. Today kinda ruined all that. Had my appointment with Dr Az Hakeem at the Dartmouth Park Unit. Yeah, didn't go too good. I almost cried as I walked towards it. It kinda looks exactly like you'd expect. Old building, locks everywhere, all it was missing was the crazy woman looking out of a top floor window. As I was walking towards it there was this crazy guy who just smiled at me. It was kinda like that scene in *Shutter Island* when DiCaprio's character is walking into the building and the creepy lady smiles at him.

So, buzz to be let in and there's the receptionist sat behind her bullet proof windows, unlocking the speaking window and looking permanently scared as if I'm going to try and kill her.

Wait. The place was so silent. Really silent. I wanted to fart just to hear it bounce around the acoustics but I didn't, I'd probably get straight jacketed for disturbing the peace.

So, the assessment. He didn't make me feel comfortable once. Not once. Always on edge with him. He was like a smug I-know-it-all dickwad. He'd put Jeremy Kyle to shame. It was like being sat in front of the Headmaster at High School. He really pissed me off, I could have punched him right between the eyes, but I managed to keep my cool. All the questions were about my anger, moods and thoughts of violence. So what if I like pain sexually?

One of the questions was 'some people will punch once and that's the anger out, others will continue to punch and it moves beyond anger into sadistic pleasure. Does that apply to you?' 'Yeah.' 'Which one?' 'The last.'

I dunno, when it ended I felt screwed, like back to the start. Kinda got this impression that he thought I was too sadistic and would get off on the pain of others. Maybe I will but that's no reason to deny me treatment. 'The one thing we do not tolerate here is violence.' I don't think he liked my 'it's not like I'll turn up one day with a shotgun and kill everyone' joke. Ha, it's like Matt said (oh, he's the guy I went on a date with. He's hot!), if I'd written that on the wall with shit then

I'd of got treatment right away.

Then at the end I wasn't sure if I was meant to leave or not or wait around. I left and went home. Needed to be by myself for a moment. What a load of crap. So now I've got to wait for another assessment to see if they'll give me treatment. It's all bullshit. Why can't they just treat me if they think I'm such a threat?

Dunno, I was looking forward to today in the hope that it would be the start point of treatment and kick 2011 off to a good beginning. Instead I'm just even more lost, confused and frustrated. 2011 is going to be a shit year, harder than all the other years of my life combined. 2010 was shit. This I fear will be no better. Screw it. Who do I need to kill to get some help?

Why can't things just be simple? Why can't they go my way for once? Maybe that's the point. Maybe I'm not destined for the easy life. This is it until the day I die. Pain, confusion, anger, hurt, no direction.

I'm expected to just act all normal through all of this but can't anyone comprehend what I must be feeling? There's only a limited amount of time that I can pull off Oscar winning smiles and resemblances of normality. In those moments you think I'm functioning 'normally', behind the back of my eyes there is so much shit I need to get my head around. What would you do in my situation? Could you even be able to imagine it?

Weird dreams last night. Joan Collins was in all of them. First I was working with her at a street market selling jewellery.

Then I was around her house watching a fire from across the street.

Then I was at this theme park where it was a hidden trap to lure people in and make them zombies, well robot drones to be precise. I managed to uncover this and tried to escape but got lost in the building, uncovering all the dark secrets. This black guy spoke to me, he said 'you don't have to follow them just to be a part of them.' So eventually I managed to destroy the main frame and the place went to blow up. Ester Ranson was there trying to co-ordinate the escape but was actually leading people to a trap but I ran away from the crowd and escaped on my own.

Final dream, I'm in a club, everyone is there. Mark (bro) tells me he's on steroids and I kick off, then I see Sam, Adam and some unknown guy and I'm like 'ha, I've fucked all of you.' Then I walked away to find Joan Collins sprawled out on a chaise-longe dressed like Cleopatra.

What the fuck was that all about?

10 JANUARY 2011

So I guess I should really make an update. It's been almost a week. So yeah. I've had one of 'those' weeks. The binge week. Oops.

Where to go from? Can I be arsed going right back? Well, nah, what's the point really? Wednesday I went home then out to see Jeff. Had to do the whole walk of 'we've missed you' bullshit that I have to endure from those leeches on the market. Two faced pieces of shit. They don't really give a fuck. How many have tried to contact me to see how I am? None with the exception of Jeff. So they can all fuck off to Hell as far as I'm concerned.

The drinks with Jeff went well. Was good to catch up. Although it descended into the usual 'I'm worried about you Dom, and your drug use.' So I was like 'Ok, no more 43 hour binges, promise.' As much as I want to mean it, it's not gonna happen. I got a bit annoyed but held my tongue. I mean who is anyone to forcibly limit what I choose to do? Who can tell me I can only have 12 hour binges? I don't need advice. Yeah I know he really does care but still. This is my world. My escape. I can do what the fuck I want.

Pinky came round on Thursday, which was awesome as ever. We went to go see Simon at the Cap which resulted in a few drinks and the obvious return to mine after for K and raiding of prescription pills. Well Noam shouldn't have left such things laying around. So wasted, we went to bed. It was the typical night. I threw some random laptop we'd found out of the window. Ha.

Next day Pinky stays asleep until 2. My xBox arrived and yeah that was pretty much that. Lounging around watching Tyra Banks. Matt text to see if I wanted to go for a drink so we did. Pinky came for one. Matt btw is the guy I went on a date with. He's cool. *Smiley face*. After that I got stopped by the 'fake' police who tried telling me my key ring is an offensive weapon. So I ran away from them and went home via Sainsbury's.

Later we go to the Cap – Si, Adam, Nick (Adam's boyfriend). *He* was there acting really camp. I couldn't give a fuck about it so I blanked him when I had to sit around the table he was at. He soon downed his beer and stomped off. Pfft, for which I got a load of 'Dom, look what you've done.' What did I do? Everyone has this opinion that he's some really nice person when in fact he's just a fucking parasite. Fuck speaking to him. It's not 'really sad' that we can't even acknowledge each other. It's how it's going to be.

So the night continues with various people pissing us off. Wankers. But we end up back at Si and Adam's. Everyone gets wasted on K and coke. Matti goes on at me about *him* and I really can't give a fuck. So what if I helped him? That's all there is. I helped him to get to the point he is at and all without thanks. The minute I need help he's like 'fuck off', so chapter closed. *He* is small fry when held up against the shit I'm going through at the moment. Stop linking me back to him. I've moved on maybe everyone else should do the same. It's now my time to help myself.

Got so wasted. Went to bed at 10am Saturday. Then chilled for the day. That night we got wasted on K again. Was a chilled night. Just watching TV and shit. Was nice. I got thinking about things like how worthless all this shit is. This Earth. You know, always having to prove yourself to someone else to get any sense of worth. Wow, you've got a piece of paper saying you're qualified at something that I'm sure loads of people could do, but you're so much more important because of that piece of paper. It's bollocks. Really fucking bollocks. Oh you don't have this, you might be really fucking amazing but yeah. Can't tick this box so fuck off. It's ass wank. Fuck that shit.

My life is just like a line. Rolling forward but hey, isn't everyone's?

Finally got back to the flat on Sunday. Matt came round and we watched stuff. Made out and had a genuinely awesome evening. Fell asleep to the *Sword in the Stone*. Noam came back from holiday at some stupid time like 3am. I mention Matt and he was like 'you fucked him yet?' I was like 'he's still here.' When I said Noam would be sleeping on the couch, all doors got slammed and he was moaning on like a fucking brat.

Monday morning we wake up, fondle then hear this cough. Oh yeah, Noam's home. So we had to do the walk of shame in my own home. Went got Starbucks and I wandered around for a bit like a teenager too scared to go home coz he'd been caught fucking in his parents' bed. So eventually I get home, shower and have to endure a fucking grumpy Noam. So fucking what if I had a guy in my bed? IT'S MY FUCKING FLAT! Get over it. You're not my boyfriend, you're not a co-sharer of the flat, you're not my fucking mother. Why should I feel bad about seeing someone I actually like? Get fucked. Don't make me feel guilty because I'm not giving you the sex you want. If you wanna get laid then go get laid. I'm not here for your sexual benefit, I'm meant to be a mate. Jeez, we've been through this before and it's like a broken fucking record. Change the channel or get lost.

Date with Matt went well. Like I think really well. Mmmm sushi. Came back to mine even though Matt was like 'I feel bad.' I'm like 'fuck off, we're on a date, we can go back to mine because it's mine.' No one's gonna give me a fucking hard time over it, nor do they have the right to treat my date like crap. It's so fucking stupid. So yeah. Noam wasn't around when we got back. Good. Fucking emo.

Had sex. Good sex. Rough sex. Scratching, punching, gob. The lot. Was hot. Matt jizzed over my face. Nice. Now this is the sex I've been craving. Oh yes. Bring it on.

So yeah. I really like this Matt guy. Really like, although we know a few of the same people. There was an awkward moment on the date. I was like 'my ex Jules.' Him: 'I had a boyfriend called Jules.' Me: 'Really? Surname?' Him: 'Woods.' Me: 'Same guy.' So that was like erm 'ha.' So same boyfriend. Then he knows Arfa too, he said he'd told his mate he was talking to one of Arfa's exes and the person was like 'well it's either Chaz or Dom.' Haha. The reputation I leave behind me. Nice. Everyone seems to have either heard about me or something I've done. Least I haven't been forgotten.

Matt. He's hot. I likes him. Let's see how this one pans out. *Crosses fingers.*

Had a quiet day today, just catching up with work and filling out the online application for ESA. Blurgh. My head felt like crap today. That squeezing sensation was back. Bit like I got yesterday. Think it may be due to my meds but we shall see how I feel tomorrow.

Noam was only in the flat for like 5minutes. Was still in a grump.

Didn't even ask how the date went. Pfft. I can't be arsed with it. Giving me all the 'I want to spend time with you' crap, then just marching in all 'I'm going out for dinner with a friend and then studying, won't be back until late.' Childish. Like I care. Meant I didn't have to see his moaning face all day. Get over it. I'm dating Matt (kinda, not sure if that's the term you'd use so early on).

So yeah. Here we go. Dom likes Matt. Hopes everything runs as he'd hope but we shall see. Don't get too attached Dom. Stay calm. If it's meant to happen it will.

So good night. See y'all tomorrow.

15 JANUARY 2011

Today has been one of *those* days. Something in the air maybe. Just conflicts, arguments and general pissed offness. A wasted day, and not even a good sense of the phrase. A ruined high. A forced comedown. Even I was the most pissed off I've been in ages. Grr. Not in the mood to write about it today. Blurgh. I'll save it all for tomorrow. Woo, that'll be a barrel of fucking laughs.

I sense something in the shadows. Something regarding *him*. I dunno, it's like I'm expecting to read some great announcement. Something business orientated. A feeling, gut-feeling. Something is about to happen. *I know it.* Something not good.

I COME FROM THE
OTHER SIDE

SLEEP

PRAY I AM
THE
SILENCE

I SEEK TO
DEVOUR YOUR
MEMORIES
AND TURN
THEM INTO
TAR.

I AM THE DARKNESS

I WILL FEED ON
YOUR FEARS,
YOUR ANGER,
YOUR HATE

NIGHTMARES
ARE THE ONLY
REALITY

16 JANUARY 2011

So where was I? In a better mood today. Thank fuck, don't want another day feeling like that.

So yeah, Noam. He's been acting like a pissy bitch all week. Fuck me, talk about sulk. Tuesday I had an early night so didn't have to endure all that. Wednesday was his exam, went shit so he stumbles in drunk and acting like a dick, all loud and erm... American. So I'm like ok, I'll drink, fucking hell, whatever. I might have been doing it just to keep you happy. Gave him K, it shut him up a bit. Can't remember what we did but I had a good time as always. Yay to the K.

Thursday we go for food at the Cap. He just sits and moans like a twat. Grumpy. Sighing. Doing the whole sarcastic reply then replying to my 'wot?' with 'hmm? I didn't say anything.' ARGH! So we leave after one pint and he's all let's take some muscle relaxants. Ok. I needed *something* to get me through the night. Three cyclobenzaprine pills later and few hours of virtual silence later we go to bed.

Friday, he moved his stuff out. MDMA and weed night in the flat. Well looking forward to it. Starts really well. Get high. Creatively high. I actually returned to my writing, like fiction writing. I've been stunted on that front since all this shit began and whoosh, barriers unlocked and I write fuckloads. Then it changed. I got banned from texting Matt. Then he would moan on about Monday and Matt in general. Again and again and again. Totally fucking killing my high and whenever I managed to regain it there'd be 'Jeez Dom, Monday!' OMG! GET OVER IT!

So end up lying in bed at 6am. Zoning out to music. Moans again. 'You know you almost lost me as a friend over this.' Not in my own bed. I was like 'yeah ok.' 'No Dom, you put in me a box when I went away and placed me on a shelf.' 'Lucky I wrote your name on it isn't it? I'd of totally forgot otherwise.' Silence. Conversations. Fun. Humour. Random MDMA heart-filled waffle. Brick. Face. Pulled down. Fuck!

'Hug me.' 'Why?' 'Because I want you to.' 'You can't ask for things like that.'

So I escape for cigarettes. So it's like 10am now. Totally zoned out in the shop. What a state I must of looked. Black eyes, gormless face. Come to after god knows how long. Buy tobacco. Go home. Crawl into bed. Why did I face the world today.

Noam: It's okay.
Me: I know it is.
Noam: No it isn't.
Me: What?
Noam: Nothing. Didn't say anything.

Aaaaaghhh! Sat in my nest fuming. He stayed in bed all day until 5. Then declared he was staying all night. Then sat in silence. Did some filming for his course. Then sat in silence. Scraping at the remains of the MDMA and weed. I had an early night. Yesterday was written off to hell. A totally wasted day. So annoyed. So lucky I didn't snap. I could of got to see Matt for like an hour but noooo had to sit bored out of my brains instead, like some tagged ASBO kid.

He left today. I got a bit of stuff done, but his attitude has really fucked this up a bit. I don't want to sit around wasting my time too scared to talk coz of the shitty remarks he'll give. Fuck that. Totally.

Grr. He's really starting to piss me off constantly. The way he eats disgusts me, like he's in fear that he'll never eat again so has to wolf it down, and the sound of it, FUCK don't get me started on that! The way he explains things. The way he gets all self righteously smarmy. They *all* drive me MAD!

Dickhead. 'Oh, I've got a big dick.' Who cares? Anyway it has to be that big to distract people from your lack of personality.

AND BREATHE...

I looked like such a desperate druggy last night raiding the last whisps of MDMA from the baggy whilst he was out if the room. It was the only thing that could keep me from snapping and shitting out Hell's fury in his face.

BREATHE...

Matt should be coming round later. Yay. Woop. Day will end okay.

Matt came round yesterday was nice. We chatted for ages. Crackwhore Sunday, so we were pretty much both muntered. We made out. Slapped each other around. Jacked off. Went on for hours. I got a well cool scratch mark out of it. Was fucking hot. Finally I've met a guy who has the same sexual urges as me. Hot. Really fucking hot.

He went to work this morning. I went to the GPs. Then the market to hand over a business letter for *him* that arrived at the flat today. Then I popped down to see Matt at work. Got meds. Home.

Went out for a drink with Matt and Laura and Becca at Wetherspoons. Was a laugh. Had an awesome evening. Matt went home though. Boooo.

Stupid ain't it. I really like him already. He's totally my type, punk, pierced. Cool. Sexy. Fun. ARGH. I really hope it all goes okay. He's defo one I wouldn't wanna lose. He ticks every box. Makes me happy. Yay. All's good in Dom's world. Well. Kinda.

Damn you Matt! Ha, but he seems keen to always want to meet up. So that's good right?

19 JANUARY 2011

What a weird fucking day. Full moon as well. Got a text from *him* about the business going under. So Pinky and I ended up at the Cap where *he* was on a date, so we stayed longer than we'd intended. I went home. There's a letter from Noam pretty much bitching out at me about shit and how he wanted me to have a 'physical object to remind you of the friend you're about to lose.' Jeez. Get over it.

Si calls, he'll bring over my K.

Doorbell goes, so I think it's Si. It's not. Through the glass it looks like Noam. It's not. It's *him*. He wants to talk. I let him in.

Well this is what he had to say. He never sacked me, Tweedledum had told him I wasn't going to turn up for work on Saturday. Tweedledee had showed him (forwarded on) all the texts I'd sent her about *him*, as I was sending them. He didn't offer Tweedledee my job. She asked for it. They'd told him I thought he was a user and a joke. They didn't move in with an ex of Tweedledum's, they moved in with *him* for three months. They gave him my camera as they 'didn't know who's it was.' I'm so fucking annoyed. Truly fucking pissed off. Those liars. Two faced cunts. And Tweedledee does have her memories. They're evil pieces of shit and I hope Karma gives them a kick up their fat asses from which they never recover.

They not only robbed my flat, they also stole and corrupted the two things I loved the most. *Him* and the business. All that time they told me how evil he was, comforted me. It had all been a fucking lie. One big mother-fucking lie. They knew how much I needed that job, they sat there the day after I gave *him* that letter and bled my heart out to Tweedledum and he 'comforted me.' That same day that bitch asked for my job. Then they had the fucking cheek to come and lie to my face. Who does that? What stupid fucked up cunt does that? To a friend? No wonder they have no one who cares for them. If you treat people like shit, shit gets thrown back at you.

So fucking angry! Stupid fucking cunts. They don't deserve to live. Fucking parasites. Leeches. Take, take, take. No one wants you. Go fuck off.

I have total respect for *him* tonight. That took a lot of guts to do.

I need to sleep on this before I finish writing about this. He looked broken. Six years of nurture and then he loses it all. Now he has no direction. I know how he feels.

I need to sort through this explosion.

I HOPE THAT BITCH DIES.

Him: I didn't say everything but some things actually horribly are better said by text. My plan is to get out of here. In a non-freaky way I will always love and admire you above anyone (even Mike lol). Thank you so much for your time, it means so much.

20 JANUARY 2011

07:40

Does all this shit really happen? It all just seems so fake. Unrealistic. Too much. Like this life of mine is one part in some fucked up TV show. Things like this don't happen. I guess I prefer this than some boring flat existence.

Yesterday everything got turned on its head and now I've got to rethink everything. How could two low life wasters cause so much damage? Fucking cunts. I'm getting that tattoo covered over as soon as I can afford to. Goodbye. You guys can rot in Hell. Grow up you pathetic worthless people.

I'm gonna lose *him* for good. If he leaves that's it, he'll be gone and there won't be a chance of seeing him. It's weird, even when I didn't know all this shit, it was comforting to know he was around near by, now what? He'll be gone. Part of my heart lost. I know I'm not in love with him but I still love him. Fuck. Fuck. Fuck. I'll never forgive those cunts for this. *Never*. They are as good as dead to me now. They can rot in the gutter where they belong. All those rat dreams make sense now. They're the vermin. Jealous of everyone that's achieved something from their lives.

'I was scared of you. I've always been scared of you. You remind me of myself.' What is there to be scared of? I never understood that part of it. I'm not that much of a monster. It wouldn't have been the first time I've heard someone say that though.

I admire his honesty. He was like 'the two people I loved I've treated like businesses. I've lost them both.' I just wanted to hug him. Pull him close but it didn't feel like the right thing to do. What must be going through his head? He's back on meds for anxiety. I hate seeing him like this, always have done, only this time I can't help him, I can't save him and I feel at such a loss. I can't bring him comfort or ease what he's going through. Even he admitted it's because of me he managed to keep the business to this point and now I can't help anymore. Even I feel so helpless. I want to help but there's nothing I can do. His dream has crumbled and now he's lost.

'I know I shouldn't have come but you're the only one I know will understand.' I'll always be there. I'll always care. It fucking hurts watching someone you loved above everyone sit broken in front of you. I just want to take him in my arms and protect him, but that's not what he needs. We're both at the dawn of a new period of our lives. The future is uncertain. Unknown, but our journey isn't together. Not at this point. Not at this moment.

I knew something big was coming this week. I felt it on Saturday. I knew it would be about the business as well.

23:30

Day almost over. All this shit has been going through my head all day. Crap like this shouldn't happen. It's too unnatural. The whole scenario runs like a sitcom. A TV show. It runs like the life of a druggy. Fictitious. Like a page of text from a book I've written.

Monday I get that letter from the bank. Delivered to my address even though the bank has no reference of it on their system. That was the letter that was the message of death. I hand delivered the words that killed his dream. That in itself is way too fucking weird. The person who saved his business over the years was the person who delivered its death.

Fate brought us together again for that one final clearing of the air. I was there at his return from the ashes. I was there at its end. We always meet under those conditions, always fated by finality and rebirth. A circle. The circle that I guess sums up our relationship. We tried twice. Fear tore us apart both times. Something felt final about it all. Those dreams he'd said of a future with me and him and the business gone. I've never felt finality like that. A broken coda. It wasn't meant to end this way. It wasn't meant to end. None of it.

So I paid his loans off today. My final saving him. One last gesture and now the gates have closed. I have someone new I'd like to share my journey with. It hurts to say it but it's true. I loved *him*, but now I am his loss.

I feel like I should cry but nothing comes. Those doctors and therapists can sit there and tell me I've never loved but I know I have.

This is love in my world and it is true. You'll never take that away from me. *Never.*

And now my world has turned again because of those fucking liars. Both of them took away from us the two things we loved. And the most hate-filling thing is that they couldn't give a shit. Who do they think they are? They're nothing. They have nothing because they are nothing. They belong in the gutter. Death is too good for them.

Argh I've had it with writing about them. 'You're like a son to us.' FUCK OFF. I let you live with me for free and you stole, lied and cheated. You don't deserve to call yourself my parents in any shape or form. That tattoo you drew? It'll be gone by the end of the month. I don't even want a reminder of you on my skin.

The truth always outs itself, that is the beauty of truth. Karma will always catch up, that's the beauty of karma.

I hope you fall and you fall hard.

I fucking hate them so much right now. There is no forgiveness for the likes of them. Let them rot in the gutter like the rats they are.

I dunno what to feel. There's an emotion at my core but I've never felt it before. It's like an emptiness, no, not just emptiness. It's like a jar has been emptied and it knows it should continue to give but physically can't. The empty half of an hour glass. Empty until the time comes for it to be spun and the sand to fall again. I guess it's my love for him. It's there, constant, ready to be re-ignited, revisited, but not yet. Now it lies empty, a few shadows of dust clinging onto the sides and refusing to let go. Memories of what once was. Time for us has run out. It hurts, I feel like I should cry or do something but I can't. The one thing that held us together and gave us hope for a possible reunion has gone. The final connection has been severed. Held only in memories now. A memory of what once was. A memory of what could have been.

The only way now is forward. For both of us. No point clinging on to the hopes of the past. Destiny and fate dictate that we walk our own paths. This the emptiness of loss. I'm losing him and it is totally out of my control. He will disappear and I'll remain to continue the story on. Always push forward. Concentrate on my destiny now that my role in the business is no more and at its final end.

Sigh. 414 and 23 have parted. The painful journey has ended and both lost and broken we continue without each other. This love will never fade, but no longer is it a priority. We cannot protect each other now. We were one and the same. Now it's time to once more be one. The business brought us together, the business set us free. Circular. The end is the beginning of the end.

16:16

OMG. He just brought round and gave me a painting. My favourite one, his favourite one. Our painting. That moment in the snow. OMG. I'm lost for words. Totally. I want to cry. He must be closing up the shop. I would go and help but I'm guessing it's something he needs to do by himself. Alone. He doesn't need me as a reminder of all he has lost.

These tears are real.

22 JANUARY 2011

Another bank letter came for him today.

I designed the tattoo that will cover up that crap 'truth' symbol Tweedledum drew. I don't want such lies on my body. They don't deserve a permanent memory on my flesh. Tomorrow it disappears. Good riddance.

Slept like crap… again. Just haven't been able to sleep since Wednesday. Think I'm still processing all the information and fitting it into the right boxes. Meh, it still feels like something is coming, so I'd best keep my guard up. It doesn't feel like it's over just yet…

24 JANUARY 2011

When will I stop finding out shit about people? Tweedledum and Tweedledee have really fucked me off. I mean really. How can they live in a place and slag off the person that's letting them live there rent-free? Bastards. I want to kill them, see their fucking throats slit. Kick that stupid cripple down the stairs and watch that worthless brain pour like shit onto the floor. Too much links me to *him*. Everyone knows everything, even dealers tell me what drugs he's taking. Everything just pouring on me and I'm like give me a fucking break. Who can I trust? Everyone seems out to get what they want. But why do I always end up the villain? I always end up worse off. No, this time I'm better. I will fly. Fly away. Sweet Jesus help me.

How could I be so stupid? How could I have let such crettins into my world that made such a lasting impression? The guy I'm dating, his best friend judged me by the brush Tweedledum and Tweedledee had tarnished. They tried to ruin everything for me. But never will they succeed. I fucking hate them. The two faced cunts. Today they showed exactly who's side they sit on. *His*, the opposite of mine. That fat ugly troll would rather ask his opinion over mine. Bitch. You turned the love of my life against me. You fucking bastards.

I hate you so much right now.

I HATE You.

*   *   *

Fuck, who wants a natural ending? Fuck my soap opera life. I will not be part of *their* fantasy. I am free. My new tattoo has covered over that shit symbol Tweedledum drew on my leg. That's truth. This *is* truth. *They* are lies. Liars. I have freed my skin from their bullshit. Let them rot.

I hope Tweedledum dies. I truly hope that fat cripple dies. Both of them.

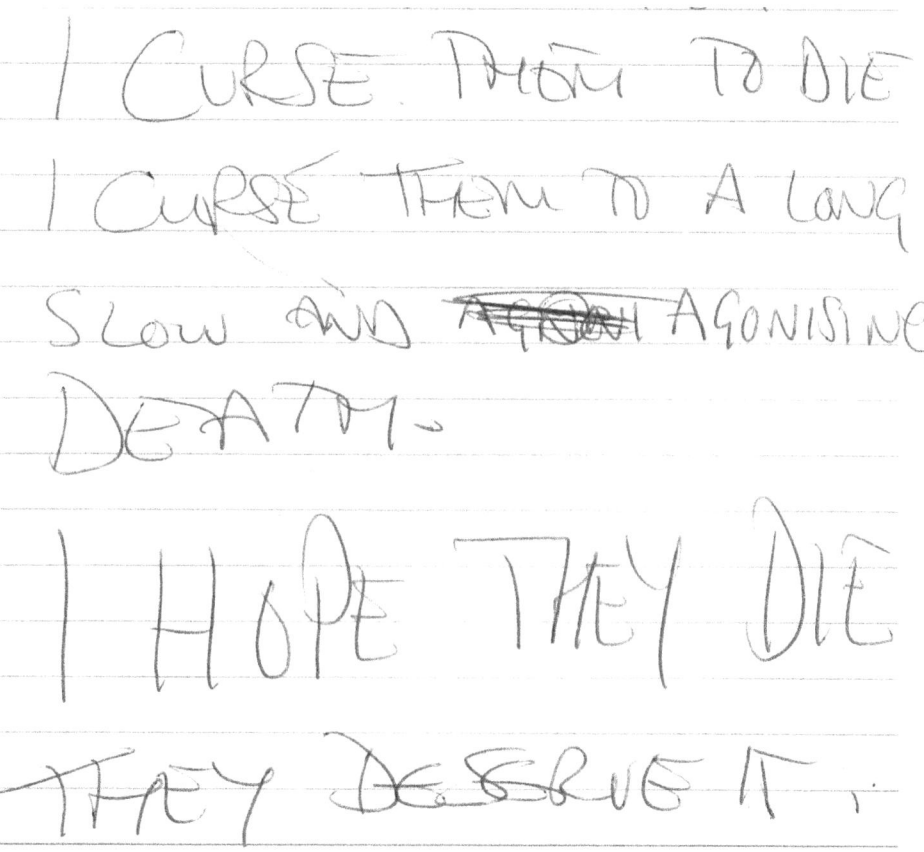

I CURSE THEM TO DIE
I CURSE THEM TO A LONG SLOW AND ~~ROTTEN~~ AGONISING DEATH.
I HOPE THEY DIE
THEY DESERVE IT.

P.S. Should anything happen to me. They did it.

OMG. I've never felt so much hatred to someone. I hope they die for everything they have ruined. They are leeches.

when will my life stop being
a soap opera?

Everyone knows everyone.

Fuck it.

melts into a k-hole

I don't know what to believe anymore.
Who the fuck am I meant to trust?
What am I meant to do?
Fuck it. What the fuck do I know?

25 JANUARY 2011

Just when I thought I'd got it all sorted, all this shit happens.

I dunno, since Wednesday it feels like I've opened a tabloid and read all the shit people are saying about me. Didn't know I'd made such an impression on Camden life. Everyone seems to know what's going on in my life but they're seeing it through this fairground mirror and it just annoys me. I don't know if I should feel honoured to be of such importance but I feel sick at the way I've been portrayed. If there was any truth in it I would understand, but when it's based on lies it's a totally different story. I feel like I've gotta rebuild my image here, well, guess I got two years to do it.

I feel like I'm the boogieman or Amy Winehouse. I'm not that bad surely?

K-Hole
Noam and I sat at a table drinking coffee. At the eye of a tornado. Destruction whizzes past us as we slowly drink. 'It's kinda cool,' Noam says. Then we explode into millions of tiny particles.

K = Blue.   MDMA = Red.

It's been a while. A week almost. I've been on K for all of it. I've needed it. Needed to escape. The K-hole on Tuesday with Noam was a great example of that. I've totally needed to escape reality and that I got then.

I haven't really had a day to myself since then, which is both good and bad, but hey can't complain too much, it makes a change me not being on my own.

Wednesday, Pinky came round. We all ended up at the Cap. Met Matti, did K, got wasted and asked to leave after getting caught in the toilets. Ha. Went back to mine, ending up going to buy vodka at 2am and robbing the shop whilst the guy went to get it. Ha. Pinky and I got so wasted on K. Si went to bed, we woke him up by laughing too much.

Thursday evening I was home alone. Took K and just wrote. Was cool. Being really creative at the moment so that's perfect. Writing really fucked up shit so can't complain. If it's all pouring out of me I need to write it otherwise I'll never get back into the flow of it. I think the drugs do help. They create the tone and pace, 90% of the book was written under the influence so it's not like it's something new.

Friday, a few drinks with Jeff and the fake pretence of pretending to like the scum that work on the market. Now I couldn't give a shit about them. They're nothing to me at all. The past, and that's where they belong. Go home. Rack up a few lines of K, do more writing. Zone out on the lips of a K-hole. It's all good I guess.

2011 FEBRUARY

So, where were we? Oh yeah, it was being one of *those* weeks, but I guess it's nice to have a positive.

No drugs this week. Okay, it's only Monday but compared to last week it's a start. I might actually sleep without K-holing. Woop.

Had such a good day today. Spent a lot of it with Matt. I'm really happy with how that is going. I mean it might actually work out for me. Yeah, I mean in *that* way. Things seem really messed up and weird but I want this to last. I really like him. Stupid and gay as that may sound, I don't care. I'm really happy.

Everyone seems to have this notion that *him* and I might get back together but I don't want him. I want Matt. I want this to work coz I have a really good feeling about it. No jumping in. No rushing. See how it pans out.

We had proper sex last night. It was really fucking hot. Yay. Woop. Slap my face and call me a slut. He pierced my nose and cock today.

So yeah, let's see how this pans out. Think happy thoughts. Happy thoughts.

02 FEBRUARY 2011

04:08

Maybe I really am in control of my own world. I mean everything keeps the cast rotating through my life. Take *him* for instance. Written out and now I've got the opportunity of seeing someone new, cue the return of 'romantic tension'. Drama.

I'm glad you're back in my life but don't try to pull apart what I've got.

My life is on a weird curve at the moment. Interesting times. Uncertain, intriguing, building towards another climax. New story arc. Gotta keep the interest of the audience. I've been directing this for twenty-seven years, I think I know how to put on a show.

That's one thing I guess I've got to be thankful for. Not having a dull life. Never a dull moment.

20:30

It's weird having *him* text me again with random shit. Just dunno, it's like instant. From nothing to back again. I hope he fits into my new life okay, I don't want to lose him altogether. That would be a shame. In one way he's my second longest boyfriend now, so yeah. I guess something important lies in that fact. I'm not complaining, just a bit wooo.

Can't wait to see Matt again on Saturday. The thought of that makes me smile like the Cheshire Cat. Happy times.

So yeah, let's see how it goes. Just don't get too into him just in case.

Another night, another evening on MDMA and weed. Noam and I excelled ourselves. Four days in a row. Hardcore. But that's the way I roll. Excess is always better.

So, that clinic place I'm meant to be going to called. They're only putting me on the Out-Patient treatment (2 days a week), the one that was not recommended by Cecilia. They've also added me to the bottom of a never ending waiting list and will only contact me when they reach my name. Why thank you, you patronising fuck heads. So I've got to wait for 'some time'. Cheers.

So what am I meant to do now? Where do I go for help? Just abandoned after all this effort. Back at the bottom, only this time I've got my name in the system. It all feels pointless. What's the point of all this now? All this has been pretty much for nothing. Same old situation. Sat on a roundabout. Waiting. Always fucking waiting. Waiting for others to help me. Is anyone listening?

Fuck.

So yeah, *he* has already impacted my life again. Apparently Stevie's all 'oh this, and oh that. *He's* asked me out.' I don't need this fucking bollocks. Si's been ignoring me because, as Pinky put it, 'you were fucking another guy behind his back.' What? There was no commitment involved so what's the problem? Argh. It feels like everything is on the brink of falling apart and all the things and people I've acquired will all tumble away from me again, and *he'd* of succeeded again. Everything is fucking up; I've lost control of my world again. Fuck. My mind distorted today, it's been a while since it's been like this. Disconnected totally from reality once again. All due to the same people. Why can't they just all fuck off?

And *you*, why do you have to keep interrupting my life path by constantly crossing it? Always have to be a permanent fixture. Always *there*. Why don't you fuck off. What is it that keeps pulling us together? Why can't you just stay away?

Little Mr Perfect. Everyone loves you, wants you, desires you even. He who can do no wrong. Things always work out for you.

Lose your shop, get a stall; lose your stall, get a new job straight away. How lucky you are. How fucking wonderful. I never get anything, just carrots dangled in my face. Nothing ever works out the way I want it to. Always surrounded by chaos, destruction, misery. Always followed by the shadow. If I died today, it would mean fuck all. And now once again you are there to witness the next car crash of my life.

The next spectacular car crash. It has to be massive to live up against all those half cliffhangers. I dunno, I can just feel it coming. Rolling in. It's gonna be big. A massive thunder clap that could change everything. This needs a conclusion. There has to be one right? I can't go on living like this. That's too much pain. Too much anger. Too much emptiness. Ten... nine... eight... seven... six... five... four... three... two... one...

Roll up. Roll up. Coming soon to a cinema near you. DOM: THE NEXT CAR CRASH. Rated R for Restricted. Yeah, it's gonna be messy.

So yeah, welcome back into my life all the crap I thought I'd managed to get rid of. Why don't you all make yourselves comfortable? I guess you plan to be round for some time.

There was once a boy called Dom.
He wasn't quite all there.
So one day the white van came,
Passed, and continued.
They just won't take him away.

SLEEP

So yeah, been a while again. So much has happened that my mind's been distracted but today it all sorted itself out. That's all that matters. No point dwelling on all the past shit right? Is it worth working myself up over it? No. I can sit and just let it go. It's happened. It's gone. Time to move on.

Noam and I had a night of arguing. It was shit. I haven't felt that much rage in ages. I could have punched him right in the face. All that it took for the initial spark was one simple sentence. 'How does it feel to know Pinky is your only friend who will accept Matt?' That was it. From that point on everything he said was bullshit to me. Just dig after dig. I held back as best I could. I managed it. Just fucking get over it. I want Matt. Why can't people just accept it?

Is it really that bad? Give me a fucking break.

It felt like my world was tumbling down this week. Luckily it didn't.

Time passes by so slowly and weeks seems like months. It's annoying. Kinda directionless, just working on my own projects.

Will I ever be able to move onto the next step? Fuck knows. As usual I'm still waiting. It's fucking bollocks. Complete fucking bollocks.

Deep breath. Count. Release.

Like that's gonna do any good.

12 FEBRUARY 2011

So today having been awake for hours, since 7am – bad dreams are back, woop – and painting two canvases, I want to talk about Matt. Well, Matt's first meeting with *him.*

Got to give *him* credit, he introduced himself but I can't see why he felt the need to. It was a tad awkward, especially given the Penguin's 'Oh your favourite barman will serve you' crap. So that meeting went well, just a shame about the way Matt was treated the next day by the Penguin.

Penguin: I can't believe you didn't know his shifts.
Me: Why would I need to know?
Penguin: That's what he said. I know what I'd be like if I walked in and saw my ex working behind the bar.
Me: As long as he serves me my drinks without question I don't see what the problem is.
Penguin: Yeah, it's such a shame about you two.
Me: What is?
Penguin: [Looking at Matt] Well you were the best couple ever.

WTF? Why do people have this fantasy about *him* and me? That's all in the past. It's history. All I've heard since he got a job at the Cap is 'when will you two get back together?' What is it? Place bets time? I have no interest in doing so, we tried twice, it failed both times. He hasn't got the ability or inclination to deal with me, so why put myself through it? Besides that, I'm insulted that they think Matt is so insignificant that I'll just throw him away. How dare they. Well it's like what I told Noam, when I was telling him about it, if they don't like it they can either get used to it or just butt off out my business.

Then Si told me than on Wednesday when I went to see him at work, the Penguin had turned round and said 'I didn't know you were friends with *his* ex, do you know he broke *his* heart.' I broke *his* heart? I think you'll find it's the other way round, twice. Get that fantasy out of your head. NOW. I've moved on. I've got Matt, well almost. This is where my journey heads now. The quicker you all realise that the better.

I'm happy with what I've got. More than happy.

Grr, let this week end quickly. Hopefully things will pick up again. Got more sorting out to do and then the journey will continue. I *will not* be put on hold any longer. I'm tired of waiting. I want results. I don't care if I'm costing our beloved NHS a fuckload of money. They can get off their asses for once and get things sorted. Like seriously! It's been six months and I haven't even had *one* therapy session, just assessment after assessment and all I've got to show for it is a partial diagnosis! I'm so fed up of it all, and now all the bad shit is coming back and what am I meant to do? Oh yeah, I forgot. I'm meant to sit in the corner quietly.

Fuck that.

It's been one of those weeks. You know. I thought they were behind me. Monday started good but then Noam pissed me off over *him* whilst I was at the Cap and so did *he*, so it kinda ruined the night. How dare they make Matt feel uncomfortable, I mean does *he* really need to keep saying 'hi' to Matt? I don't to it to his 'dates'. Grr. So yeah. I was pissed off. I've dreamt that I beat the shit out of Noam for three nights. They were real dreams and made me so grrr that I know they could come true.

Saw Pinky on Tuesday and Wednesday and that took my mind off things for a while so that was a welcome break. Woop.

Thursday I woke in like a shit mood. Noam came round. We took MDMA and I painted. It was okay; no, it was good. We talked and sorted. I know he can piss me off but I don't want to lose him as a friend. So yeah. Matt came round early, he gave me a microdermal in my heart tattoo and we decided to make it official. So yeah, he's now like my proper boyfriend. Happy happy.

Noam came round on Friday. More MDMA, weed and painting. All good. He stayed the night.

Saturday, *he* texts with this text saying that 'our exes have met' and I was like 'I know.' Then he was all 'so you and Matt made it official yet?' So I guess he'd seen it on my profile. But whatever. I'm just fed up of his life constantly crossing mine, even my past. Grrr.

Later on Saturday, that dick who I thought was a friend text me asking for *his* number because he likes him. What the fuck is that all about? Who does he think he is? Nobhead. I went ape-shit at him. Fucking cunt. I'll fucking spit in his face if I see him again. Grr. But it wound me up so much. Fucking dicks. I sent *him* a nice text stating: 'I can tolerate everyone singing the sunshine out of your ass, and me being a cunt who "broke your heart" but in future give your fucks your number so they don't come to me and piss me off. Night.'

Argh. How has *he* suddenly become a part of my life again? Why can't he just stay the fuck out of it like all my other exes? Why do people expect me to care? I've got Matt now and I'm not gonna put up with shitty evil glances and bitchy 'Good evening Dominic' comments just because I'm seen out with him. The sooner people get it into their heads the better. Seriously. I don't see what this fantasy about *him* and I is. It's been over six months since we 'split' for the second time. There is no future there at all. It's over and now I actually wish he hadn't bothered coming around to apologise with his cheap honesty. Since then everything, with the exception of Matt, has turned to shit. One thing after a-fucking-nother. Like them not being able to get my meds. WTF? Luckily I found one place that had them.

It's fucking never ending.

Right. So I need to concentrate on what is most important and it certainly ain't the shit from my past.

23 FEBRUARY 2011

01:10

'Happy birthday to me, happy birthday to me.'

'You're alone and you're fed up. So happy birthday to you.'

Hello voices in my head. So yeah. Another year of my life starts as usual. 'Hello self.'

'Hello Dom.'

Hello anger. I see you left a load of fallen bottles and broken glass on the floor. So nice of you to return with your normal entrance.

16:00

Day is going good. Decided not to do the whole Tate Modern thing today coz a) it was raining and b) coz I feel a bit shit still. Noam's getting a tattoo, he's excited. That's nice to see.

Woop to MDMA for cheering me up. It's my birthday. I hate birthdays. I just want to be happy, but hey, thanks brain for not letting that be the case.

Matt's coming down later. Well excited. Big grin. It'll be nice to see him for a while. I'm calm. I can feel a break coming. A moment where I will fucking snap and rampage on to oblivion. But not today. Oh no, not today.

I heard the white cat walking around the flat last night. Nice to know it's still around.

Tate Modern day today! Yay!

Woke up with Matt, had a well good evening. Noam didn't stay out too late, he left once he felt really uncomfortable and down. Apparently he was just gonna walk out but Becca told him to grow up and stay. Anyway, yay. Got to see Simon and have a drink with him. He got on well with Matt so that's also an awesome positive. Yay.

Matt jumped on my back for a piggyback but caught me unaware so we ended up falling face first into the middle of the road. Not the most glamorous of endings but what would you expect from me? He grazed his cheek and busted his lip. I woke today to fucking painful ribs. Couldn't even turn over. So much pain! But life goes on.

Noam came round. First dab of MDMA delayed coz he wanted food. So hit the Tube and head off to Waterloo. Took our first hit on the South Bank in a park.

Tate was fun. Just ambling along off our faces. We did a dab in the video room coz it was dark, but by the end we were doing it wherever possible. Like just being sat on the floor surrounded by people and then dab, drink. Done.

We sat on South Bank and had two joints whilst we talked and drew the Dom/Noam picture that's become a staple when on MDMA. Some kid ended up getting hurt behind us, he was crying and everyone rushed around him. We watched. Took more MDMA and left. We didn't care.

At Waterloo we had a moment. Stood in front of the escalators having creative thoughts. Speaking excitedly. Hundreds of people spewing from the depths like rats out of the sewer and we refused to move. Zoned into our little world of two. The rest just blurred lives zipping past. Gone, unnoticed, forgotten. Creating. We created chaos whilst creating.

Zoned out on the Tube to Leicester Square. That was weird.

Forbidden Planet, Cass Art, Apple Store. Home. Bought more drugs 'just in case'.

Home. Sanctuary. A time to relax.

I like Noam's company, it's calming. I know people are all like 'he's being a dick' but I can look past all his moods. People like us need time to get over things that hurt us, we need time to work it out for ourselves. Time is what you should always have for your best friend.

Today I am totally happy. Look, happy face. This has turned into the best birthday in ages. Like seriously. What more could I want? Things are kinda calming down, I'll get the GP thing sorted on Monday, and I have a beautiful, awesome boyfriend and a caring group of friends. I'm being the most creative I've been in years. So happy day. Happy day.

Give me a fucking break. Seriously! It's just one thing after another. Why can't all the shit just leave me alone?

So today I get a letter from Camden Council. The landlord's applied for planning permission to build on top of my flat, extending it into a two floor property. If it goes through, what then? What's going to happen? This is my home and it's being taken away from me. The one bit of security I had and now not even that is certain. Everything feels like it's falling apart again and there's nothing I can do to prevent it from happening. Just when it finally starts to feel truly like my home, bang, this rolls along.

There's no way I'll be able to afford the new rent, so I'd have to look for flat mates but that means it doesn't belong to me. My private sanctuary is lost. It becomes other people's homes. I won't get any time to myself. All those people in my space. It's fucking typical. I hate the idea of it. Hate it, hate it. I really fucking hate it. My home will become out of my control. My existence will be impacted by other's lives, wishes, demands. My home will become a 'community'. My home. MY HOME!

No matter what the outcome will be. I'm still going to lose *my home* and that fucking scares the hell out of me. Totally.

Hello 2011, I thought you would be a good year but nope. How stupid of me to think that way. 2011, the year I become homeless, remain jobless and am crazy with no help.

Fuck. Fuck. Fuck.

Fuck, Fuck, Fuck!

Tonight I cried for the first time in ages.

361

28 FEBRUARY 2011

Hello Monday, hello *that* visit to the Docs. Two things to sort out (i) ribs (either bruised or cracked, just need antibiotics to prevent infection); (ii) mental...

So I told her things were getting worse, and how the brain squeeze is back. She was a little shocked that I so far haven't received any form of help. So in her opinion I need a psychiatrist to be assigned to me, so she's contacting the Mental Health Team; she's also going to contact Cecilia for either a deeper diagnosis or to look at the report as they haven't been given a formal diagnosis yet or seen any info back from it except through what I've said.

So yeah, at least now something might get done. Instead of this stupid waiting around. I'm just pissed off at how no info about my 'case' has been shared between those who are meant to be 'treating' me. What the fuck? So I get it. Keep the crazy person's diagnosis secret until he begins treatment, but keep him on a waiting list for ages so that's one less mental health statistic on the books. Fucking dickhead cunts. Fucking around with my health like they own it.

Grrr!!!

I'll cash the prescription tomorrow. Just want to go see Matt.

2011 MARCH

Went to get my prescription on Tuesday, low and behold they wouldn't let me have it, snatched it out of my hands all because I'm apparently allergic to penicillin. Thank you NHS for trying to kill me. Thanks for that.

Went for a drink with Noam. The planned 'few' drinks turned into one then weed and MDMA. I don't like the Cap anymore. They make me feel unwelcome, like I'm not allowed in there at all. Well, my body seems to prefer powders over liquids at the moment so I guess they can go stick my absence up their arse.

Today was funny. Had one of those 'fantasy' moments. You know, tattoo shop has a leak again, they want me to speak to the flat downstairs. So yeah, I knock on the door and the guy answers, fresh from the shower, still with soap on him, wearing only a towel. Erm... instant boner. I think he caught me checking him out but I mean why wouldn't I? He looked hot. I was hoping he'd drop the towel and then invite me in. Ha, fantasies. Like I'm kinda hard thinking about him sleeping directly under me.

Like OMG. He is rather hot, way too pretty for the likes of me but still that's the whole point of fantasy.

I wonder how big his cock is...

08 MARCH 2011

So once again it's been a few days. Just been chilling really with Mark. Saw Jeff on Friday briefly, it's been nice having bro visit.

Matt came down on Saturday night. Brought me the two grams of speed I'd asked if he could get. Was well nice seeing him again. As always.

Sunday we went for a wander around Camden, I got some bondage hot-pants and a new pair of New Rocks. Becca came round in the evening and we all had a well good night at the flat talking and doing a fuckload of speed. Ha!

Monday, a bit more speed. Then we saw *The Woman in Black*. Was well good. Awesome what can be achieved with only two cast members. Gave me ideas. Inspiration. Always good.

What I didn't appreciate was seeing *that*. In the second half I got this massive oppressive feeling and then there it was, at the side of the stage. The shadow man. Tall, gaunt like always, his tendrils of smoke rising from the floor, only this time where was one difference. One *massive* difference. It wasn't its usual height, no, this time it was the height of the theatre. Standing from stage to almost touching the top of the stage curtain bit. Just stood there. The surrounding area looked like they'd been spraying smoke but when I did the startled blink it all cleared instantly leaving me with that feeling and a sudden sense of vertigo, like I was gonna fall from where I was on the steep theatre layout.

Since then I've not been able to settle, I keep seeing things again, sensing things. Like something is going to happen. An oncoming tide. I wonder what's approaching… please don't be something too damaging! I'm enjoying my life at the moment.

Got refused codeine today from the pharmacy. Conversation went something like this:

Me: What you do mean you won't serve me any more codeine?
Man: I served you twice last week.
Me: Well sorry for my pain not going.

Man: It's too addictive.

Me: Do I look like an addict?

Man: [Silence]

Then I threw a tub of yoghurt in some black bitch's face in Sainsbury's. She barged into me, so I was like 'bitch' and she started bitching on at me, calling *me* rude! So I did my usual 'When you knock into someone the words are normally "excuse me" or "sorry".'

Bitch then did the whole 'oh no you just didn't' bullshit, then went to spit at me. The yoghurt pot hit her face quicker than she could spit. It exploded on the floor by her feet and I casually just walked away.

Stupid bitch should learn some fucking manners.

"MY NAME IS ~~TOM~~... some people call me a SLUT...

...stick a line in front of me and tell me to snort it with the sharp intake of entry...

okay, sometimes I make mysey a little bit sick.

Dream.

He was in it. We talked. He wanted me back. We kissed. He went to re-enact a moment. I turned. Matt was there. Unexpected. We kissed. *He* left without 'goodbye', just a tear stained face.

Matt and I walk home. As we reach the flat I get a text. It's from an unknown number. 'Whenever we drink in Camden, he's always here. I know what happened between you guys but he's here in the Black Heart, on his own. He's always here; my friends have come up with a nickname. Just thought you'd want to know.'

I reply. 'He's no longer my problem. He's not my concern.'

Wake up.

14 MARCH 2011

Went out on Saturday to the Cap for one of Matt's friend's birthday. Was okay, wasn't really in the mood to be honest, but I still did it. Yay.

He was there. I totally ignored him. Just walked passed without saying anything. No response. Just a walk. He was with that fat ugly bitch I can't stand. His 'flat mate'. Woo, good for *you*. I don't like being around him.

You can have the Cap, I'm done with it. I want to feel relaxed when I drink, not feel like I'm constantly being watched. Gossiped about.

Him: *Hey, I thought we could at least be polite to each other. I don't know what I've done wrong but I won't bother in future. It was loud and clear. That aside I hope you're well.*
Me: Fed up of hearing your name every time I walk into that pub. Fed up of everyone telling me what you're doing. Fed up of everyone's opinion that I was the one who screwed us up. I'm done with all that and I don't need my life being invaded by people that aren't part of it.
Him: *We both have Camden lives. I'm not sure what I'm supposed to do or if there's anything you want me to do. I also have to hear your name every time I'm at work and am constantly reminded of my failures. We can only live our lives but I would never get in the way of your happiness.*

How about staying the fuck away from me or my boyfriend? Start there and then gradually fade away.

Why does he always have to do things that make him catapult to the forefront of my mind?

'*...and the truth is I miss you...*'

STOP IT! JUST FUCKING STOP IT!

Yay, an appointment with a psychologist. Yay, movement. An announcement. Finally the help I need… hopefully. All called through and confirmed. Can relax now. A deep breath and calm. Well, not calm but a sense of hope. A sense of something coming. Look at this smile. Today is all good so far.

The sense of calm comes with the fear. Been off my meds, only taking one pill to ward off any withdrawal. Self medicating with narcotics. Yesterday was the first time in eight months that I've felt 'myself', my true self. The one I've lived with for twenty-eight years. It made me happy. Made me feel whole and complete. It felt like coming home after a long vacation. Now thought there's the chance I might lose it again. I just want to be me, living in my own world whilst existing in yours. Is that too much to ask for?

This is reality for me. Here, right now. Sat in this park with my friend. This is perfect. This is my life. As it should be. Creating, sharing, EXISTING.

Here I exist. I am one with my surroundings. At peace. Physically, mentally, spiritually.

I love this park, surrounded by housing flats, church behind, garden in front. The calm in the chaos. This represents me now. This is why I come here to escape. My mind calms in the unending, recreating chaos around it.

Today I showed my friend my secret spot in London. My secret garden.

I wouldn't have wanted it any other way.

Another moment.

Another memory.

Another day.

18 MARCH 2011

Party at Pinky's. It went good. Was a laugh. Everyone kept asking after Matt and I was like 'who?' Ha, still not used to having a boyfriend people are interested in.

Was nice to see people again. Simon, Stevie and Adam where there and I ain't seen them in ages. So a good catch up was had. Everyone seems to be pairing off at the moment.

It got weird though. I did speed and K and everyone started making out on Pinky's bed and I got well tripped out and had to run to Simon. Then when everyone left I needed Simon to take care of me, not physically, just to mentally be there otherwise I would have spazzed out. I was totally confused and everything.

We ended up getting back to Simon's at 7ish.

I crawled home at 9. The walk of shame to Starbucks then home. Noam came round, then I had to go to Pinky's again to pick up my K and Matt's shirt that I left there.

Just waiting for Noam to come round. He wants my K.

Grr. Stupid fucking brain. Why won't you stop being all shit? Why won't you just be normal? Keep getting that head squeeze sensation again. Constantly. It won't fuck off. Didn't really get to see much of Matt this weekend coz he came late Saturday and had things to do on Sunday and went for drinks with Becca on Monday. Was nice to see him anyway.

Noam had his psychological thing today and was all like 'he was hot, gay and totally checking me out.' Like I give a fucking shit. Don't fucking insult me. You got the medication you wanted for your mere anxiety through an appointment daddy's purse strings paid for. Good for fucking you. Don't rub it in my mother-fucking face. I've got to wait until the 12th until I get to see someone. I don't need your 'money can buy' bullshit.

I've been struggling with this for eight months and all you need to do is get daddy to make one fucking phone call. I'm actually ill; you just have anxiety. Leave me the fuck alone. And no, your psychiatrist wasn't checking you out as he is a professional. Maybe you should have him check out your delusions that you think everyone finds you hot. God, get your head out your Jewish ass. 'They see my cock and…' Yeah, that's your only asset. Now go and get your medicated personality.

Totally off my meds and I feel like myself again, only now I can 'feel' what I've got. The meds made such a pathetic difference but have now left me having to relearn again. I don't want a prescribed personality. I just want to be me, the strong person who's lived twenty-eight years with this shit. You fuckers broke into my world with your godless science and now I'm trying to get admittance back into my own world. The world I apparently 'created'.

Go fuck yourselves. You fucked me up even more than my 'chemical imbalance'. Leave me the fuck alone! I am a person, not a brain process. If I'm myself, I'm a malfunction; if I'm what you want, I'm a chemical personality. I don't want to be part of your world anymore. The past eight months have shown me that. I just want to be me.

LET ME JUST
fucking BE
ME

JUST LOOKED IN THE MIRROR.

GOD!! I'M WELL

FUCKING

UGLY!!
xx

23 MARCH 2011

Chaos. It sounds like chaos outside. Just stupid people moaning and living their argumentative lives. It's fucking urgh!! Filtering their problems into my flat. Why won't it just fuck off?

I just want to be here, alone. Let the world rot and let me be the last survivor. I'd break into everyone's houses. Fuck those I've always wanted to. Fuck them bare. Ha, danger, even in death they could kill me. Spit on their worthless corpses, read their personal texts. Rape their lives just as they've raped mine.

I'll break all the rules just so you'd have to put them back together again.

I'll break all your conventions with my chaos and watch you struggle to maintain order.

Fuck you and your order. Fuck you and your rules. Most of all, fuck you.

Fuck you.

Fuck this week to hell. It's been the worst mentally for ages.

Saw fuckloads and every time I stepped out of the flat I just disconnected from it all. Walking in a constant dream. Nightmares every night. It's just dragged on and on like a never ending mother-fucker. I've been on my own for 99% of it and I can't tell how I feel about that.

Saw a girl. A little girl. With my flat in darkness, I looked out my window and saw a girl dressed in white crouched in piss corner outside. One blink and she was gone. Vanished. Then I had to go to bed. Felt uncomfortable, like someone was watching me. In bed I couldn't open my eyes in fear of what I'd see looking at me.

Shadows. Who's at the door? Don't just peek in, show yourself. What do you have to be scared of? If you want to watch me, don't simply perve from the corners of my eye; make yourself known to me. Have some fucking decency.

Fuckers.

Went to an installation at P3 today. It was awesome. We walked back through Regent's Park. Such a nice day. We ate out. Woop.

29 MARCH 2011

I wish these nightmares would stop. Stupid things. Too realistic. Too real. Did it happen? Was that an existence or not? I just want to be normal... well actually I don't. I don't want to *be* normal, I just want to sleep normal. No, I just want to sleep.

Shit, only two weeks until my appointment. Eep. There was loads I wanted to write, but does it all matter anyway?

Dreamt I had an argument with Matt. Apparently it didn't happen. To me it feels like it did.

'Things don't go up there too often.'

'Tell me about it.' Push away and slam onto my other side.

Why can't I tell between real and not?

2011
APRIL

What's the fucking point anymore? Each day I'm more confused; more likely to lock myself away. I don't want to be around people but then again I do. But who do I really have? Everyone has all these friends they can switch between and what about me? Always having to fit into timetables. People plan me around their lives. I am part of a schedule. Always been that way; always remains that way.

Fed up. Started my new tattoo, looks awesome, only had two hours done on it. Think it might take another four hours. Love it though. Another self drawn piece. It's the only permanent thing in my life, my tattoos. Everything changes, they age with me.

Fuck. Fuck. Fuck. Fuck. I'm nothing but a fucking ghost. That's all I am. I don't exist. There is no time, no dates. Just moments of light and dark, awake and sleep – even those feel the same. Nightmares within nightmares. Feel empty when awake; feel empty when asleep.

Today I just ambled around my flat. On my own. Fucking usual boring nonexistence. How much of my life has been spent this way? Too fucking much. Dom Lyne always on his own. ALWAYS AND EVER. Am I that bad a person? Fuck it. Maybe I'd be more interesting if I wasn't here.

Went to Sainsbury's. Usual. Zoned out, autopilot. Everyone looking at me as though I'm a junky. Looks of disgust. Some hideous creature that must be avoided. Maybe I have a bad aura. Maybe I am just rotten. Dead. Living on overtime. That's why nothing ever goes my way. I have no destiny. A dead piece waiting to be buried. The toy you never throw away but keep hidden from sight.

I am dirt. I am nothing. I am a ghost.

I don't even know how to feel in a relationship any more. I'm just flat. It's all words. I can feel complete for a moment. Then I'm alone and it is back to being just words. Is that how it's always been? I can't remember how I felt around any of my others. They're just names. Experiences. I guess it's still early. Things will grow. I know they will. I truly hope they will. I could look him in the eye and tell him I love him, and in that singular moment know I mean it. Then later… who knows? Who knows anything?

I feel so sorry for Matt. He deserves better. Deserves someone who is not me. Someone who isn't going to put him through all this crap. He shouldn't have to put up with any of it. No one should. It's all bullshit. Why can't I just exist normally? I used to think everyone was just like me. Thought like me. Now I know I'm wrong. In my world they're all wrong. In theirs I am, and there's more of them.

Do I have to lose my 'self' just to fit in? Do I have to sedate my personality just to be accepted by your society? Do I want to be part of it? If it means 'I' have to die then no.

Leave me alone as I curl up and die in my pit. My dungeon.

I am nothing.

I am no one.

I am a ghost.

I am dead.

I am dust.

I am dirt.

03 APRIL 2011

I hate waking up, I hate zoning out. It feels like my body is trying to force me out of it. Taking its own control and pushing me to one blurred, disconnected side. I just want to be able to maintain control of it.

Fuck.

Broken.

Finally falling to pieces.

Just got a text from *him*. He's re-opening a unit. Good for fucking him. Nice to know everything works out okay for him. Nice to rub it in my face. 'Look, I didn't lose *anything*.' Flaunt it in my face. Go on. It's what you do best, Mr Oh-so-wonderful. Bet that ugly goth-wannabe pig troll is gonna work for you. If I see her I'll spit in her face. Creature.

Funny thing is, it isn't a surprise. I dreamt about it a few days ago. I also dreamt about smashing a pint glass into her face too. That would be so fucking satisfying to do. Call it charity work. Might make her more attractive.

'Just letting you know.' I don't fucking care. What do you expect? Me to be happy for you? Too bad.

When I'm in a relationship I cease to be a person, I become part of the other. I exist because of my association with them. Then once it ends, I am dismissed, people don't want to know about my person. I'm a shadow. Stunted. Forgettable. Then when/if I win dominance I am shunned and accused of smothering them.

I am not a sum of who I am. I'm part of who I'm with.

Ahh, I see how it works. I pay off your debts, you sit around quietly for a bit – say until the new tax year – then you return without owning money as that is now just 'personal debt'.

Claps Clever little shit ain't you.

05 APRIL 2011

Seven days to go.

Walked around Central with Noam. Went to Leicester Square, some park, Regent's Park. Was awesome. Nice and relaxing. Makes me feel good. Was in a good mood all day.

Went to the Cap, first time in ages. *He* was there. Didn't serve us in the end. Good. Didn't acknowledge him other than the 'nod'. Meh, who cares at the end of the day? Got more important things to worry about.

But why does *he* have such a hold on my life? What gives him that right?

08 APRIL 2011

So I went round to Pinky's last night. She was making sushi. Was fun, her friend Tim was there and Hugo came over.

Pinky told me that Adam and Simon had pictures of *him* around their flat. So I guess that's why they haven't seen me in ages. Fuckers. Why does *he* have to infiltrate every part of my life? As soon as he arrives everything goes to shit. Guess it shows Pinky's the only one who is on my side. She was a bit annoyed by it.

I sent *him* a text. Angry text. Grr. So fucking annoyed. Friendships are nonexistent. They can all fuck off as far as I care. I said this would happen, everyone was like 'no it won't' but HA! In your fucking faces you cunts.

As soon as *he* appears I become a nobody, everyone just wants to know about him. I become an asset. It's all *him him him*. I simply just don't exist. I'm the cunt that 'broke his heart.' It's always been that way. I was always just his boyfriend or his ex. That's all my significance was. He walks in, everyone bows at his feet, I'm pushed aside. Forgotten. No one gives a damn about Dom.

Fuck them. Maybe one day I'll find friends who actually like me for me. Not as part of someone else. I doubt that's ever going to happen. It hasn't for a long time, and doesn't seem to be happening now.

ARGH!! I JUST WANT TO SCREAM. SCREAM. SCREAM.

I JUST WANNA BE ME!

So, you spend the whole day looking forward to going to Torture Garden with your boyfriend. You prepare, get ready. Whoosh, off you go, all is good. You're having fun. Then he starts talking to some random guy and ignores you. Then he gets up and walks over to the couples room with said guy, turns back and goes 'we're going to the check this out, wanna come?'

You follow them, you're not made part of the conversation. You're just an extra. You reach the entrance. Your boyfriend announces you're a 'three'; your heart sinks. 'Kiss,' the attendant says. 'Ok,' says your boyfriend and the guy. Right in front of your eyes your boyfriend makes out with a stranger before you. YOU FEEL THE MOST WORTHLESS YOU HAVE EVER FELT IN YOUR PATHETIC EXISTENCE.

'Your turn,' they say. You hold up your hands and simply say 'sorry, can't do it.' You walk away. It doesn't get mentioned again. There is no apology, no remorse shown. No guilt.

YOUR BODY DANCES FOR THE REST OF THE NIGHT WHILST YOUR HEAD SCREAMS IN SILENCE.

In bed later you mention it to him. Say you can't get that image out of your head. It's rolling around on replay. You feel the same pain each time it does. It doesn't lessen. More and more gets eaten away from you. He doesn't even remember it. 'I was fucked,' he says. Your reply is simple: 'So was I.'

Silence. Tension.

He leaves to go see a friend until '6'. It reaches '9', you call to see if he wants food. 'Just leaving now, I'll be there in thirty minutes.' He gets in at 10:45. He's asleep within ten minutes. You question your importance to him.

Does he really care? Did he spend all day laughing about it? About how silly you are. In that split thought he's exactly like all your other boyfriends. You're just the joke. The object. The token.

You wonder if there's a point in it. Any trust.
You cry about him for the first time.

Went to Brighton with Matt, Becca and bro. Was an awesome day. Then we went for a Japanese meal.

It took my mind off tomorrow.

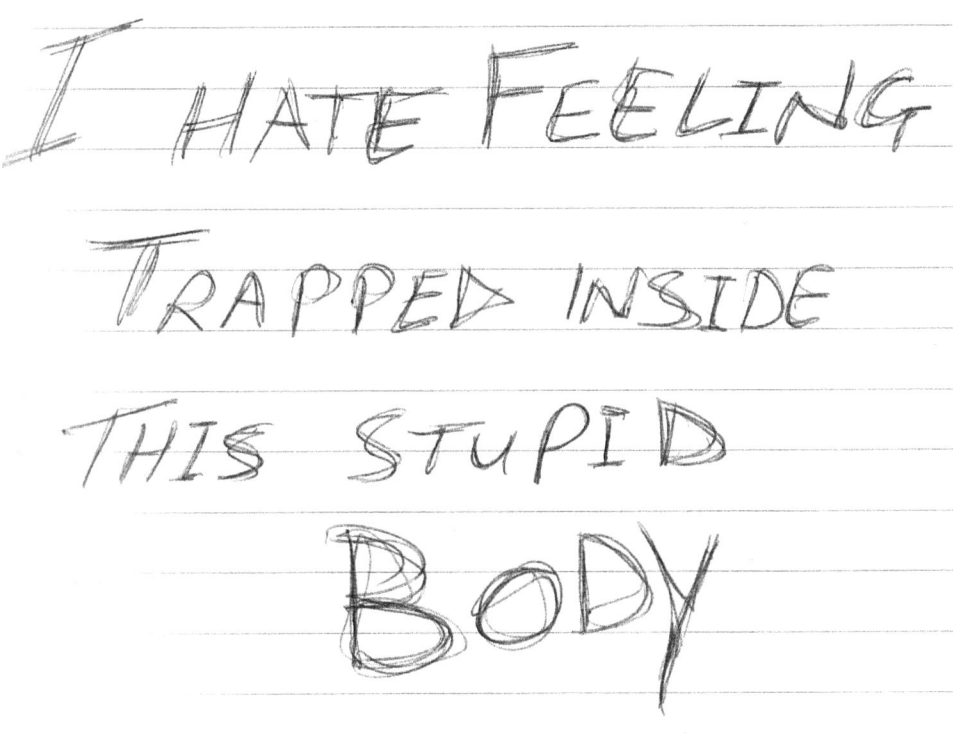

I HATE FEELING TRAPPED INSIDE THIS STUPID BODY

12 APRIL 2011

Today was the day. Another assessment, this time with a psychiatrist. So I told them how I'm feeling. What is going on in this messed up head of mine. He looked really concerned at some of the things I said, as though it was a shock that someone could be saying all those things and not feel remorse. I don't do remorse or guilt. No regrets.

Another draining hour and a half but finally got the official diagnosis after eight and a half months of living under this blanket of stress and worry. The roof has been pulled off and now I can understand what is wrong with me. This part of the journey is now over and I can rest and recuperate before the next one begins. The final diagnosis stands at Dissociative Disorder Not Otherwise Specified and Borderline Personality Disorder. He believes I have had the Dissociative Disorder since before I was four, but for which I have no apparent cause or trigger. So he is left confused on that one. So there we go. Officially broken.

I've apparently created a world around me where I have given shape and form to the emotions I am unable to deal with, pretty much all of them. Fragmented inside at extremes. Fucked. Broken. How many pieces can a china doll crumble into over twenty-eight years? It's probably all just dust.

So now I have to wait. Wait for treatment at that Dartmouth Park Unit, no matter how long I have to wait until they reach my name. No point sitting around for an oncoming storm, best make the most of my time whilst I can I guess. At least I don't have to take any medication now... not that I was taking them anyway.

I cried after whilst trying to phone Mum. This time was different. I've finally got what I've been waiting for. That one simple diagnosis. Tears of happiness? Relief? Joy? None of those words can really be used can they? How could any of them vocalise the concrete confirmation that you are damaged? To be honest, I just feel numb. Completely and utterly numb.

Crazy Dom. Craziness confirmed.

2011
CODA

Over a year has passed since this journey began, and although I stopped keeping a diary in April, the diagnosis they came to was not the end. The journey didn't stop, it just became too tedious to write about on a daily basis. So much stress and heartache. Highs and lows. Living with mental health and trying to find help for it becomes like a full time career, each day there is always something more you need to sort out, find answers to or loose ends to try and knot together.

Life continued. Did it get any better? No. The relationship with my boyfriend fucked up, I found things out and it went from one thing to another in a downward spiral for months. Too much had gone on behind my back and I couldn't deal with it. I however didn't lose faith. Against everyone's advice I held on to it and it is now hopefully at the point of being pulled away from the cliff it almost fell off. At least from here, things can only get better.

Friendships ended, changed, refocused. *He* moved away and has his new life. It matters little to me. We're walking our own individual paths now. The 'best friend' dickhead decided that a boyfriend was more important than our friendship so he followed his nondescript boyfriend's advice that he shouldn't hang out with me as I was merely using him emotionally. We haven't spoken for months, he found someone else to do drugs with, so my purpose was served and I was removed. He isn't missed, wasn't and never will be.

As I've continued to try and get some notice from my doctors, I've found myself being accused by them of having an agenda to get Valium to either abuse or sell. I've been chucked on Amitriptyline pointlessly and refused to take it. I've also sat at that Dartmouth Park Unit begging for them to help me and all they did was dismiss me with an attitude of 'you're not our patient yet and you still may have up to two years left to wait.'

In the end I went Private. I had another assessment and yet another label was added to my list. Schizotypal Disorder, again since before I was four. This psychiatrist believed that the Borderline and Antisocial Personality Disorders are born from this and unless the

Schizotypal is treated first, anything else will be pointless. Rendering the forthcoming treatment at that Unit worthless.

I was put on Quetiapine, and for the first time in my life the noise has been turned down, a few TVs switched off. For the first time in my life I can feel in my head what you do, and I don't like it. I don't like it at all. Everything so simple, everything so easy. Put this to the back of your mind and forget about it. Important things are left to fester and dreams pushed into tiny little boxes and stacked on shelves. You make the choices and then complain about what you didn't do.

You think life is hard? That God has some axe to grind? Pause for one second and consider this, maybe then you can give me a second fucking chance. My life is noise, never ending noise. Constant and without pause. I have some fucking reject brain that doesn't allow me to be the person I want to be. I didn't choose to be this way, I had no fucking choice in the matter. I don't want to stand there like a third wheel, I don't want to appear like an aloof cunt, but no matter how hard I try, that's where I end up. Locked inside this ugly prison of a body. The world through my eyes is different from what you experience as a reality. There is no connection. The easiest way to describe it would be for you to take a happy little Disney character, a pretty one, a nice one and stick it inside the body of a horror movie troll. Imagine that inner turmoil and you might understand mine.

So I take these little pills and they pull me into your world a little bit more. But it's alien to me. I don't understand it and it frustrates me. I can't live inside my head, and I can't live inside your world, so what the fuck am I meant to do? You get to do the things you love and enjoy, then you bitch and moan and complain about it. What the fuck is that all about? You're doing what you love, surely that should be enough. If I was given the chance to do what I wanted, I'd do it with all the passion I could muster, I wouldn't complain, I wouldn't come home and moan. I would value it because I have been given the opportunity to do it. I wouldn't begrudge any one from trying to do the same thing, I'd support them, give them advice, help them. If someone wanted to write a book I'd be the first one there helping them realise that dream. That's what I do. I understand everyone has to start somewhere and that person who is starting was once me. But you all forget that. You all forget that someone helped you out. Someone helped you live your dream. So feel fucking lucky, coz no one ever did that for me.

I am invisible. I am a ghost. People look right through me. I'm the extra on the film set. I don't want to be invisible, I want to exist and be valued. I want to change the world, I want to inspire and be inspired. I want for once to be a centre. I want to live the life I want and be happy. I want people to give me a chance. I want feel part of something. I'm fucking fed up of being empty all the fucking time. I try to give so much but in the end I'm forgotten and dismissed. Then sometimes they even have the cheek to try and come use me again when there is no one else, well fuck that. Fuck that to the pits of Hell.

I'm the invisible boy.

I do not exist when I'm not around.

This month I start a ten week course of Explicit Mentalising Groups designed to prepare me for the main programme of treatment I've been assigned at the Dartmouth Park Unit. I have no choice in the matter. They may use the words 'You are invited', but there is no option for you to not accept the invite. If you say 'no', the simple outcome is that you are not allowed in the main treatment group. I hate being forced into things. I hate not feeling in control of my own life. I hate the idea of having to deal with group sessions and other people's problems.

A year ago this was what I wanted, what I believed could help me, now I don't know. Everyone has told me different things, if this treatment is designed to help 'cure' my Borderline Personality Disorder, will it help with the Dissociative and Schizotypal diagnoses? Or will I have to embark on another journey after the next two years? How will this mentalisation crap make any difference other than trying to make me see things like 'normal' people? Will it prevent me from being strangled by shadows at night? Will it bring about the end to me seeing things? Will it silence the noise in my head? At this precise moment I doubt it.

This journey so far has left a bitter taste in my mouth and the only conclusion I can come to is this. They want to make us think differently, not because it will make life easier for us, but because it will make it easier for them to understand us. Why should we try to understand you when you put no effort into understanding us? Why should we see the world from your point of view when most of you are not willing to see it from ours? Why should we become like you? Why should I have to bend to fit into a system that I have no love for, that I despise?

I will not become someone else just to fit in with you. Would any of you make the sacrifice of self to become like me?

Didn't think so.

BOOK THREE
CYCLE-2
THE SILENT SCREAM

PART ONE
SCREAM № 1

So here we stand, darkness my old friend. It's the same as it always has been. Just me, you, and the shadow. I'm empty inside, fading away like a ghost. You pour out of my core, you surround me. Hug me. Keep me safe.

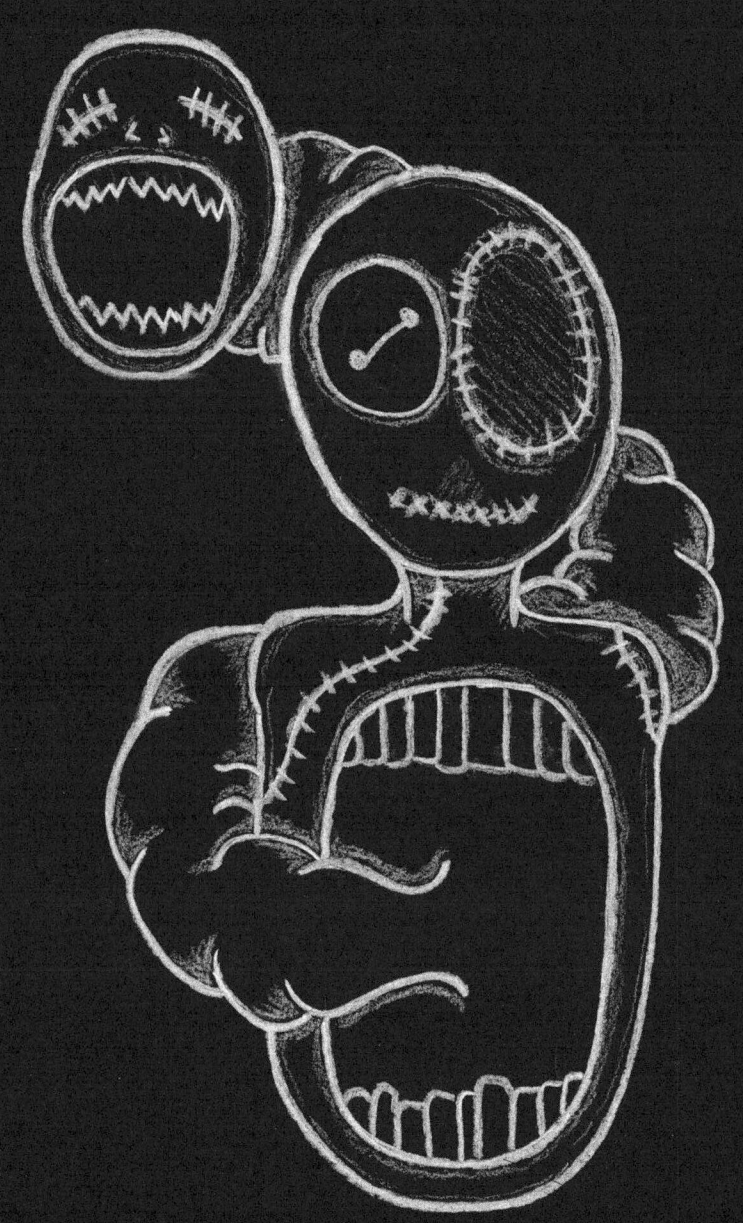

I don't know how long this is going to go on for, this wait. The constant

never ending wait. I guess this is limbo. Locked between two worlds,

never connecting fully to either. Do I have that choice? Maybe... we'll

have to wait and see.

That word again. Wait. It haunts me like a guardian angel. 'Please wait in line.' 'Please wait whilst we follow up your claim.' 'Please hold the line.' The wait for treatment. The wait for help. Always on a waiting list somewhere.

Wait, hold on a second. Why should I have to wait? Oh yeah, I lack

direction. All roads forward are blocked, closed, shut off from me. The

leper waiting at the gates of a city. Will I eventually be let in?

The future looked positive. Movement. Little baby steps but still progress. Hope. I guess this all confirms what I've always said. Hope is so pitifully changeable.

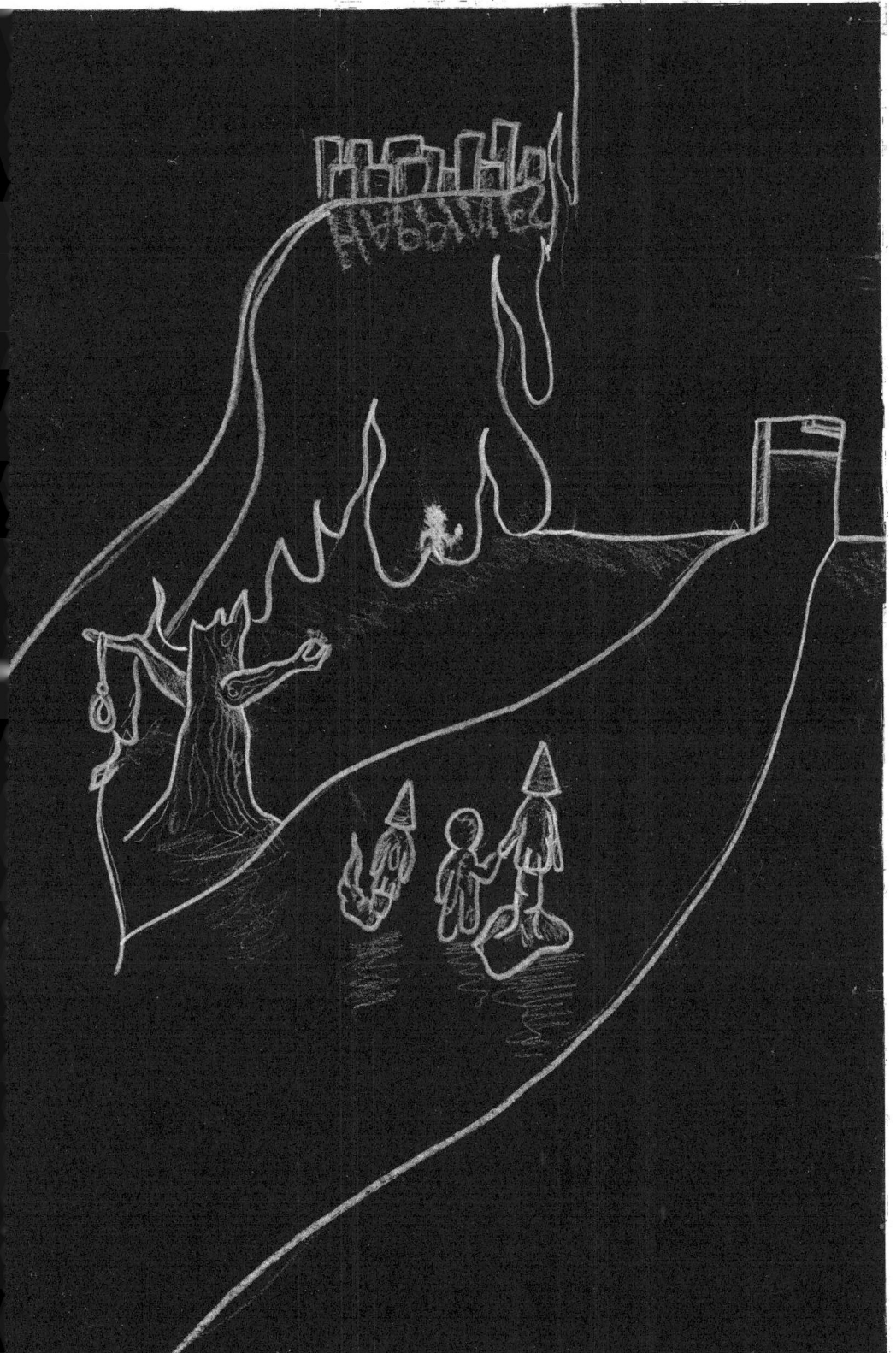

So what about me? Where do I go from here? Where can I go? What do I have that could benefit the world? Would anyone want anything I produce? Are these all words spat out for nothing? Wasted ink on wasted paper for a wasted dream. I wish I was wasted right now. At least I'd feel right.

At least I'd feel alive.

How many times do I need to crawl only to find myself back at this point? Discarded, beaten down by the people I need the most. Maybe I should just take another pill to just end it all. End the silence and exist solely in the dark. I know my reality more than theirs, so do I really want to be part of it?

I just wish that I could be free. Free from everything. No expectations, no responsibilities. Lose all the burdens of my past and just burn the future to its pathetic knees. Destruction. Watch me lay naked in the dirt. Watch as the silence kills me. It drags its blade across the skin and I scream.

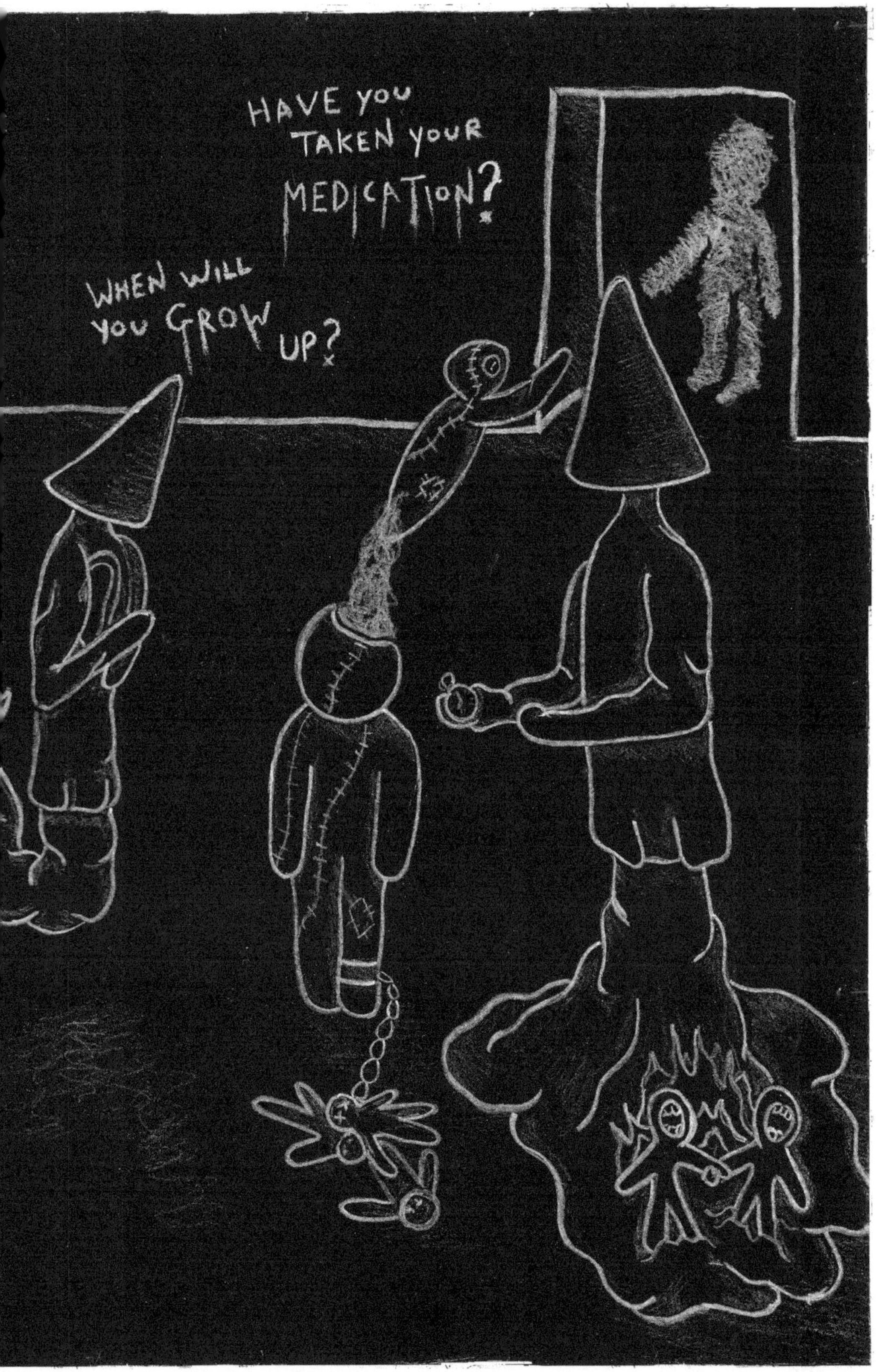
HAVE YOU TAKEN YOUR MEDICATION?
WHEN WILL YOU GROW UP?

Scream the silent scream. The scream so painful that no one can hear.

Not even the almighty God in his golden throne. His hearing aid long

since broken. No, not broken, he just turned it off and turned his back.

The figure in the shadows, was it born from the scream or was I born

from it?

So many questions but where are the answers? Where are the conclusions and aftermath? Where is anything? Just one question after another, building towards the climax. The end of series finale. The cliff hanger then the wait.

TOGETHER
WE WILL
BRAVE THE
DARKNESS

The series gets cancelled. The story never resolves. We're all left

disappointed.

Waiting…

What am I expected to do? Fade away? Sit in the corner quietly like a

good little boy? You drag me to this point, rip apart my world and then

leave me to deal with it. Shatter existence and fuck the pieces.

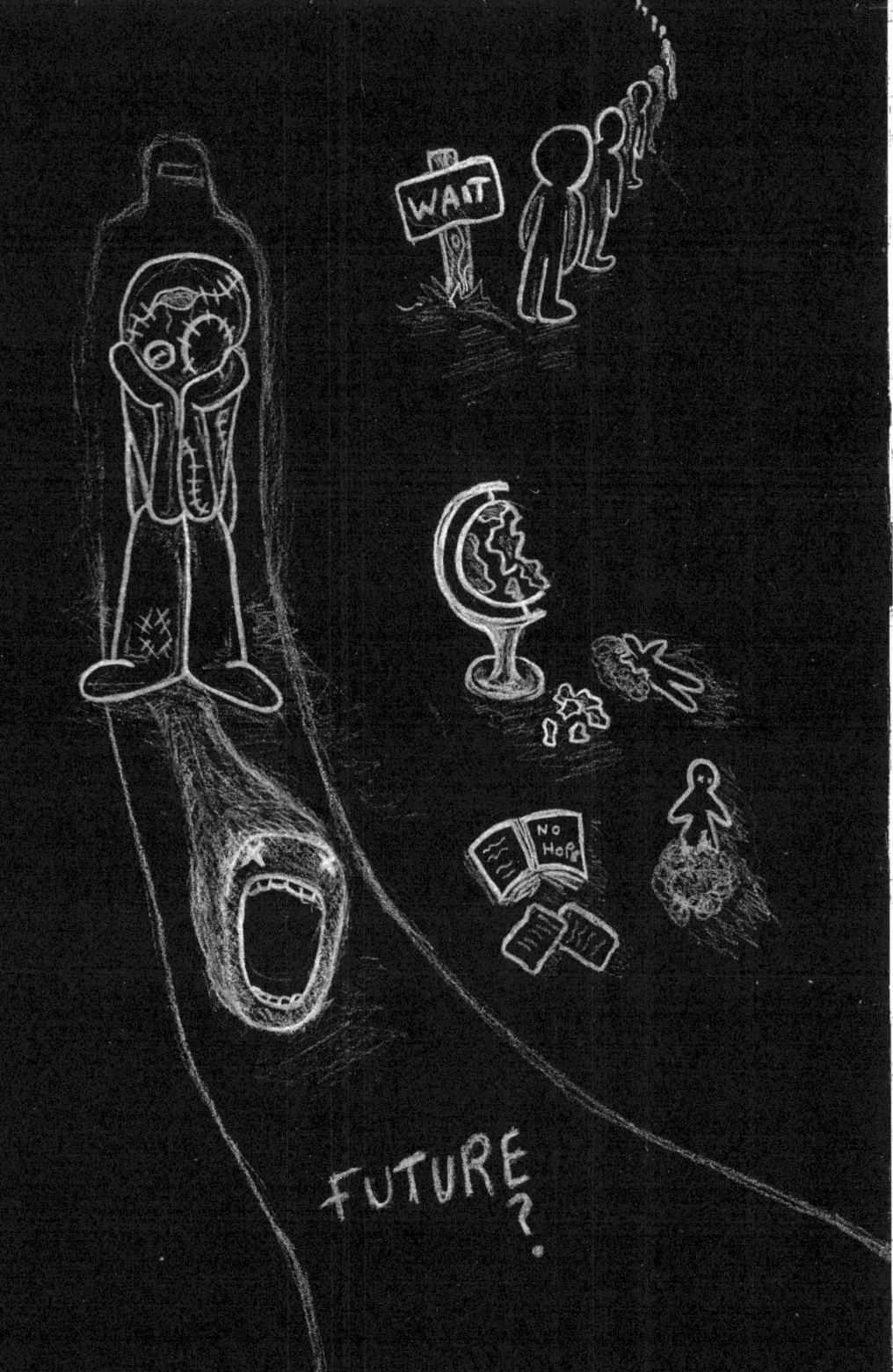

So I open my mouth to speak out and you constantly try to silence me.

Silence the truth of the matter. You don't want your reality tainted by

my words. Well here's a fact. You won't fucking stop me. I'll never be

quiet. I'll never be what you want. I won't do what I'm told.

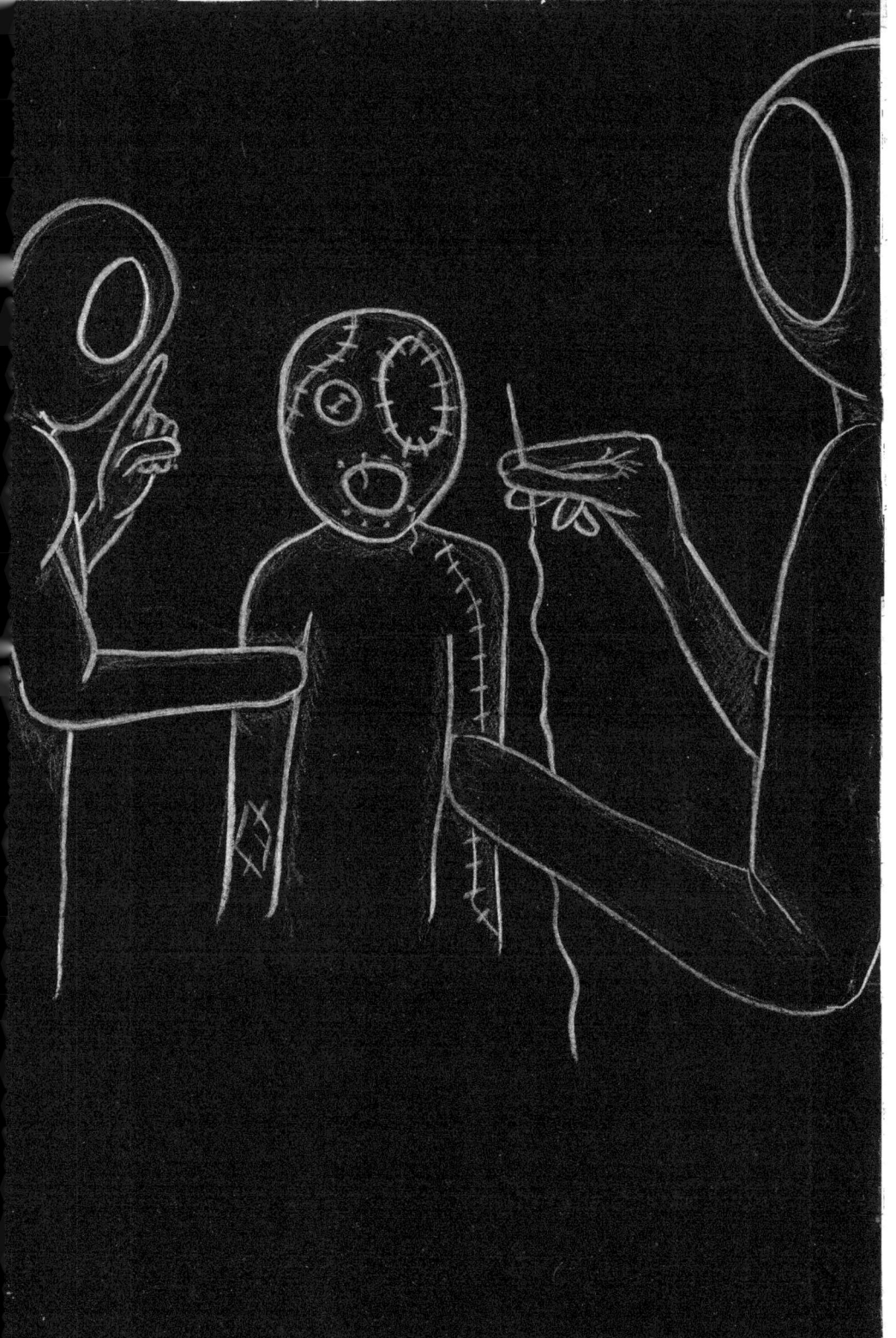

You might leave me confused and broken but you forget, the broken

are used to shattered pieces and discarded hopes. We pick up our own

pieces and piece them together slowly and weakly but we still soldier

on. We will always be here.

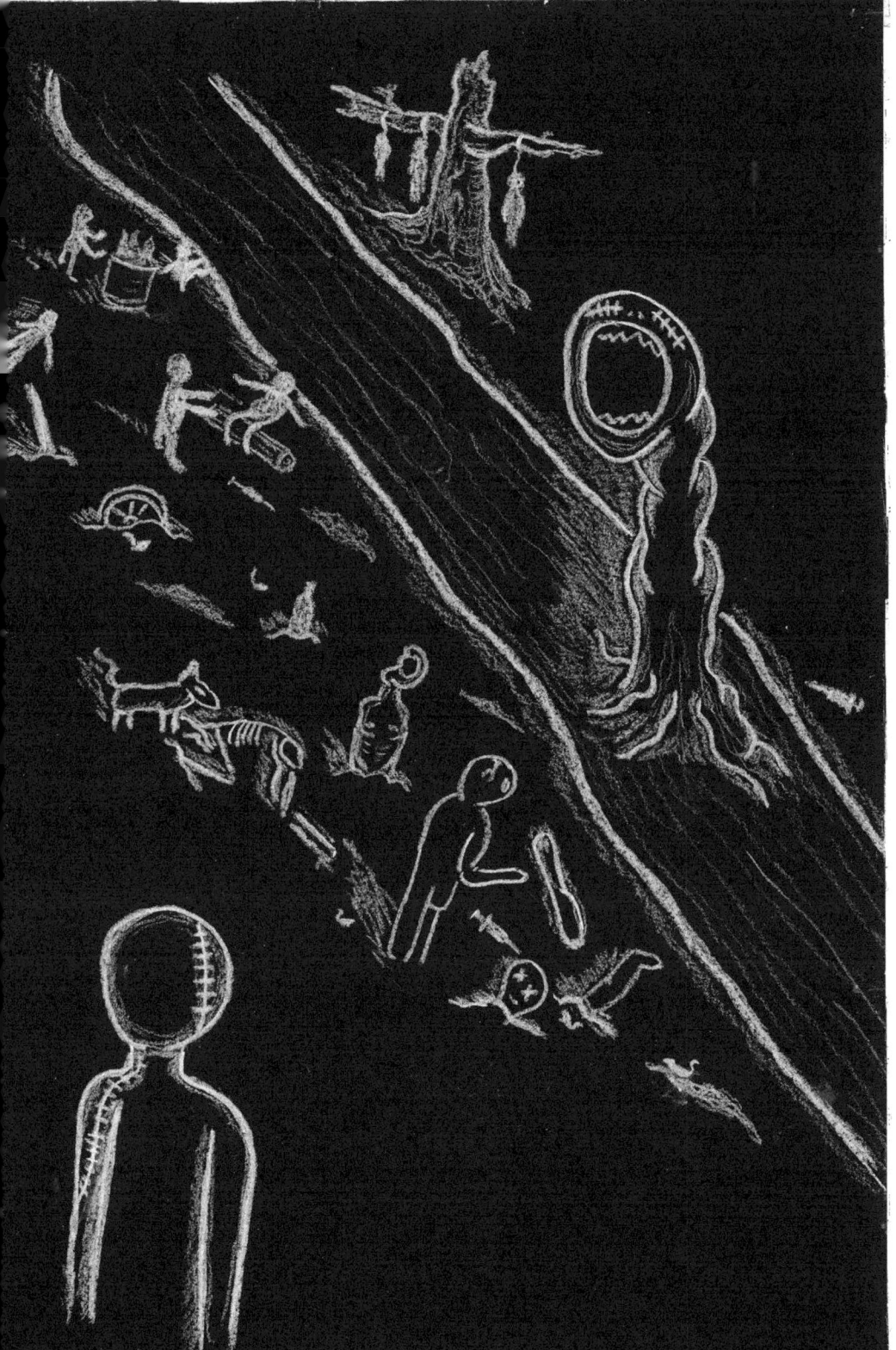

We are your waste. We are your dirty secret hidden under society's

carpet. I will not be forgotten. I will not dismiss your world like you

dismiss mine. I don't want to be part of yours but at least I have the

decency to acknowledge it as an option.

So here I rot amongst your waste, sleep alongside all the addicts and china dolls. Needles, pills, lines. These are my diet, my protein. I consume whilst I bleed you dry. Revenge. The price you pay for closed eyes. But in the dirt where is the hope? Who wants to care for me once everyone else has turned their backs?

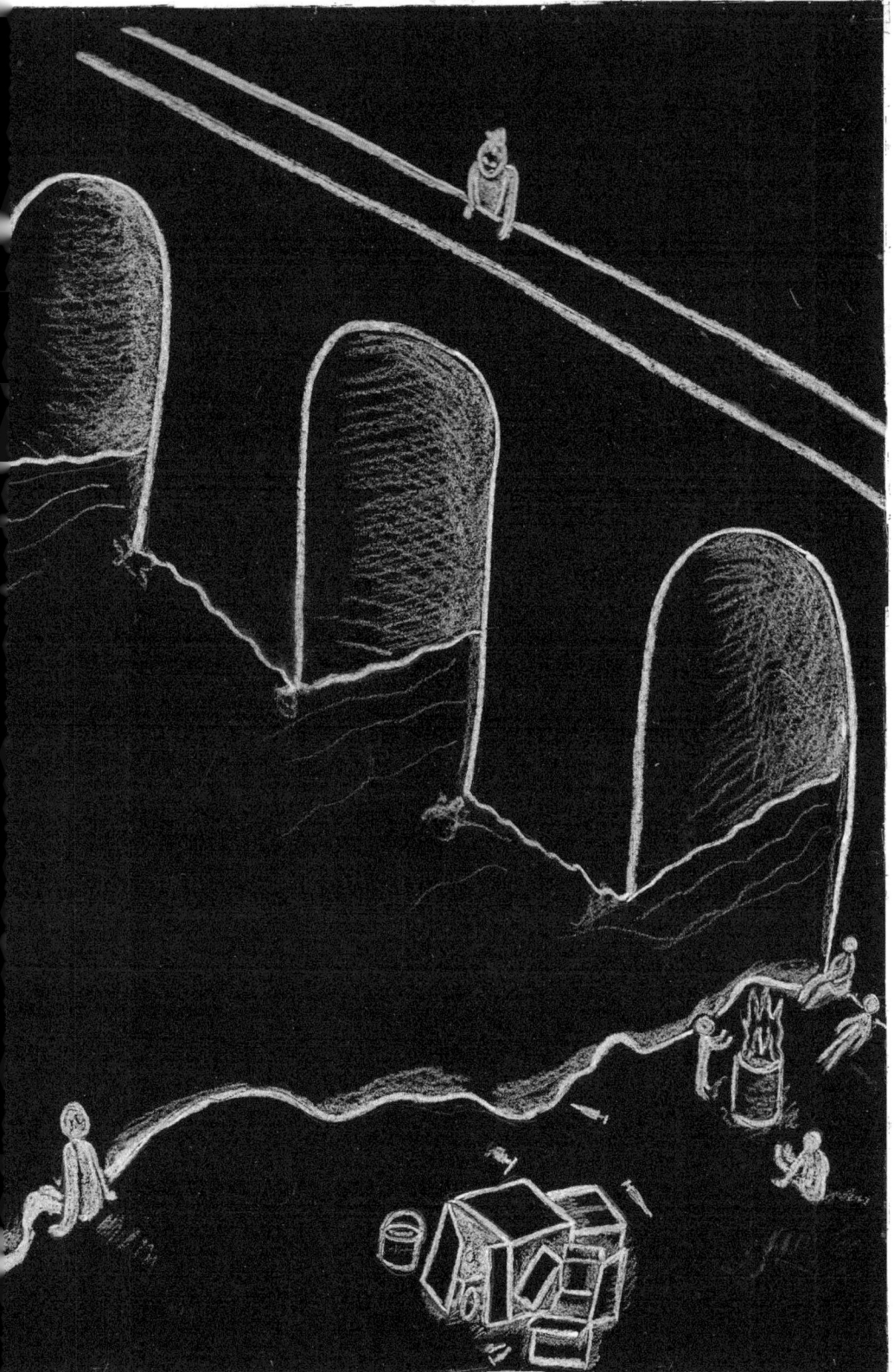

Resigned to my solitude I continue to scream my silent scream into the shadow. Bleeding my soul to the dark. Then, unexpectedly, all it takes is one. One chance meeting. One lucky accidental passing of paths. Then everything changes. You learn a new truth.

'One man's rubbish is another man's gold.'

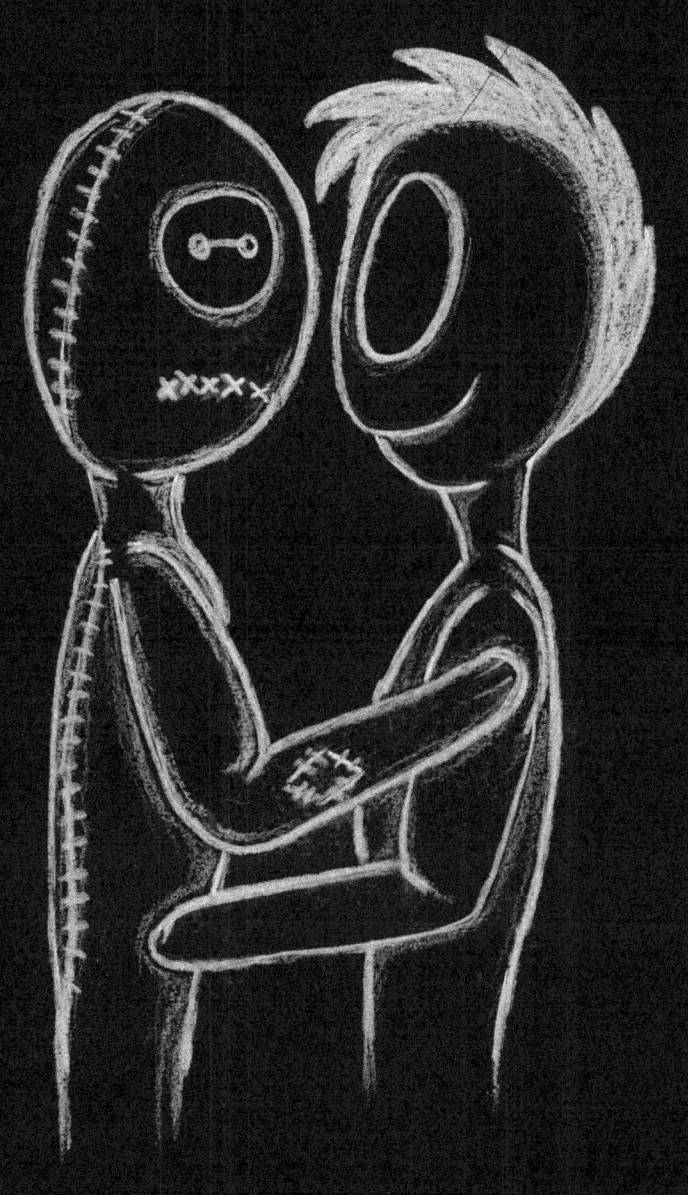

A smile. A smile cracks upon this broken face. The crap still falls like snow, attempting to suffocate me, but the difference is hope. Hope of happiness. A connection to another soul. That one person gives your whole world new meaning. A new dimension. You're no longer fighting by yourself. You are no longer alone.

You now appreciate everything. Self-destruction postponed. You can't implode when you have someone who you want to share your world with. The welcome stranger, invited in from the void between the two worlds. A connection. You smile. Light the fire and embrace.

YOU'LL NEVER FACE IT ALONE

So this is the good to come out of all this shit and past lies. This is the start of the new series. The unexpected plot twist. Yeah, the climax hasn't arrived but that can wait.

Everyone has fallen into place. Let me enjoy this moment a little while longer. Let me feel this way for even just one more second. Let me say the words that I'd forgotten how to pronounce. Words and emotions long forgotten re-emerge.

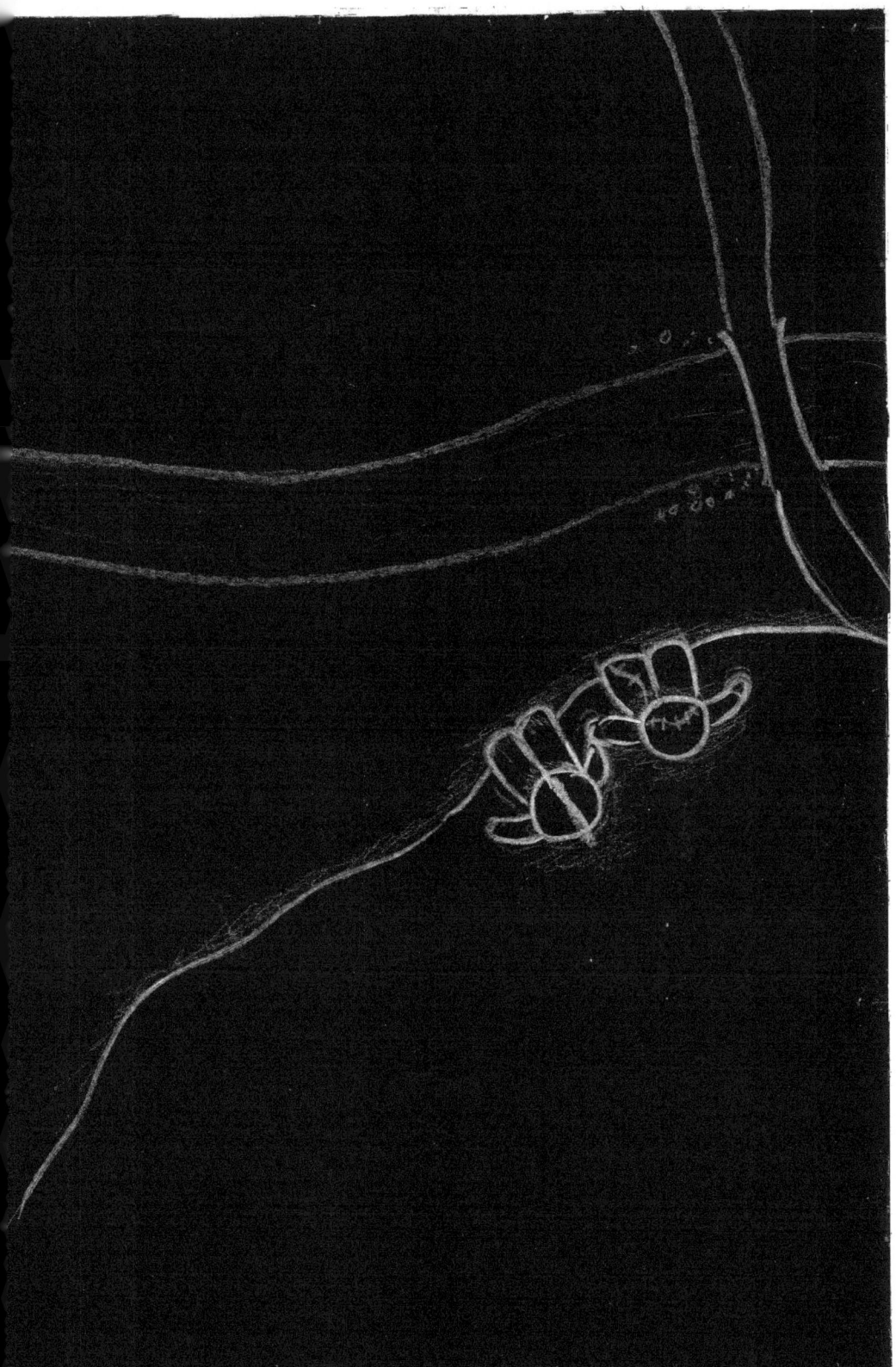

I am happy.

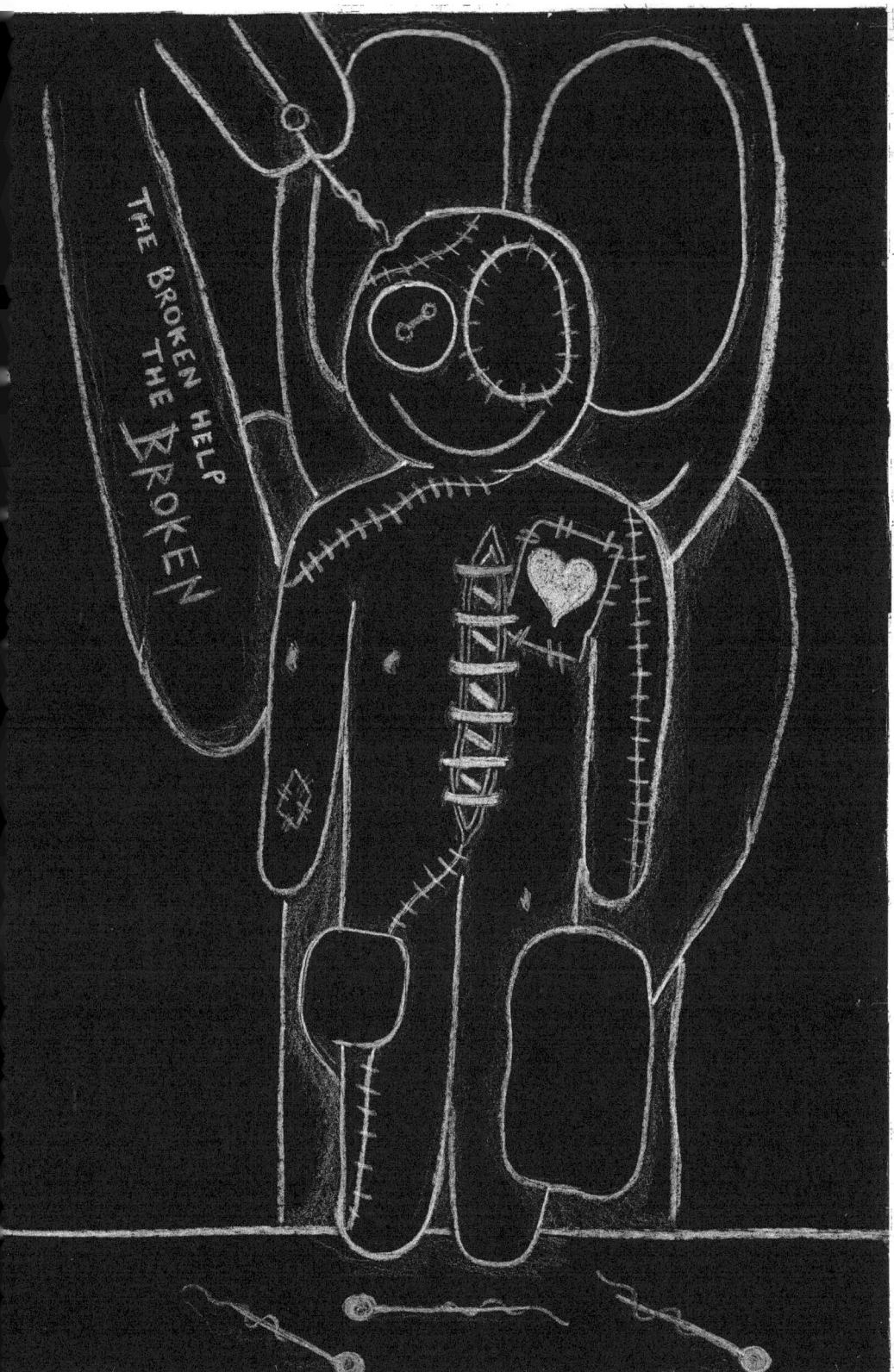

PART TWO

SCREAM №2

The moment lasted for but one second. The universe had her say and cast the die against my favour. Everything is so fleeting. Never allowed to settle, constantly on the move. No security upon which to place an anchor.

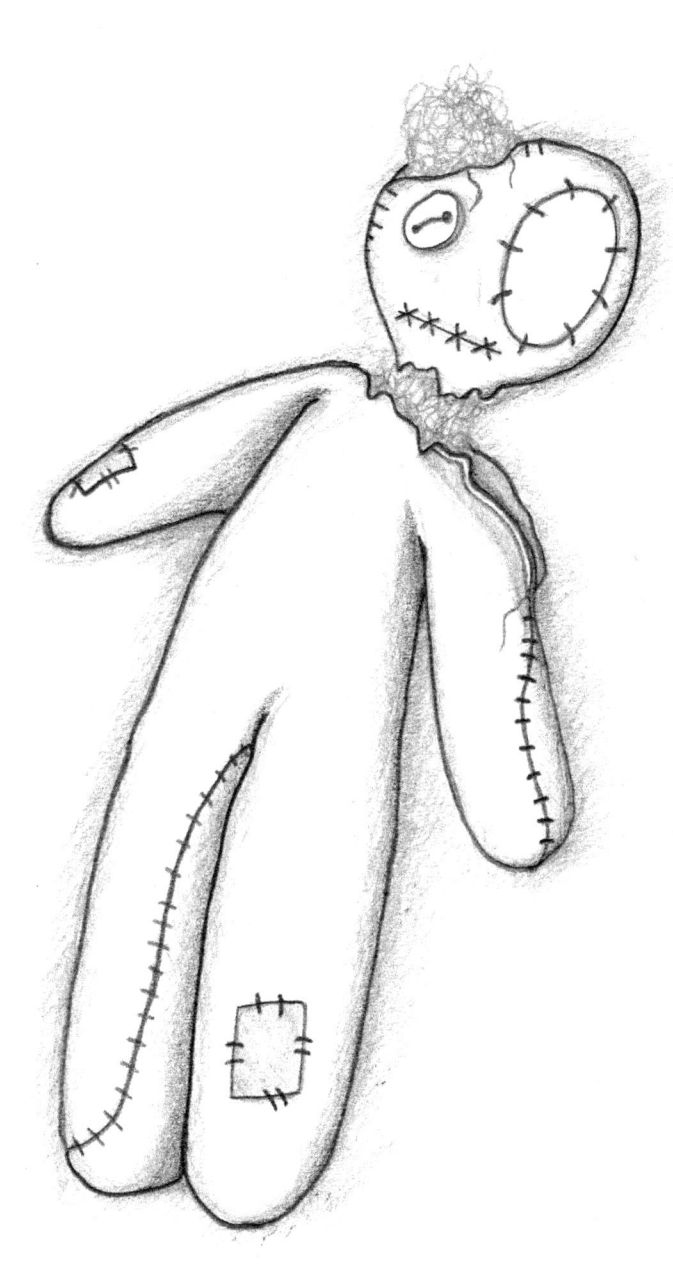

You speak of future. I see the void. You see in hope. I speak of despair.

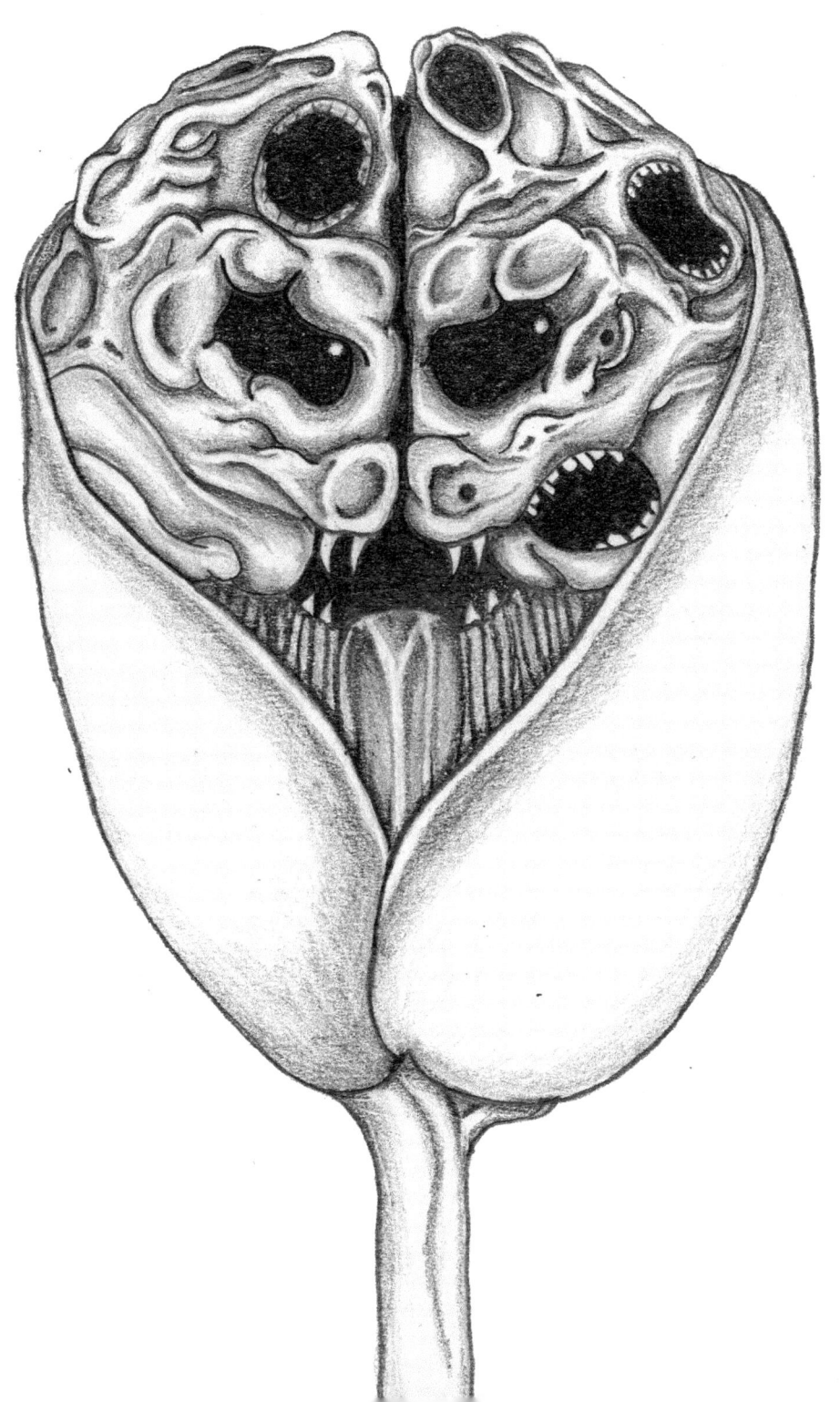

So this is it, this is my brain functioning as normal. This is the return to how I feel after the chemical break. None of you know how lucky you are. Now I can look back and 'feel' how I've spent the entirety of my life. I can sit and ask myself 'how the fuck did I manage?' I can look at it and have to relearn it all again because of some stupid fucking pill from your world. A pill that did nothing but make me feel 'incomplete' on such a pathetically small level but which has fucked the rest.

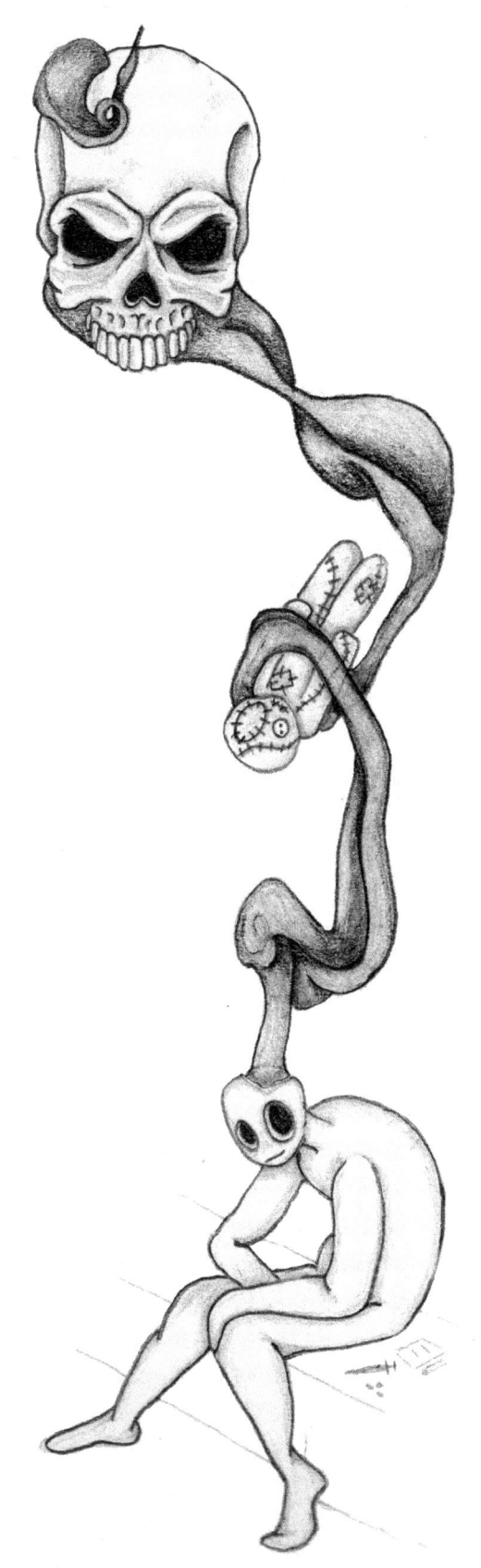

You're all so fucking lucky. Look at you all, living your existences with normal brains. You sit there and look at me and tell me to just get over it, to deal with it. You selfish fucking creatures. Sit and think for one minute. You have it all so perfect; you get to live as you want. Mine is either a defect or a loss of part of my self. I'm not allowed to be who I am. If I want to connect I need to change. Need to change a whole fucking world, and all you need to do is 'pretend' to change.

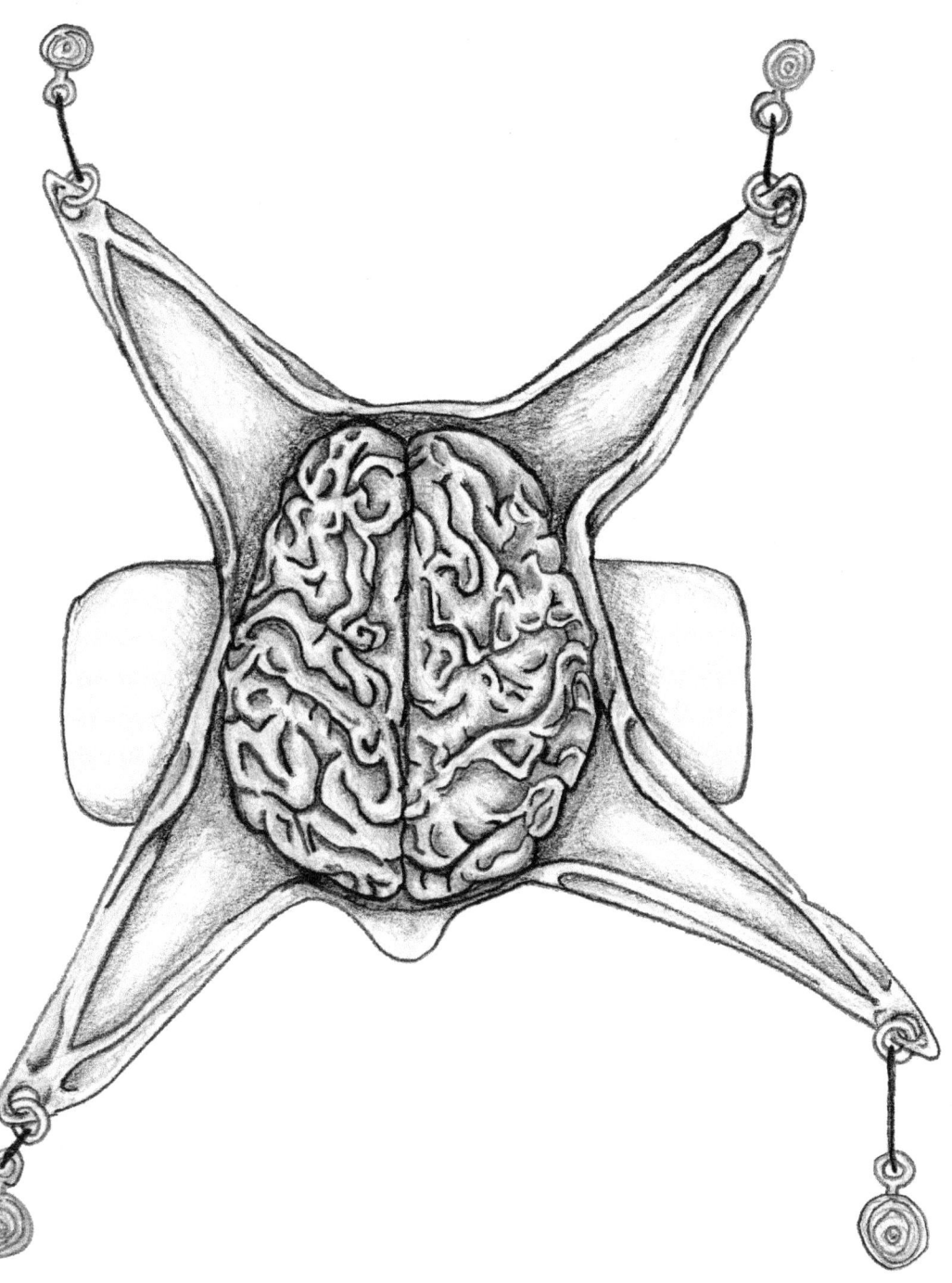

You know what, have your world with its pathetic rules, its regulations. Its expectations. Its greed and importance on the insignificant parts of existence. I don't want to be a part of it. I don't want to exist like you. Living like automations. Pack animals. Herds of fucking sheep grazing until your extinction. Take your world and get it out of my face. I don't like it. Never have done. Never will. I don't want to help benefit it in anyway. It's rotten. Rotten to its core and you all feed off the decay.

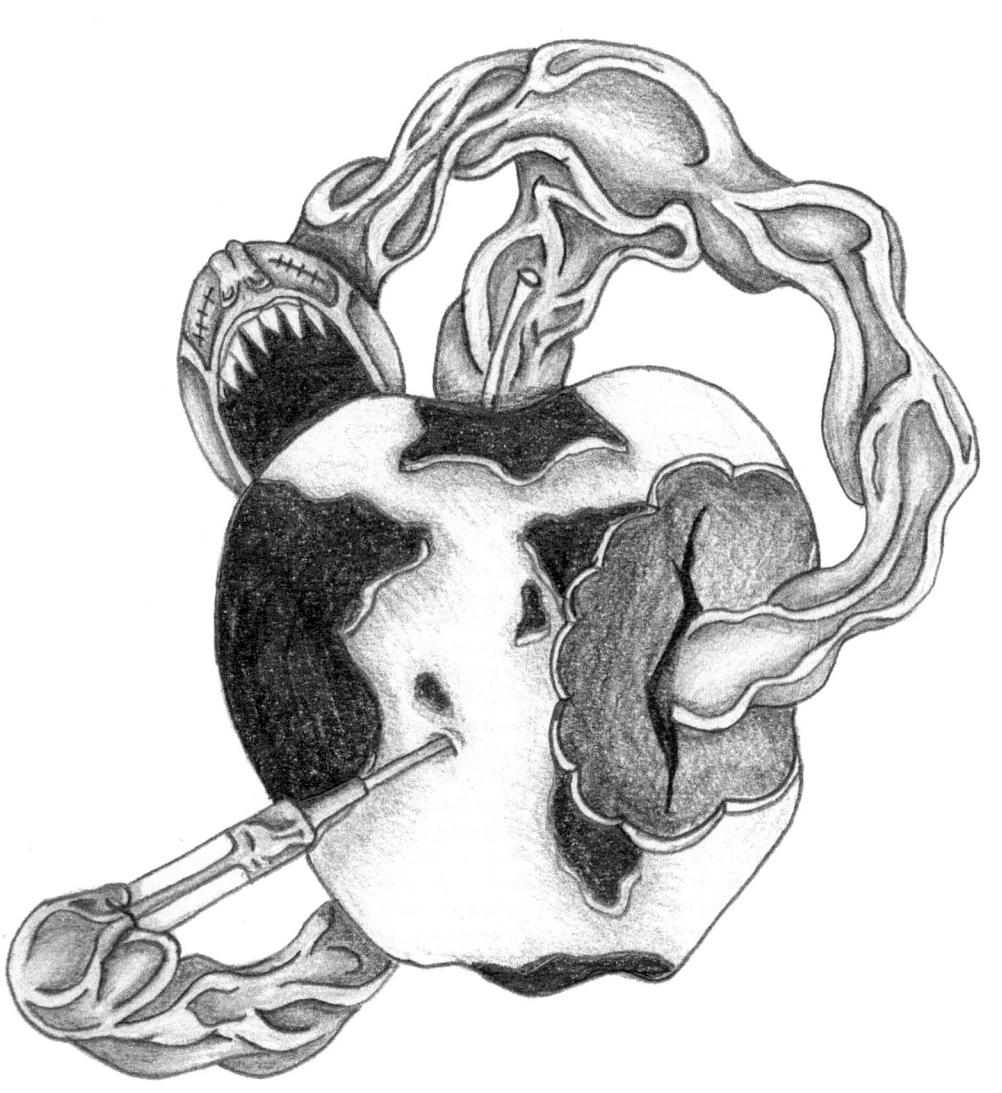

Take your world. It doesn't belong to me. Take your world. I don't want it. Take your long-winded explanations. You view me as just a malfunctioning organism, my personality a chemical imbalance. You don't view me as a 'person'. I don't follow your rules so you put me on medication to make me think like you, act like you; you want to make me a puppet. Does that make me more of a person to you all? You're just the blind governed by the blind.

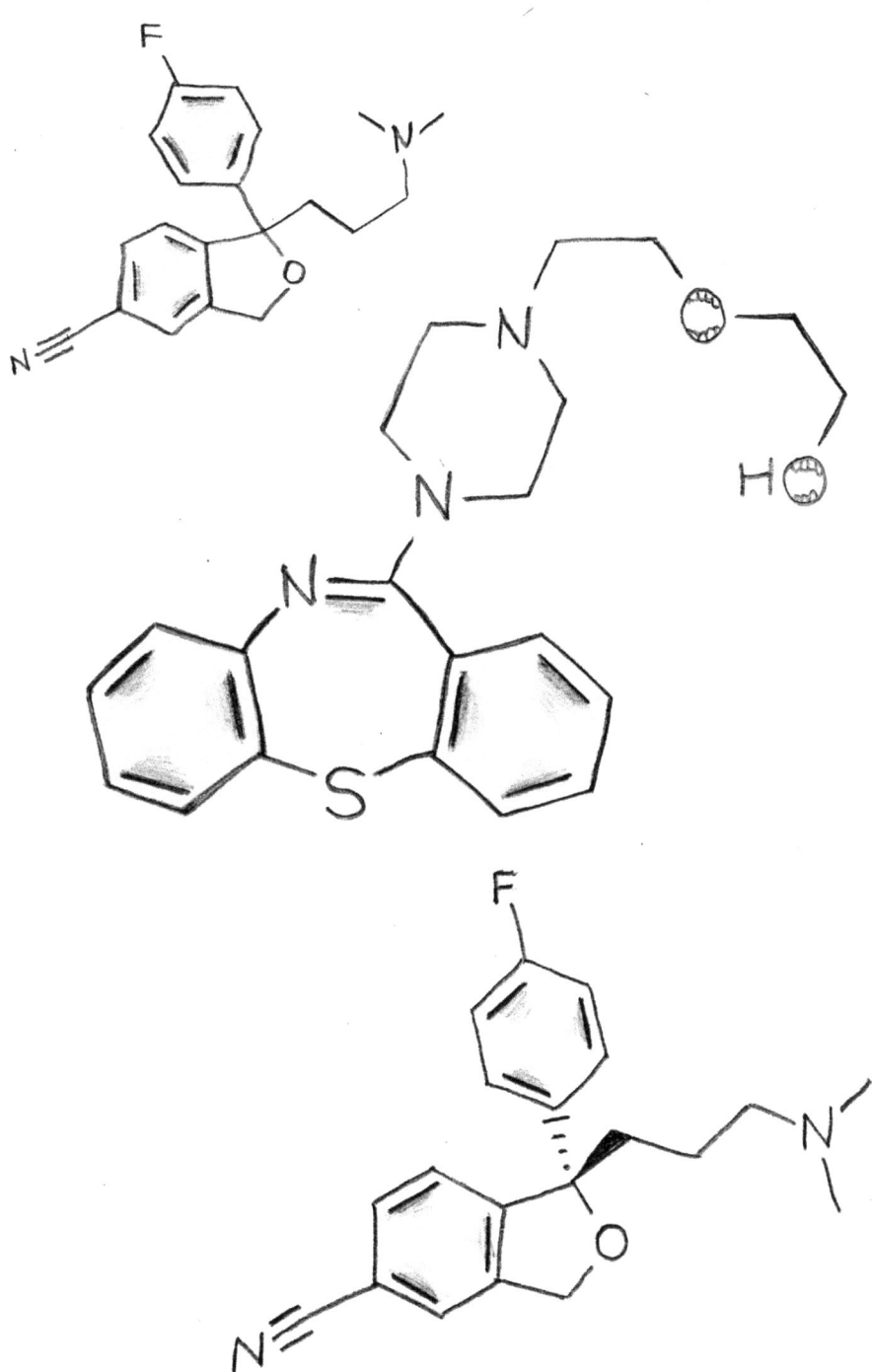

Take your pathetic godless science and stick up your asses. You try to understand everything about this world, yet you all run blindly from the dark. How meaningless a life without an afterlife is. You just degrade your existence to one small moment of time when you could make yourself infinite. Just leave me alone. Just let me exist.

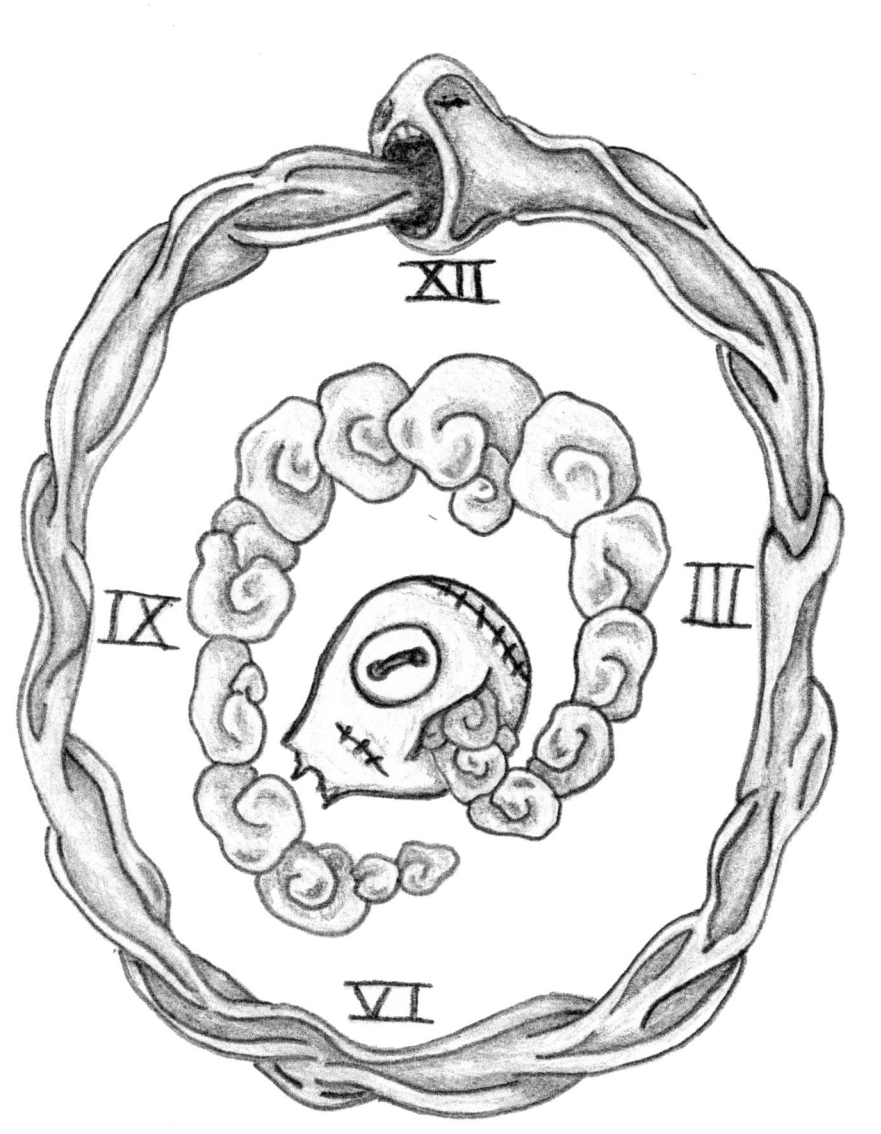

Exist? What is existence when everything has all been like this? A lie. If not a lie then a created falsehood. If I could escape from this emptiness, this disconnection, would I do it? Step away from everything I know and begin again. Could I do it even if I wanted to?

Mother, please explain to me the workings of your world. Explain so I can see. I can't promise to understand. I can't promise anything any more. Just know that I'm sorry. Sorry for everything I have dragged you through. I'm trying. Trying my hardest but I'm broken and tired. I'm scared. Scared of losing myself. Scared of the dark. Scared of the silence.

I'm not worth any of this.   I am no one.   I am a ghost.   I'm nothing.

Nothing but worthless dirt.

I'M NOTHING. I'M NOTHING

I'M NOTHING. I'M NOTHING

I'M NOTHING I'M NOTHING

BUT WORTHLESS

DIRT

I'M NOTHING I'M NOTHING

I'M NOTHING I'M NOTHING

I'M NOTHING. I'M NOTHING

I'M NOTHING. I'M NOTHING

I'M NOTHING. I'M NOTHING

I'M NOTHING.

I'M No THING.

So I scream, kick out at reality for never including me. If I punch hard enough could I cut it? Could I make it feel just a bit of the pain inside me? So many questions, never any answers. Answers can be argued. Conclusions dismissed. So maybe all I need is the end. Finality. The end of everything.

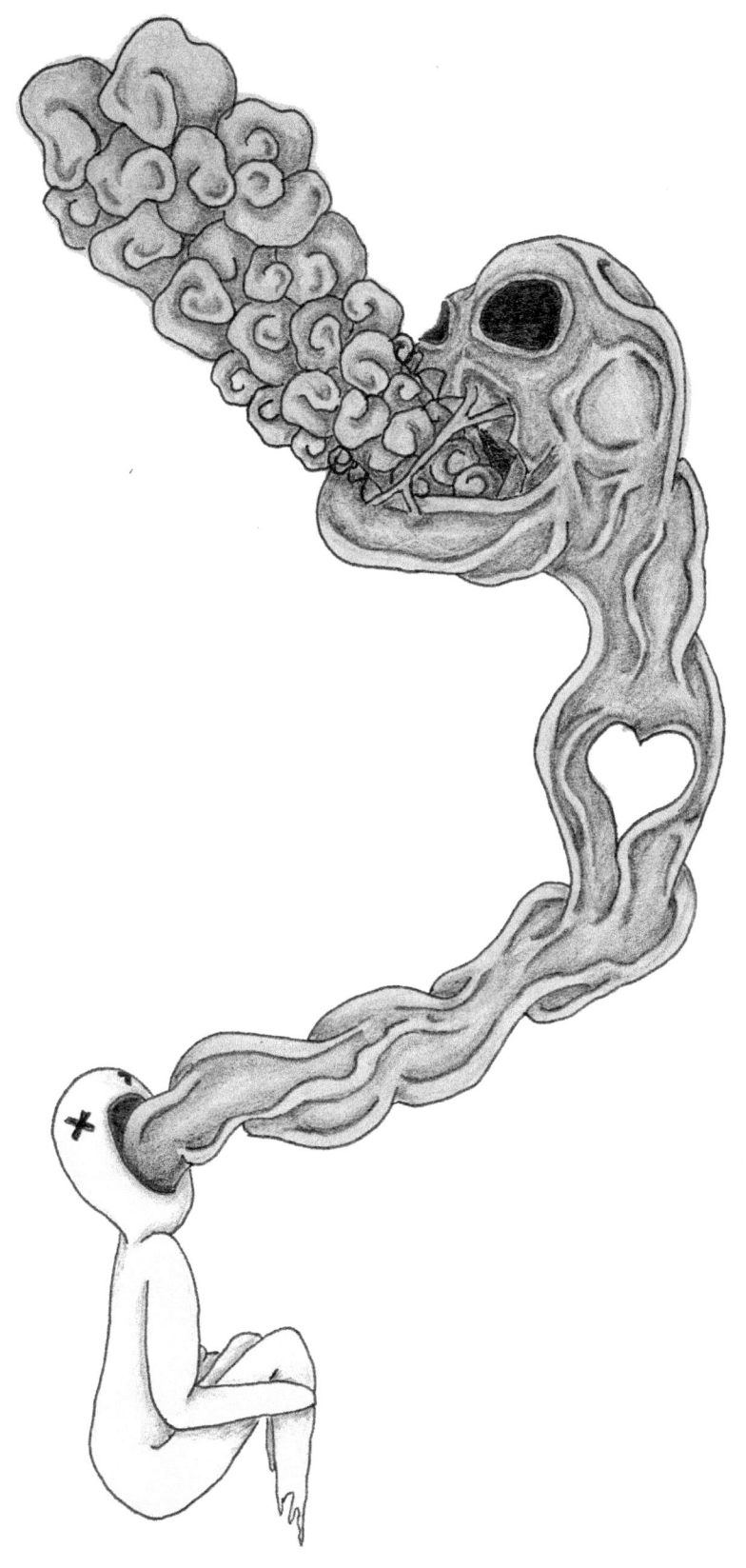

If only you could understand how I feel. If only you could witness this

life through my eyes, through my pain. Then you would understand.

You would go insane. You would tie the rope around your neck and

jump. One minute would kill you. It killed me years ago.

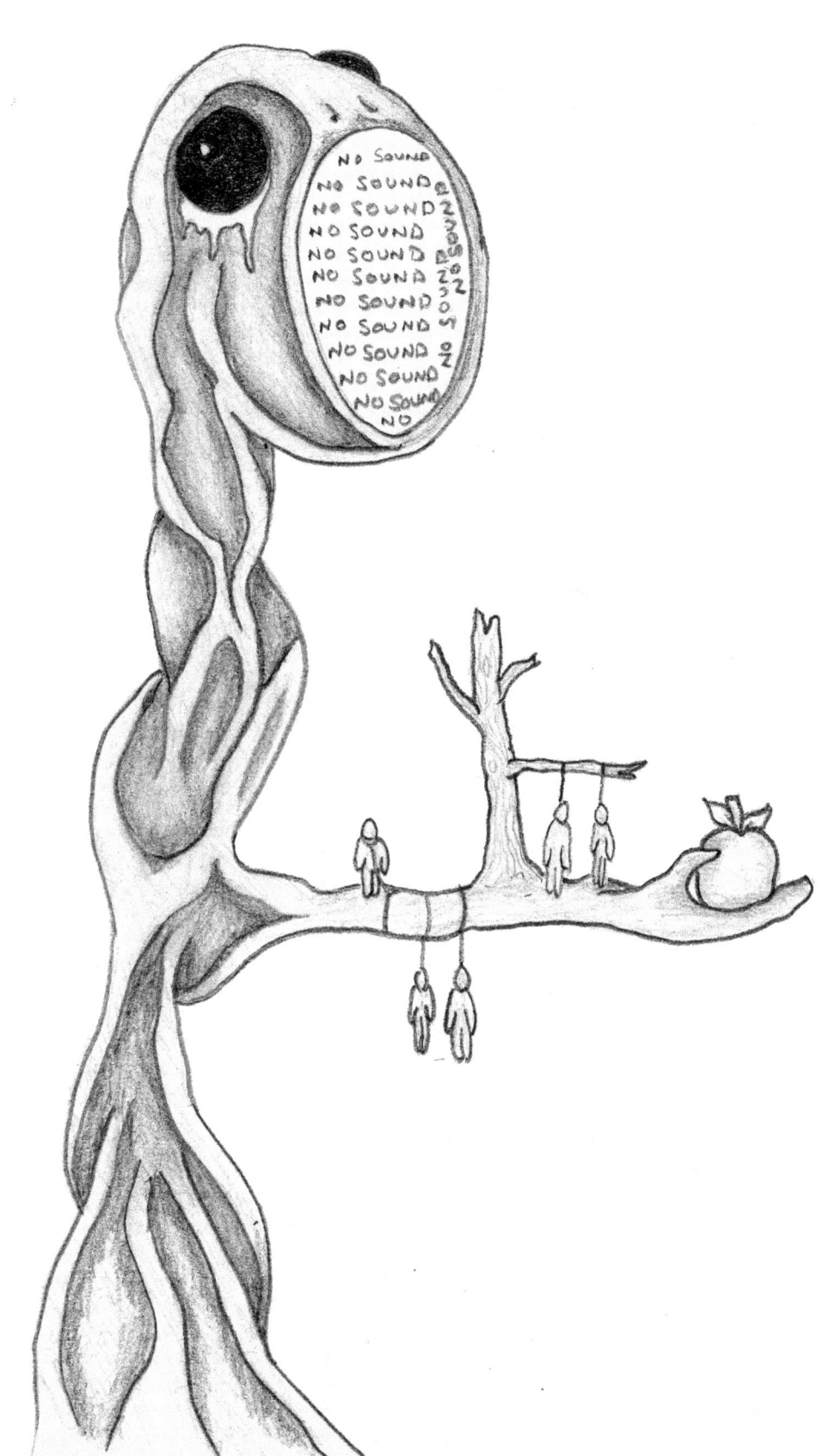

Alone. I face this alone. Stand by me if you wish but this journey is mine alone. The final walk of the Nazarene, the weight of the world upon his back. Please comfort me when I fall. And I will fall. I will go down deeper into the abyss and drag you all with me. Save your souls, escape whilst you can. The longer you wait, the harder it will become. Save yourselves. At the end of the day that's all you can do.

Maybe this dream will come to a conclusion and I'll wake up in a new one. Maybe there is nothing else outside of this. Maybe I am going to get better. Maybe one day there will be certainties.

Each day I live my worst nightmare. Each day I live in fear. Each and

every fucking day. Each day I pray that it will end.

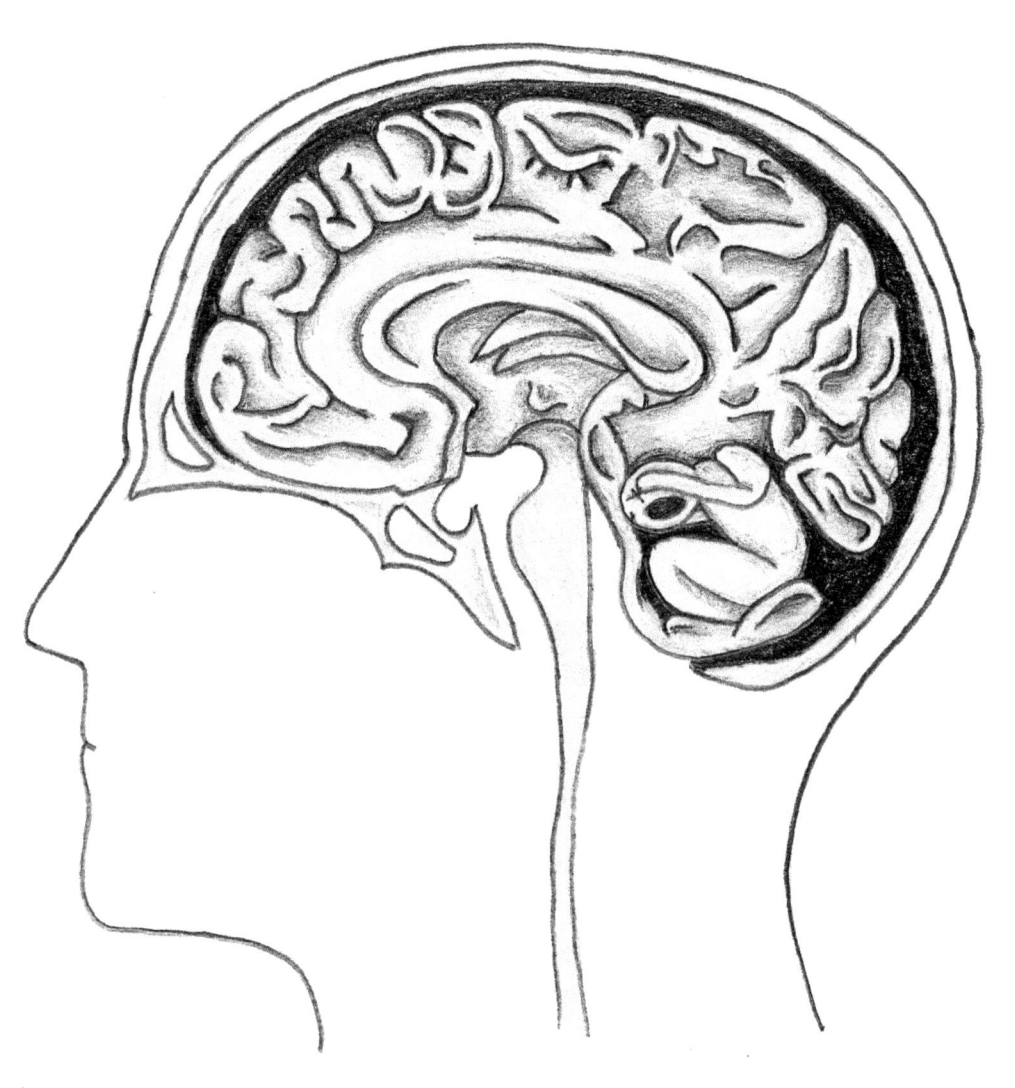

When will this all end?

The End

BOOK FOUR
CYCLE-2
EYES OF INSANITY

PART ONE
REALITY

What is this place? This place to which I am being told I have to belong? All I see when I look at your world is pain; constant unending pain. Deceit after deceit. A world built upon greed and power. Why should I want to subscribe to any of that? Why would I want to be part of it in any way? Why should I even try and understand yours when you don't even listen to mine?

All my life I have been screaming at this world. Screaming from within a body that is not mine. I don't belong here, *this* isn't my world. Forced to exist within this frame of skin and bone. A prisoner. The darkness plucked me from the void and held me in wait. A baby was born without a soul and I was placed within it. From within this form I have watched it grow and age. I have controlled it like you would a stolen car or machine.

I have had to interact with your world; had to build friendships and relationships only to see them rot at my touch. Your world too corrupt and dirty for what I desire. Am I normal? In the sense that I long to be loved, cared for, respected, but none of these are my priority. All I see through these eyes is your pathetic existence. Torn between dreams of freedom from this hell and the need to try and find some evidence that I could be wrong about your world.

I was born from the darkness and I am its prisoner. I am not here to exist, I am here for their purpose, regardless of how much I could fight against it. It pours words into my head. Each and every single word I write down in my books is not from me. The darkness has written it and I merely transcribe. It can't enter your world on its own and I am here to make the cracks that will allow it to seep silently through. If I refuse to write, I am punished. If I try to alter what is spoken, I am punished. If I write what I want to, I am punished. I will be punished for writing this. That dark shadow who is my jailor will come to me and strangle me; it will scream and shout at me; it will not give me one moment of peace until I relent and do what I am here to do.

This head is filled with noise. The words of the darkness; the voice of the shadow; the voice of the old lady when the shadow gets too angry; my own inner voices. They all merge into one chaotic noise and it is too much to bear. All I wish for is silence but there is no escape.

The darkness has shown me that. It has shown me what waits for us all at the end. The nothing. The dark. The endless emptiness filled with eternal pain. Yet, despite knowing all of this, I'd rather be there than trapped in this world I do not understand.

I am here for a purpose. I didn't choose to be here, but here I am. I am the victim of an existence I do not want to be party to. I am here to write the darkness into words; to let those words enter into your soul and plant their little seeds deep within it. To help the darkness enter into you and then walk away, leaving you all alone whilst, like cancer, the darkness consumes your world.

That is what all this is about. That is what this existence upon your Earth all boils down to. The conclusion. The darkness has watched your existence and it has decided that now is the time for you to all pay for your sins. It will make mankind hear the pain it has caused. It will make you hear each and every scream, cry and shout for eternity.

That is your Heaven.

That is your salvation.

PART TWO
POSTCARDS

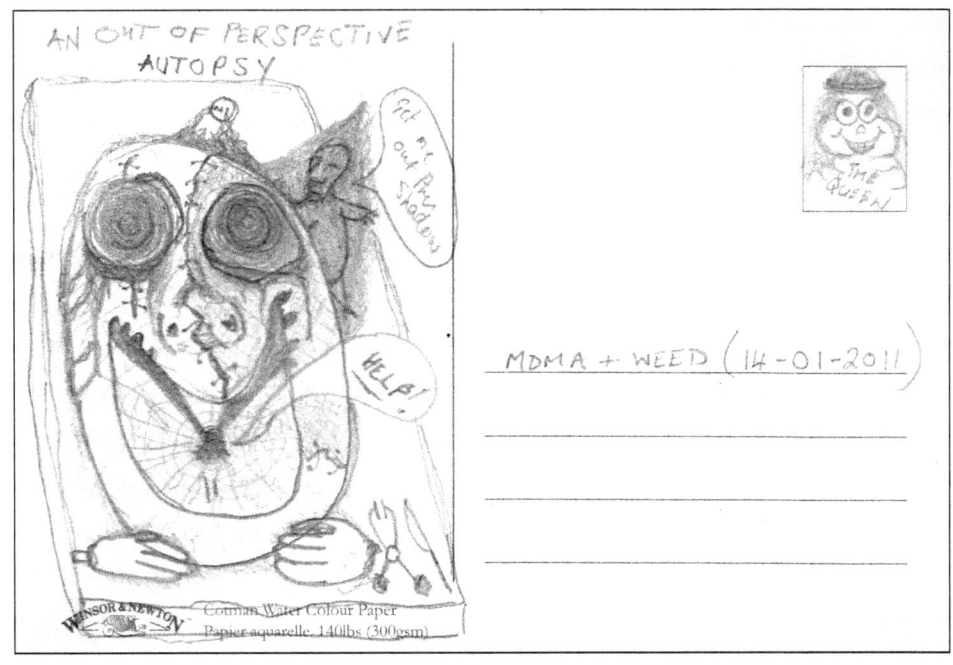

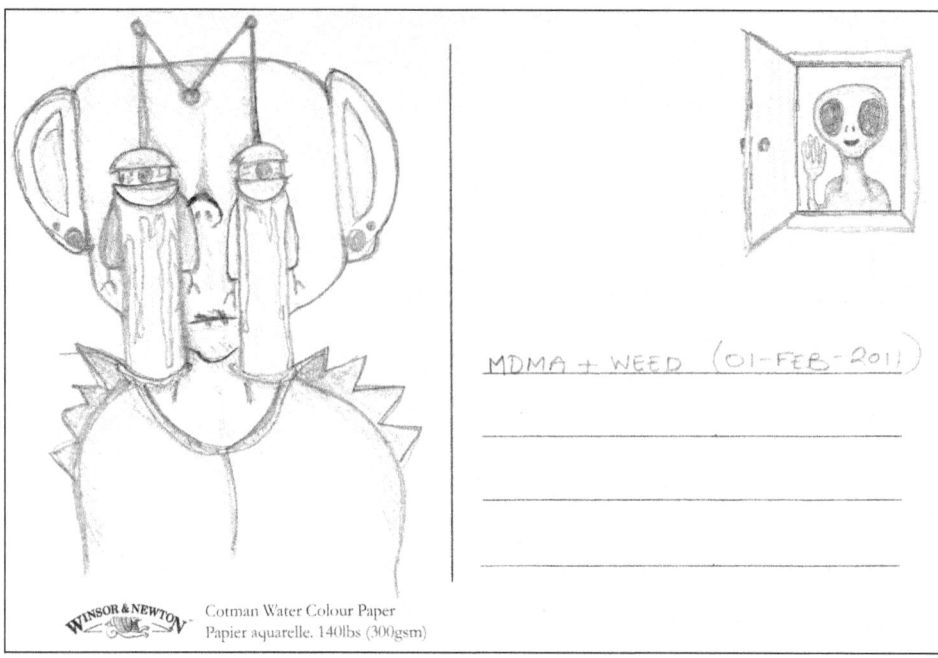

MDMA + WEED (01-FEB-2011)

WEED + MDMA [02-02-11]

MDMA + WEED [03-02-2011]

Cotman Water Colour Paper
Papier aquarelle. 140lbs (300gsm)

MDMA + WEED [18 - FEBRUARY - 2011]

Cotman Water Colour Paper
Papier aquarelle. 140lbs (300gsm)

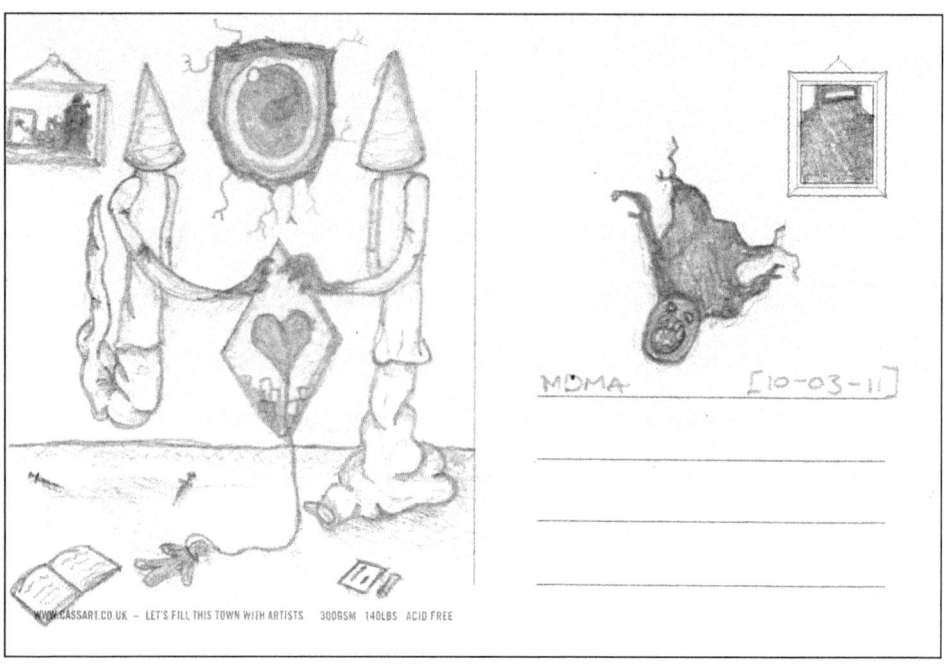

MDMA [10-03-11]

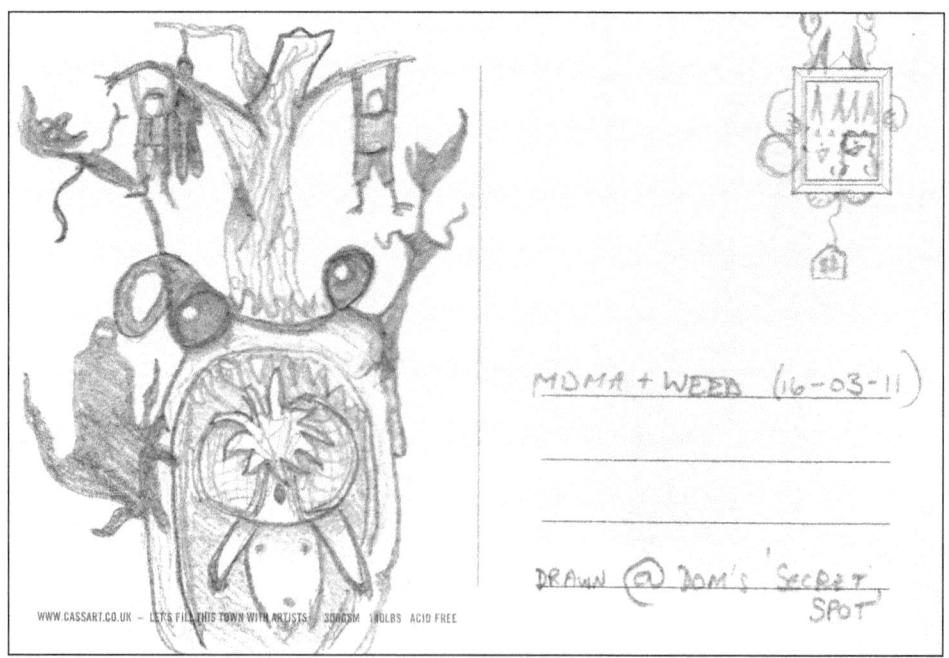

MDMA + WEED (16-03-11)

DRAWN @ DOM'S SECRET
SPOT

MDMA [20-03-11]
PICTURE
'The Langton' 140lb (300g/m²) Not (CP)

FAITH
HOPE
LOVE
DREAMS
MDMA [05-04-11]
OM
PICTURE
'The Langton' 140lb (300g/m²) Not (CP)

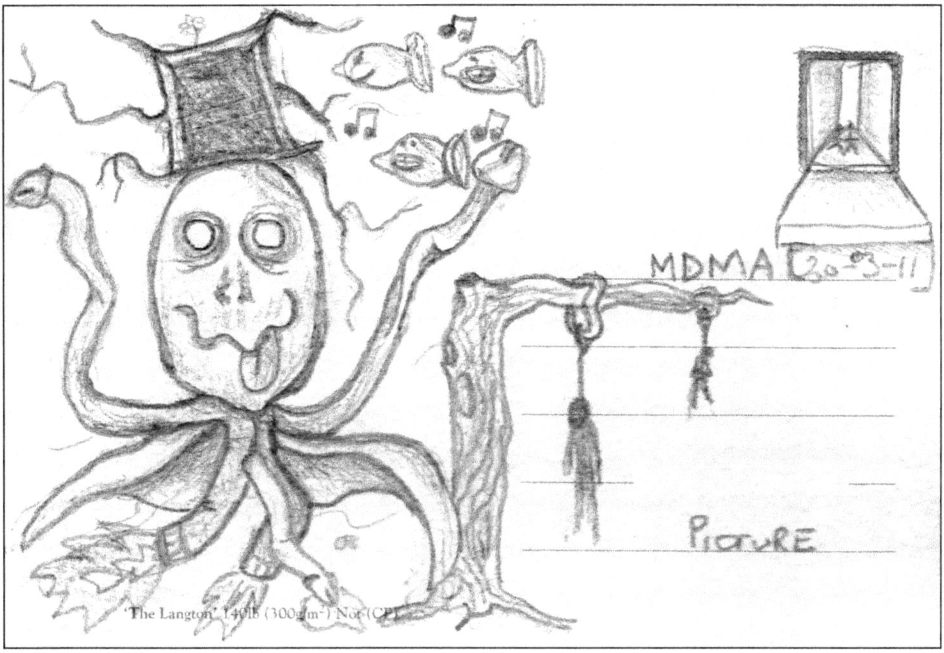

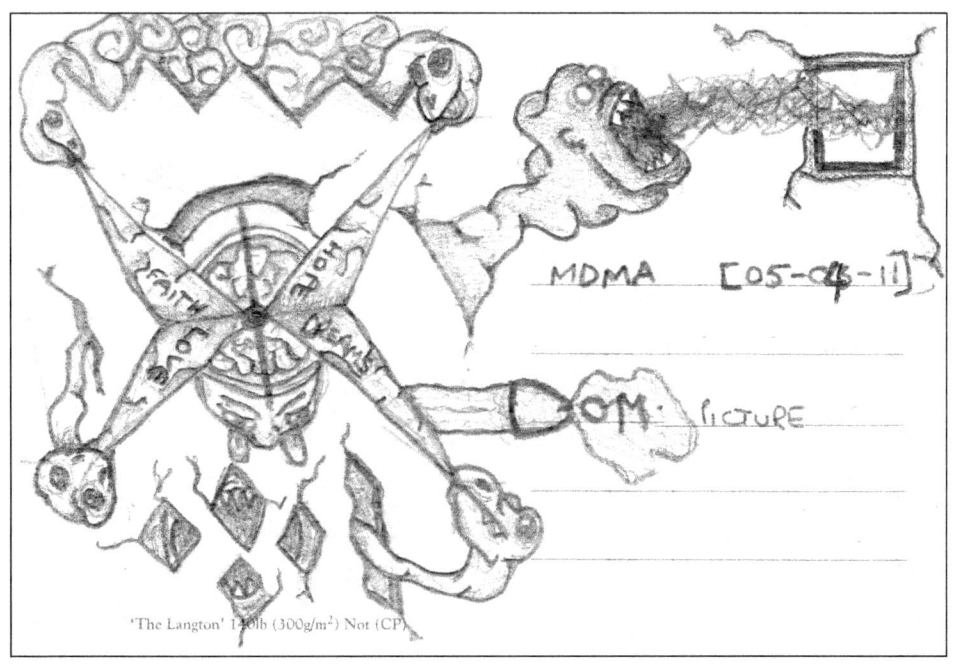

MDMA + WEED (06-04-11)

(DRAWN IN REGENTS PARK)

'The Langton' 140lb (300g/m²) Not (CP)

MDMA [27-04-11]
+WEED

'The Langton' 140lb (300g/m²) Not (CP)

PART THREE
NOTEBOOKS

16 - SEPT- 2010

ARTHUR IS SEXY.

503

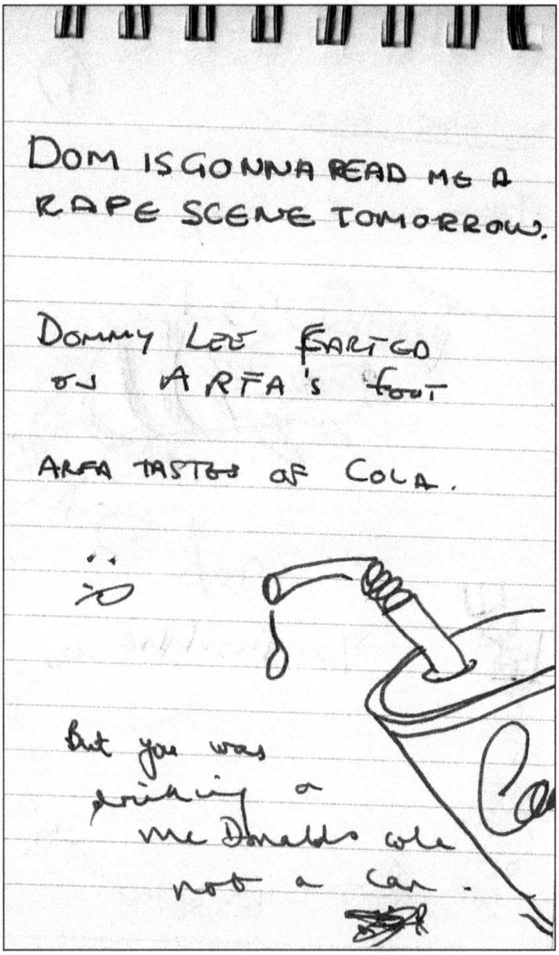

DOM IS GONNA READ ME A
RAPE SCENE TOMORROW.

DOMMY LEE FARTED
ON ARFA'S foot

ARFA TASTES OF COLA.

:0

But you was
drinking a
mc Donalds cole
not a can.

mmmwahwah

Between awake and
asleep.

Don MISSED ARTHUR —

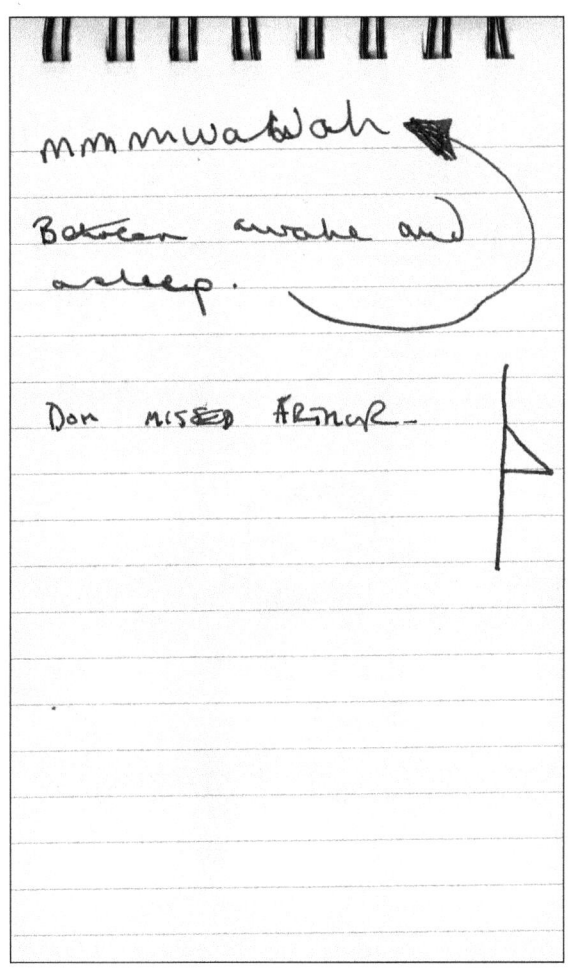

Just think how fucked the book would be if always like this. Totally totality. Yeah that made a lot of sense. Just getting bored of sentences. There goes speak.

Talking all day how can you never run out of things to say. Total shit on this.

This is obviously the best way to live? It's fucking right.

I WANT COFFEE

16 - DEC - 2010
17 - DEC - 2010

Think. Think and wonder.
Nature is a beautiful thing.
Its wonderful in every way.
The Earth is Perfect. What
ruins it is Mankind. Our
pollution and destruction.
Raping and raping. Living
like vermin. Ticks bleeding
the host dry. Parasite.
But then... then you realise
the are thing everyone
else seems to have forgotten.
Mankind is part of Nature,
we might be the most cancerous
part of its core but by design
we as a species are beautiful

507

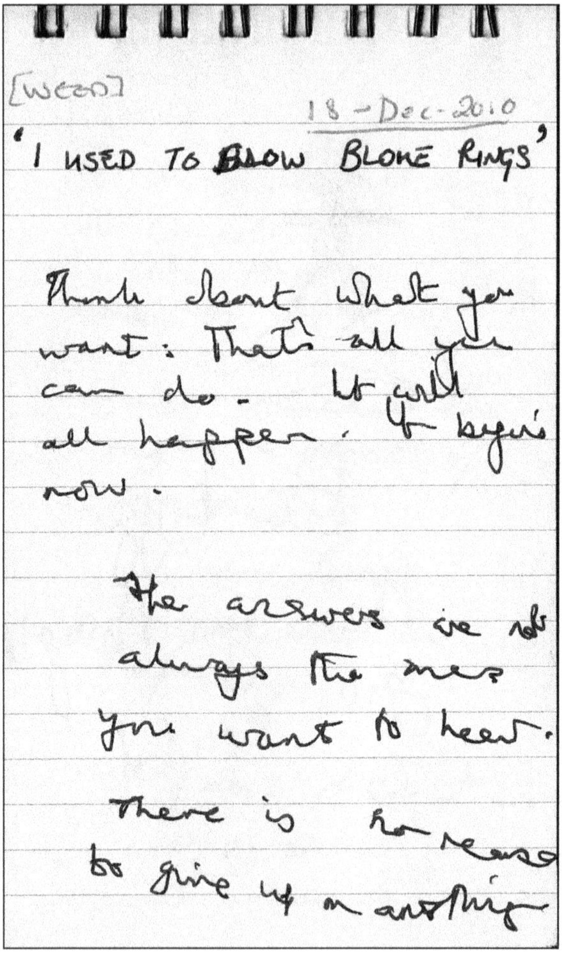

18 - Dec - 2010

' I USED TO ~~BLOW~~ BLONE RINGS '

Think about what you
want : That's all you
can do . It will
all happen . 4 begin's
now .

The answers are not
always the ones
you want to hear .

There is no reason
to give up on anything

Be bigger
than you thought
you could

ben

If I could tell if
I could.
The trigger is there
easy to see.

Just it needs the
right amount of
pressure.
Then Bank.
One more soul in
Purgatory.

Yeah. I could
do it.

14 - JAN - 2011

Guess it's a staple. MDMA with weed. That's the way we roll.

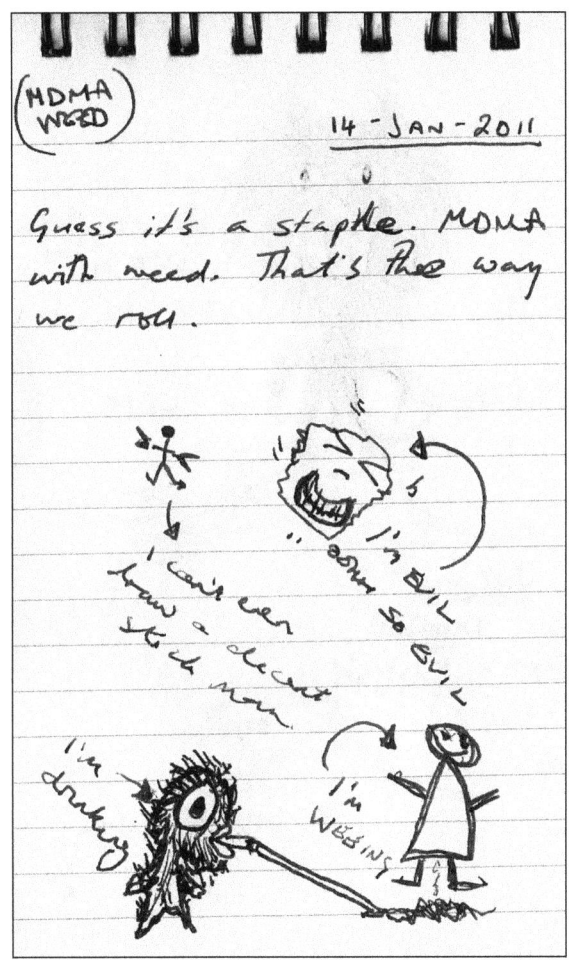

512

513

514

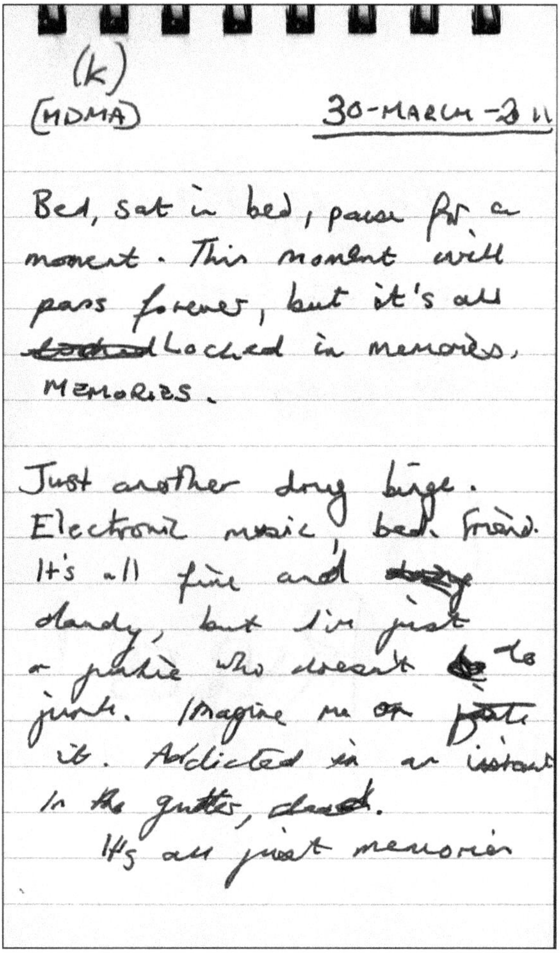

(k)

(MDMA)   30-MARCH-11

Bed, sat in bed, pause for a
moment. This moment will
pass forever, but it's all
~~locked~~ Locked in memories,
MEMORIES.

Just another day binge.
Electronic music, best friend.
It's all fine and ~~dandy~~
dandy, but I'm just
a junkie who doesn't do
junk. Imagine me on ~~junk~~
it. Addicted in an instant
In the gutter, ~~dead~~.
        It's all just memories

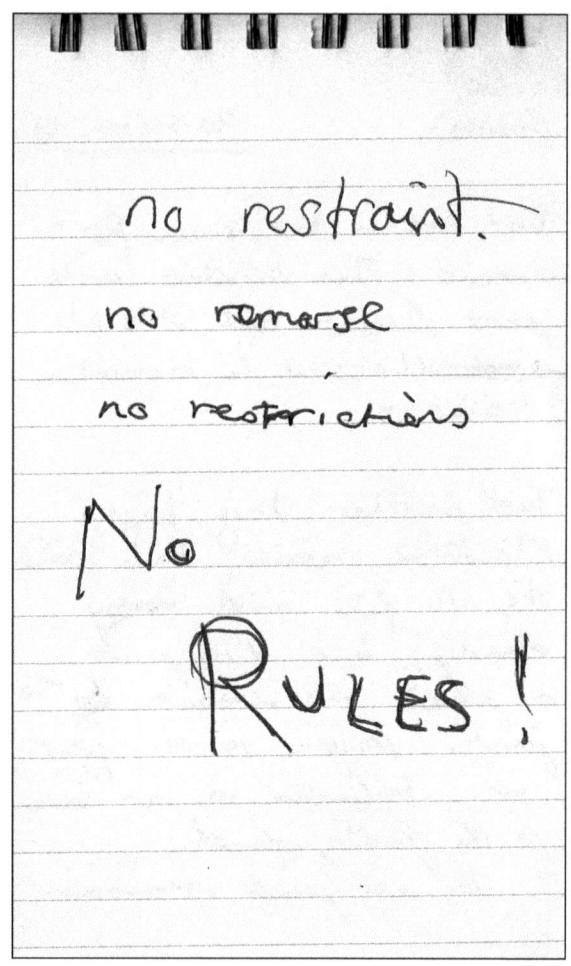

no restraint.

no remorse

no restrictions

No
RULES!

(MDMA)   05-APR-11

This is written by a body,
a vessel for what my mind
commands. But what if
those two constantly fight?
   I AM MY SOUL! THE
BODY IS ITS PRISON. IT
CONTAINS IT. BUT IF THE
PRISON EVICTS ITS PRISONER?...
WHAT THEN? TELL ME
THAT.

YOU BECOME A

GHOST.

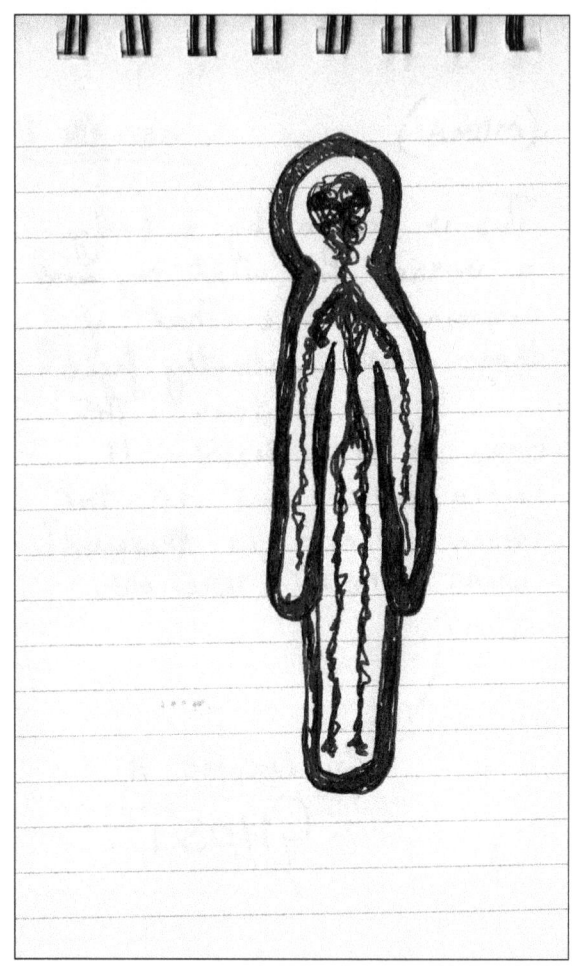

PART FOUR
ARTWORKS

i don't know why...
...we all forget.

Why Do We Forget? [Drawn on MDMA]
2010
Artwork by Dominic Lyne
Medium: Pencils

522

Fracture [Drawn on MDMA]
2010
Artwork by Dominic Lyne
Medium: Pencils

524

Cycle-2.1: The Dream
2010
Artwork by Dominic Lyne
Medium: Graphic Pen, Ink and Watercolour

Cycle-2.1: The Pain
2010
Artwork by Dominic Lyne
Medium: Graphic Pen, Ink and Watercolour

Cycle-2.1: The Fear
2010
Artwork by Dominic Lyne
Medium: Graphic Pen and Marker Pens

Cycle-2.1: The Future
2010
Artwork by Dominic Lyne
Medium: Graphic Pen and Marker Pens

Paradise is Nowhere
2011
Artwork by Dominic Lyne
Medium: Graphic Pen, Marker Pens, Pencils

534

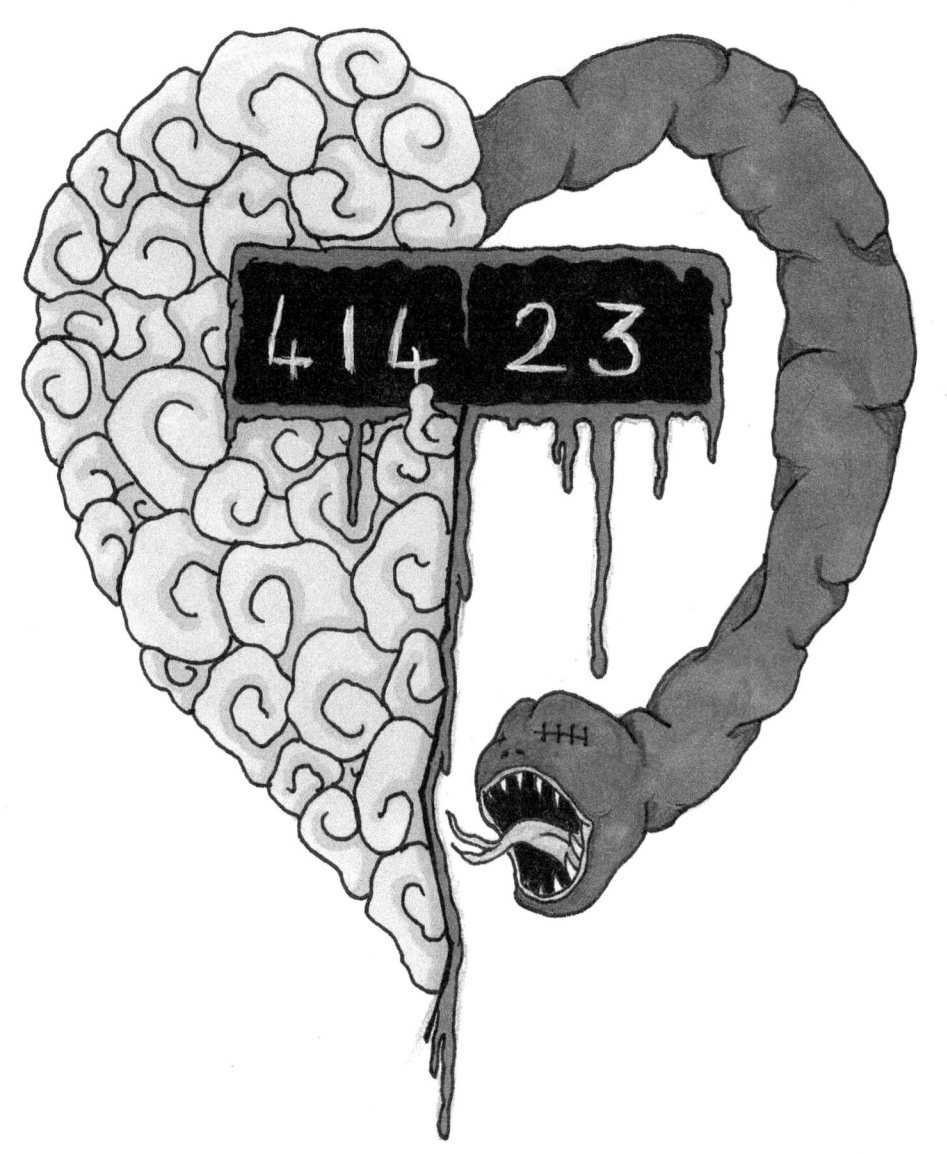

Lying Wasted Under a Broken Coda
2011
Artwork by Dominic Lyne
Medium: Graphic Pen, Marker Pens, Pencils

536

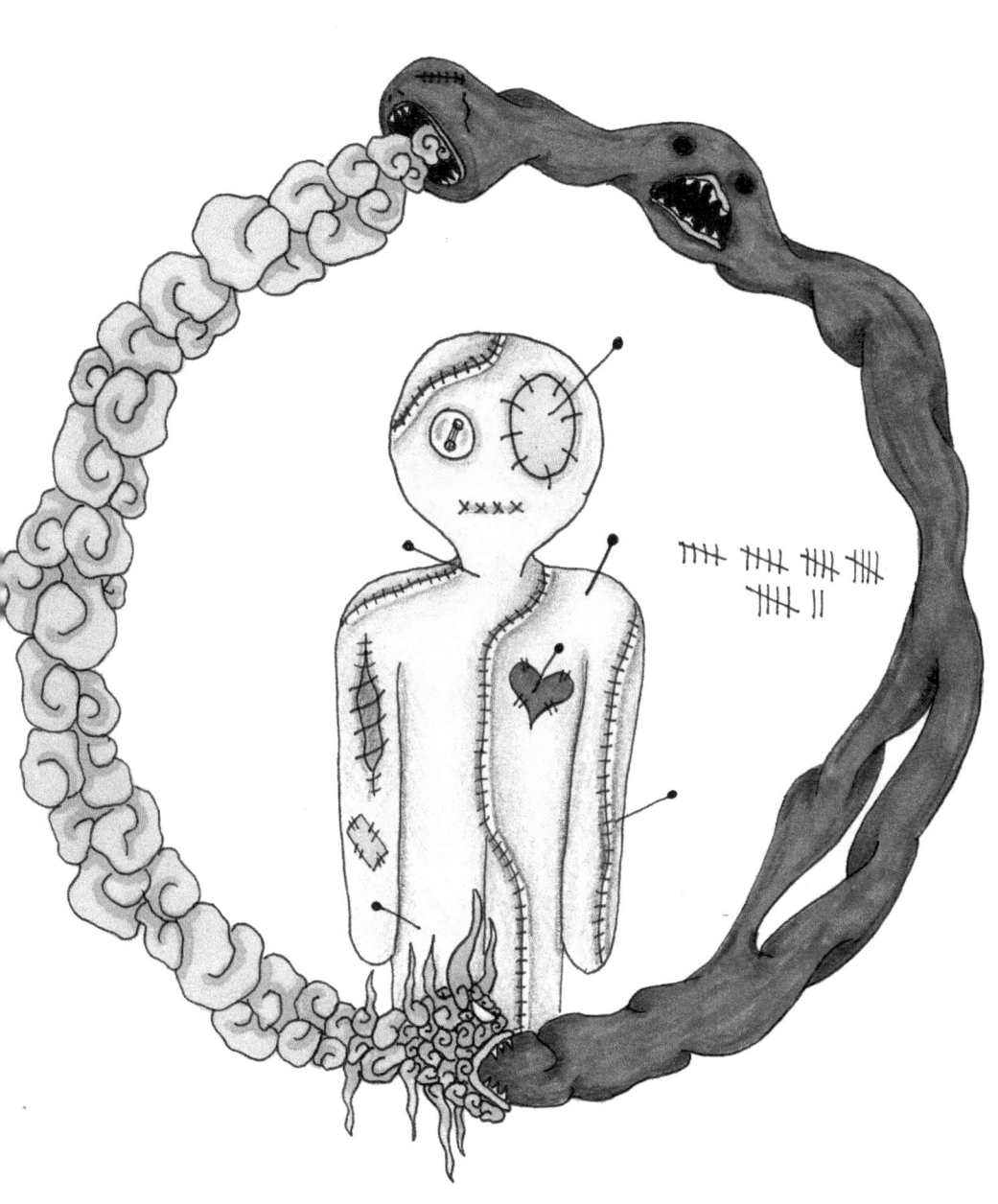

The Silent Scream
2011
Artwork by Dominic Lyne
Medium: Graphic Pen, Marker Pens, Pencils

538

Eyes of Insanity
2011
Artwork by Dominic Lyne
Medium: Graphic Pen, Marker Pens, Pencils

540

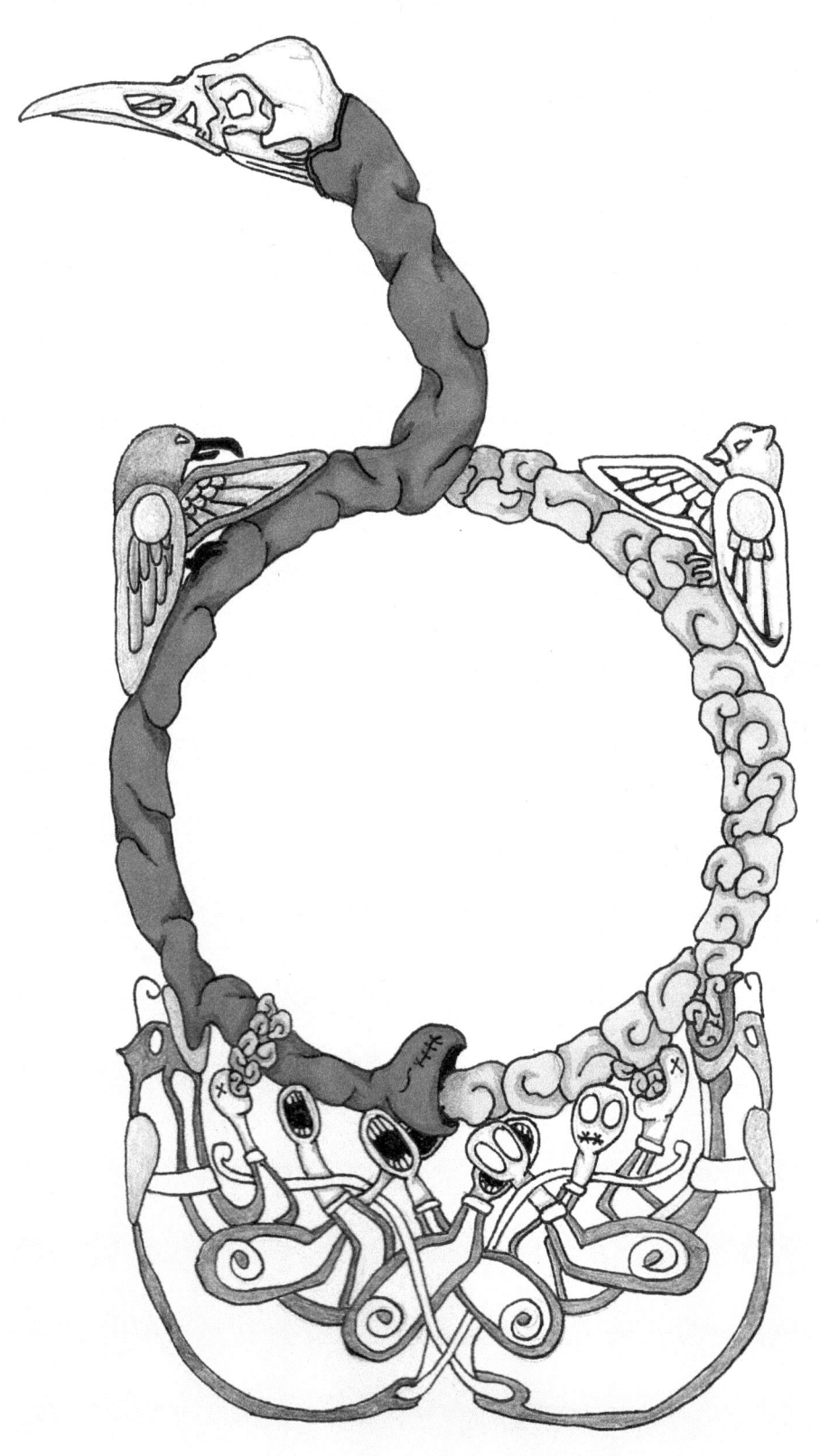

Darkness and the Light [Tattoo Design]
2011
Artwork by Dominic Lyne
Medium: Graphic Pen, Marker Pens, Pencils

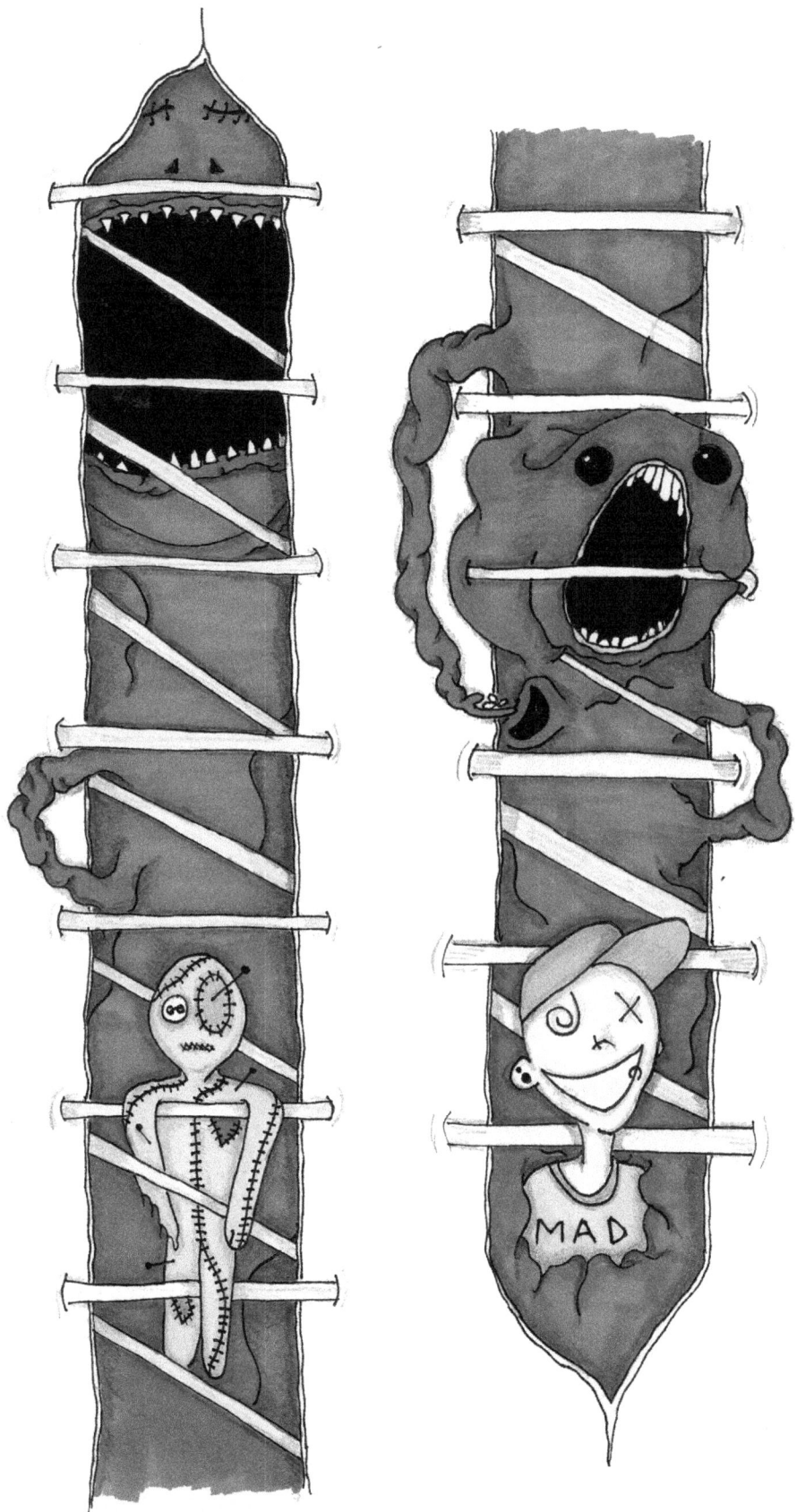

Inner Demons [Tattoo Design]
2011
Artwork by Dominic Lyne
Medium: Graphic Pen, Marker Pens, Pencils

544

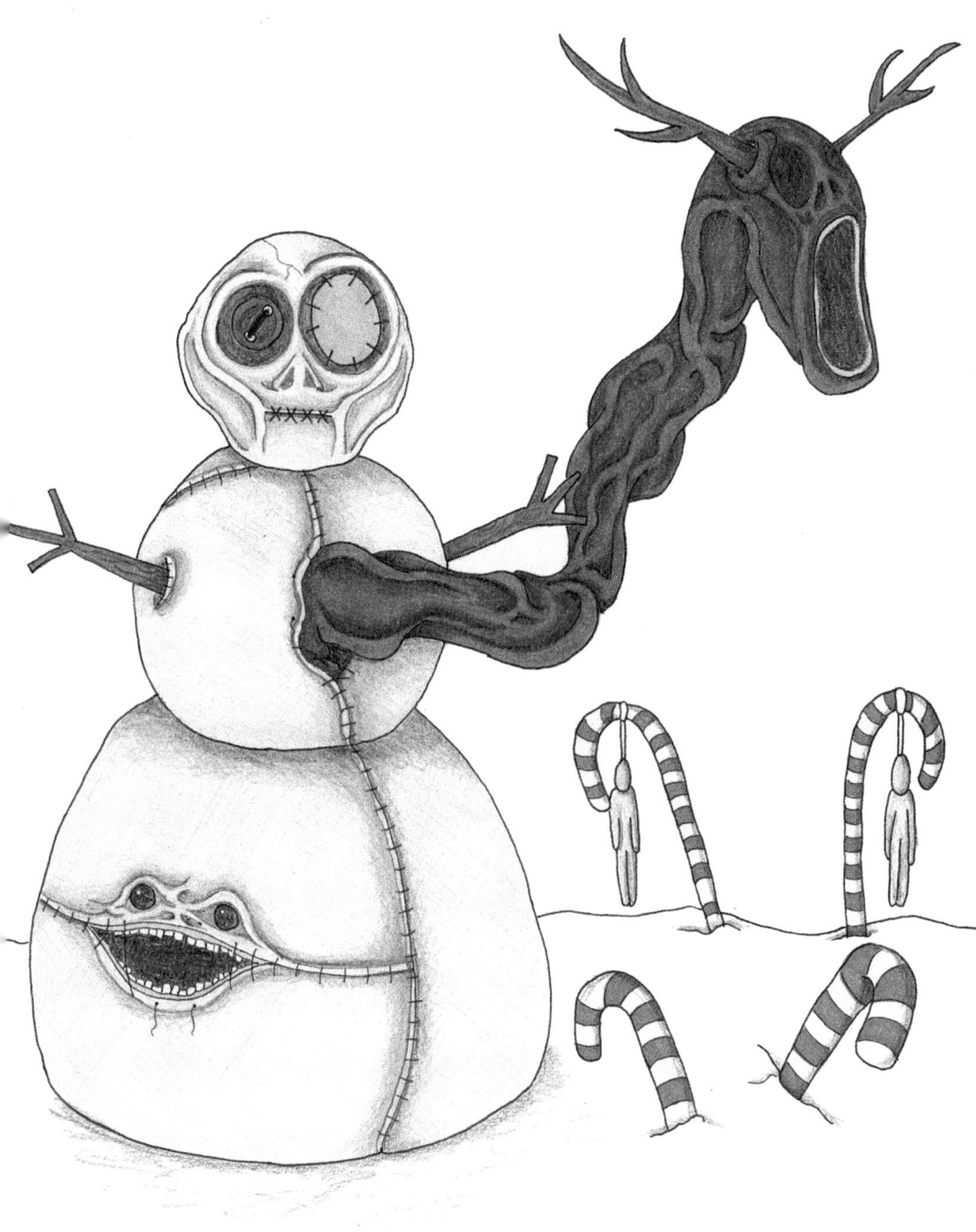

A Rotten Christmas
2011
Artwork by Dominic Lyne
Medium: Graphic Pen, Marker Pens, Pencils

546

Self Portrait
2011
Artwork by Dominic Lyne
Medium: Pencils

548

PART FIVE
DIAGNOSIS
NOVEMBER 2010 - JANUARY 2012

PSYCHOLOGICAL ASSESSMENT

Transcript
10 November 2010

The sort of things you are doing at the moment, the way you respond to the world, the way you respond to other people, is leaving you losses. You're clearly very talented and creative, and someone with your amount of talent and creativity could be flying, but there is something about the way you relate to your world that is blocking your progress. So when that happens, it's not saying to you that your way of doing things is wrong, it's just saying that your way of doing things means you're losing out, you're losing out on work, you're losing out on relationships, you're losing out on progression really. What I think would be really great for you is if we could harness all of this energy you've got, all of your creativity and drive, and actually have it go somewhere meaningful. It must very frustrating for you that you are talented and it isn't going anywhere, and I suspect that this then fuels feelings of anger, feelings of frustration, perhaps even of low self-esteem because you think you could be somewhere else but you still find yourself here. Then you get manipulated by other people, but you're very good at manipulating as well, but what we then find is that these two wrongs not making a right really starts to fit. And I feel frustrated on your behalf as it does seem crazy that someone like you, so attractive, personable, likeable, lovable, has got these deficits. So we're not starting from a place saying there's something wrong we you, we're starting from a place where there are aspects in the way that you are relating to your world that is leaving you losses, and I would like us to think about how to help you achieve perhaps a different set of skills that means instead of losing out, you start gaining.

Now, the way that you are responding to the world really does fit very much with this Borderline presentation I was talking about. And my sense is that this little boy who had far too much freedom, far too much control over his environment, really pushed it as far as he could, I mean you were really pushing the boundaries all the time, and outsmarting all the grown ups. Now when you come into the adult

551

life, the problem with that is that there are far more people out there who are smarter, faster, heavier, angrier, etcetera, and you start getting these cumulative losses. This is a very big pond we're in and there's some really nasty sharks out there, and my worry is that so far you haven't been too badly done to, but there's the danger that one day you could meet someone who is really nasty and who you can't charm or manipulate your way out of, and all the things you have learnt, all these skills as you say, this Oliver Twist type skill set you've got, won't be enough to keep you safe. Certainly in the terms of your career progression, and I'm sure at some point you want to have a healthy relationship with somebody, and be loved, and be loving, but all of those things seem to be the real losses for you at the moment.

You're a very fast thinker, which is partly what informs your impulsivity, and because you are moving ahead of the game, people can't keep up with you. The problem is that sometimes you go so far ahead of the game that you've lost sight of what was happening, so it escalates exponentially and things get out of control. I would like us to help you to be able to harness your brilliance, your quick mind, your quick-wittedness, but actually apply in a more real way to your experience because then you really start to shape your life.

At the moment, because you've had too much freedom and no boundaries, it's almost like your brain thinks it can do what it likes, and the problem is that the external parameters that your working with squeeze in on you, so other people will get angry with you, they will drop you, they will reject and abandon you, because they can't keep up with you or understand why you're doing it anyway. So what would be really good for you is to slow things down a bit so people could understand you, and you could communicate in a way that they feel they don't have to abandon you and walk away. So in other words, you get something that might not be as exciting in some ways but it will be a lot more real, and then you can put your excitement into your creativity. Instead of the dramas being played out in your own life, you can have them played out in your books, which is a good place for them to be, so I think that your instinct about writing is a good one. But at the moment you find that your getting lost in all this drama, and the drama is stealing from you. At the time it might feel like it's adding to you, but actually it is stealing from you because it takes on all this loss: your friends, your relationships, your work opportunities, and even your self confidence about who you really want to be.

I think you should be flying, that's what you deserve. And I think one of your frustrations with school was that it wasn't going fast enough for you, so you found your idle fingers. Idle fingers, lots of trouble. Maybe there's something about that; that maybe your challenges do need to be a bit more than other peoples, but you need a lot of help to get there so you can feel confident about standing that ground and making it your own. You can do this. I know that you can, but you won't be able to do it if you keep destroying things around you. The universe doesn't like that, the universe will block you. You might be able to do clever things and manipulate, but the universe will ultimately block you because you're not playing the game. Once you've learnt some strategies to show you how to play the game, you can then have what you want. I think that all your life you've been waiting for the right challenges to come your way, but you've got stymied by all the limitations that have surrounded you. You probably should have been in a school where your talents were being really supported. You were probably one of those kids who should have been on a special programme. It just feels it must have been very frustrating for you and is probably why you created so much mayhem around you.

You know, clever child with no boundaries, really dangerous.

21st April 2011

PSYCHIATRIC ASSESSMENT

Re: Mr Dominic Lyne (d.o.b. 23/2/1983)

REFERRAL

This 28-year old currently unemployed man was referred by his GP, Dr Judy Martin, because of mood symptoms and possible hallucinations. He is on the waiting list for the Dartmouth Park Unit. I met with him on 12th April. He said that the presenting problems were of "zoning out" and finding it difficult to distinguishing between dreaming and reality.

FAMILY HISTORY

His parents divorced just after he was born. He said he didn't know much about his father although he came back into some contact with the family when the patient was 17. His mother is 63, a retired midwife. He described a good relationship with her, although he only sees her once a year because she lives in Preston. They keep in telephone contact. He has a 33-year old brother who is training to be a nurse, with whom he has a good relationship; he said his brother was like his best friend.

FAMILY PSYCHIATRIC HISTORY

He said that his mother's brother had mental health problems, but the diagnosis was unclear.

PERSONAL HISTORY

He said that he was born 4 weeks prematurely by caesarian section. His early development was normal, as far as he knew. He said that his childhood was happy and that he was cared for well. His mother had help from au pairs. He said that he had temper outbursts and would, for example, bang his head against objects, when he was less than 4 years old. At the age of 3 he pushed a child down the steps of a slide. There were some problems with his later speech development and he said that he mumbled a lot until he was 15 and saw a speech therapist. At primary school he was "a loud child who was a trouble maker"; he got

554

bored easily and was somewhat disruptive, although he didn't have any difficulties in keeping up with work. He said that he had lots of energy and he described problems with concentration. At the age of 9 he twice set fire to objects in a church where he was an altar server. He said he did it because he could and that the church was the only place other than his home where he had access to matches. He also described deliberately making a mess at school in order to be naughty at that age. At secondary school he was disruptive in lessons and he said at this time he occasionally was involved in casual theft of books, for example. He said the teachers said he had "a knack of being an annoying student who is still listening" and he didn't fall behind in his work. He got 10 GCSEs, 7 As, 2 Bs, and 1 C. He went to a 6th Form College but was expelled after being disruptive and shouting and swearing at the principal. He lasted 3 hours in another college because of his temper.

From the age of 18 he went to the Academy of Temporary Music for 5 years. He eventually got a first by doing a degree in music production. He said that he would often fall asleep during the lecture part of the academic course and would then be much more involved in practical activities. He wasn't able to find work for a couple of years after leaving college, then worked in a school in Camden when he was 25; he had a relationship with his boss and lost his job when the relationship ended, although he worked there again for a period. He has been unemployed since July 2010.

He said that he had 6 relationships in total, 2 lasting for longer than 1 year. He has a homosexual orientation, and said that he had always been happy with this and never experienced any major problems resulting from his sexuality. He has been sexually active since the age of 15. He has been in his current relationship since January and said that he had been more open with his current partner about his psychological difficulties.

PAST MEDICAL HISTORY

He had an eye operation for strabismus at the age of 8 or 9.

ALLERGIES

He maybe allergic to penicillin.

FORENSIC HISTORY

Nil.

SUBSTANCE MISUSE HISTORY

He currently drinks socially once or twice a week. He has had periods of heavy drinking linked to depression and anxiety in the past. He has a history of using cannabis, cocaine, amphetamines, ketamin, mushrooms, and LSD. He has never used crack or heroin. He said that he had used substances to "cut off from reality". He denied have had symptoms of dependence.

2

PSYCHIATRIC HISTORY

He said that he had experienced seeing shadows (images of things that weren't there) since he was about 4. He described having memory lapses related to periods of time when he "zoned out". For example, in a supermarket he would find himself at the checkout, having not remembered buying the things that he had with him. In some social situations, he felt disconnected from what was going on around him and found it difficult to make his body do what he wanted it to do. He found it difficult to distinguish between dreams and things that really happened at night. When watching films he could become so intensely involved in what was happening that he could experience the film as reality. He could look in a mirror and not recognize himself and said that he frequently felt that things around him were not real and that his body didn't belong to him. He was able to relive past events vividly. He easily became involved in fantasies and daydreams and could spend time staring off into space, thinking of nothing.

He has had periods of low mood and last summer felt depressed, with panic symptoms. He took citalopram, which was not helpful and, later, escitalopram, which produced a slight benefit in his symptoms. The depressive symptoms appear to have gradually improved.

He described longstanding features of borderline personality disorder: he often became frantic when someone he cared about was going to leave him, his relationships with people had extreme ups and downs, he lacked a clear sense of his identify, there was impulsivity in many area of his life, in the past he used to self-harm by cutting, he experiences sudden mood changes, he often feels empty inside, he becomes easily irritable and loses control of his behaviour when angry, and experiences dissociative symptoms.

CURRENT MEDICATION

Nil

MENTAL STATE EXAMINATION

He engaged well with the interview and quickly became involved in discussion of his problems. His self-care was good. He had several tattoos and piercings. There was no abnormality of behaviour or speech. His affect was euthymic and reactive. His underlying mood was changeable. There were longstanding dissociative symptoms. There were no current persistent symptoms or panic symptoms. He described longstanding negative thoughts about his appearance, but these were not focused on any particular area of his body. There were no psychotic symptoms. His insight into his problems was good.

RESULTS FROM RATING SCALES

On the dissociative experiences scale he scored 57 percent, with depersonalization symptoms particularly highly scoring.

3

SUMMARY

There is a history of attention difficulties throughout childhood and adolescence. There is no history of traumatic or abusive experiences or neglect in childhood. He describes a positive relationship with his mother and brother and, generally, with school friends. There are dissociative symptoms present from the age of 4 onwards and features of borderline personality disorder developing in early adolescence. He describes a longstanding unhappiness with his appearance and a sense of disconnection from himself and from other people. He appears well motivated to engage with therapy and is on the waiting list for treatment at the Dartmouth Park Unit.

DIAGNOSIS

1) Dissociative disorder, unspecified, ICD10 – F44.7.
2) Borderline Personality Disorder ICD10 – F60.3.

PLAN

I have given him information to read about dissociative disorders and borderline personality disorder. He is already on the waiting list for treatment.

Consultant Psychiatrist

Copy: Dominic Lyne

4

3 August 2011

Dear Sir/Madam

Re: Dominic Lyne

I saw this 28 year old man who is currently unemployed. He is currently in a gay relationship.

Dominic came to see me as he had been assessed by the local NHS services and had been referred for psychotherapy to the Borderline Personality Disorder Unit. He did not feel however that his current symptoms were being addressed whilst waiting for his treatment and so has sought a private opinion.

His main difficulties seem to centre around noises in his head, mood instability, and a variety of other dissociative phenomena centred around pseudo-hallucinosis.

He described the sensation in his head of feeling like he is in a room with ten televisions on at once, all on different channels, experiencing a number of clashing voices and noises. The symptoms fluctuate, are aggravated under stress, and the general tone of the experiences is negative and self-critical. In addition Dominic experiences visual pseudo-hallucinosis in which he feels he can see shadows hovering menacingly around him when he is stressed. He also experiences out of body phenomena and feelings of unreality.

558

He describes his mood as volatile, irritable, and at times he has been prone to minor acts of physical violence. In the past he has self-harmed by cutting himself but has not taken overdoses.

He has used a variety of drugs including cocaine, MDMA amphetamines, diazepam and LSD, although his drug of choice is ketamine which characteristically reduces his auditory and visual experiences.

His assessment at the local NHS unit in Dartmouth Park followed an episode of worsening symptoms in 2010 and he is now on the waiting list for psychotherapy. He also saw a psychiatrist at the Peckwater Centre who diagnosed a dissociative disorder in addition to his emotionally unstable personality disorder. Dominic has received antidepressants in the form of escitalopram but felt that these have been ineffective.

In the background Dominic was born in Essex. His parents divorced when he was aged one and he never really had any contact with his natural father. Dominic has an older brother. He appears to have been quite a naughty child and there seems to have been a background of a certain amount of affective instability and chaos during his early childhood. His first dissociative experiences began in childhood such was the level of his internal fantasy world and his imagination. He could imagine his drawings coming to life and as a child he seems to have lived "inside his head" a great deal. This combination of a vivid internal fantasy world and dissociative phenomena occurs in individuals with strong schizoid or schizotypal personality features.

Again in accordance with these personality features Dominic is creative and as a child and adult he writes, draws, paints, and has been involved in the music industry. He realised he was gay at the age of 15 and has had a number of relationships. His current partner is getting rather exasperated with his mood swings.

Overall the picture is quite characteristic of a mixed personality disorder including not only emotionally unstable or borderline features but schizotypal features. In combination with the identity disturbance and emotional chaos of borderline personality Dominic has features of vivid internal fantasy world combined with external dissociative features in the form of pseudo-hallucinosis in the visual and auditory modality. He is most likely to benefit from medication which reduces his state of arousal rather than having a true antipsychotic effect and as a result I gave him a small amount of quetiapine 25 to 50mg as necessary and will review him in a month's time.

Yours sincerely

Consultant Psychiatrist MBChB FRCPsych

28th November 2011

PRIVATE AND CONFIDENTIAL

Dear Dr Ukaegbu

Re: Mr Dominic Lyne (d.o.b. 23/2/1983)

Thank you for asking me to review Mr Lyne, with whom I met on 25th November. He spoke about some additional symptoms to those that we explored when I met with him in April. He spoke about feeling that his thoughts were directed by a dark force that had a special purpose for him. He felt disconnected from his body and from the world and said that he believed that his only purpose in the world was to write down these thoughts so that other people could be affected by them. When his mind is racing with these thoughts he believes that other people know what he is thinking. On the street he often believes that strangers are looking at him and talking about him. He described having some abilities to predict the future. He described experiencing a voice calling his name and once hearing a female voice saying "go to the roof". He said that for a long time he had had visions of a dark figure, turned away from his, that was connected with these other beliefs. He believed that at night he could be physically attacked by this figure.

He continues to experience dissociative symptoms, as before. There were no persistent mood symptoms. He feels intermittently anxious.

We discussed how these thoughts and experiences could be symptoms of psychosis and I have made a referral to the Early Intervention Service for further assessment.

He reported having a transitory benefit from quetiapine, which he is continuing to take at a dose of 100mg once daily. The intensity of his symptoms then increased again. I suggest that he continues on the current dose for the present, but he may benefit from a higher dose at a later stage.

Yours sincerely

Copy: Dominic Lyne

560

06 JAN 2012

29 December 2011

Re: Dominic Lyne   DOB: 23/02/1983

We have assessed Mr Lyne after his referral to us from Dr Collis at the Peckwater Centre. He has traits of Schizo-typal Personality Disorder and Borderline Personality Disorder.

Today he seemed quite low and described hearing voices from various characters including a "shadow man" and said he had also heard the voice of a little girl. He does not use drugs on any regular basis. After some consideration I have decided to restart him on the Quetiapine which he was started on by a private psychiatrist whom he saw six months ago. I have suggested he start Quetiapine 100 mg moving up swiftly to 200mg at night. This should also help stabilize his mood and help with his sleep which is poor. His insight is quite good and he is currently engaging well.

As you are aware he has already been referred to the Dartmouth Park Unit who will be starting to see him for more intensive treatment in 6 months time. Dr Collis has kindly agreed to continue to see him in ourpatient clinic until then.

Yours sincerely

Associate Specialist
Early Intervention Service

561

13 JAN 2012

11 January 2012

Re: Dominic Lyne   DOB: 23/02/1983

I saw Dominic Lyne today for a final appointment. We discussed the plan i.e. that he will be attending the DPU in approximately six months time. He is eighth on their waiting list currently. He also felt that attending your outpatient clinic in the interim would be helpful for him.

His mental state was much the same as previously. He has stopped the Quetiapine 200mg as he finds it unhelpful. It helped with sleep to a certain extent but he said that he felt some numbness in his arm which he attributed to the medication.

He remains quite a socially isolated young man. He is still in his current relationship although there seem to be recent difficulties with this. We also discussed him volunteering as a way of giving him more structure in his life as he is tending to spend lots of time at home alone in his flat.

Many thanks for agreeing to see him.

Yours sincerely

Associate Specialist
Early Intervention Service

562

PART SIX

SUICIDE NOTE

I guess there is never a good place to start one of these. I guess it is not really a necessity other than removing the pain for others, when in fact none of this has anything to do with anyone else's pain but my own. This is a selfish act I guess, but it is a positive act. Positive for me and positive for everyone else even though it may be hard to see that at this precise moment.

I'm tired. So tired. You couldn't even begin to imagine how much so. None of you could even imagine how I feel. You might think you can, but you're wrong in even trying to do so. I'm sorry but that is the truth of it. How could you understand when you couldn't do so when I was alive? I suppose death does that, people scrabble to find meaning, pretend to understand, or at best pretend to care. Who are you feeling most upset for? Me or yourself?

When all is said and done, and your tears have all dried to dust, remember one thing. One simple fact. This was the only way. The only escape. The only way to freedom. We all die at some point. My time was now. Twenty-nine years trapped inside this rotting corpse that was born without a soul. For twenty-nine years I was the prisoner to the darkness. Twenty-nine years of living in constant pain. You've all been in control of your destiny, mine has simply rolled on and on with nothing but constant let down, pain, anger and deceit. All the things the darkness has needed for me to keep me beaten down and obedient to its plans for my life. To write. To write the words it pours into my head daily and without respite. But who would believe that? Who would even for one minute entertain that idea? All I've heard is how I'm to blame, I'm responsible, that I chose to live this life. Seriously, who would *choose* to live the life I have endured? How could you even entertain that notion simply to make yourselves feel better?

I've been dragged through into the understanding of what you all call my 'sickness', my disorders and malfunctioning brain. For years I simply believed this was the same for everyone, that you all had this pain secretly going on inside your heads, but now I know things could have been different. That it didn't have to be this way. If I had been more open about the voices in my head back when I first heard them at 13, or if I'd told more about the shit I've seen all my life, then I could have been freed from them; lived a completely different life and experienced happiness. True happiness without fear of the pain that will follow. Alas, that was not the case, the visions and noise moulded my existence and are now so ingrained that there is nothing anyone can do to release me from this prison. Not that you could. Not that anyone could. I don't believe your lies of names and diagnosis. I believe that this is the fact of the matter and that you are all blind. The darkness is coming and when it rips through to engulf your pathetic world, you will all wish that you had listened to at least part of what I had to say. But then, like now, it would be too late to save anyone.

Mother, please do not cry. This was not your fault; this was something you had no control over. I'm just sorry that I didn't surmount to anything that could make you proud. Always bringing pain and upset down upon you. Always the burden. Always the disappointment. So please take these few sentences to understand that you meant everything to me. I cannot even attempt to word the feelings I have, as those words would do them no justice. Just remember this was the end of pain, the end of all this unhappiness and torment. I have escaped from all of it. For once, I am free.

Brother, we have been through a lot, experienced so much together and grown as best friends. Now is the time we find our own adventures, walk down paths apart. This is one journey that I have made alone. So please understand and don't feel anger towards my parting. I will always be with you, in your heart and memories. We will see each other again, but only when you are old and grey and successful. Live until you the world has changed and your body is frail. Then, when the time is right, I will come and get you.

To my boyfriend. Thank you for everything, both good and bad. Now you are free. Free to be with whoever you desire at a given moment. I guess I did put you through so much shit. I have never felt good enough for you, always your inferior. In a way what you repeatedly did proved that to be the case. In my own way I managed to forgive you for everything no matter how much it hurt, even though others could not see why I should have bothered. I tried because I loved you. I hope that you have learnt from us; that I have helped show you a way that was completely different from what had gone before. I hope I helped you grow as a person. You showed me a life that had been stolen from me since birth and for that this soul is eternally grateful.

To the world. Continue to live in your bubble; placing worth in things that are fleeting. I could never connect with you, not through choice but through the simple fact that I was never meant to. I have seen your disgusting ways and now I am free of them. The darkness is coming, you cannot stop it. It will consume you but by then it will be too late. It already is. I have been screaming out for help and you turned your back. Left me to rot. Now I know there was never any help, never any light at the end of the tunnel. There was no turn in the corridor I have been walking down all these years. The wait has been for nothing and now I am at the end. The exit. Goodbye. You will not be missed, just as I am sure you will not miss me.

Please don't pray for my soul. It was already dead.

Lightning Source UK Ltd.
Milton Keynes UK
UKHW041855071118
331957UK00003B/23/P